PENGUIN BOOKS

THE ART OF HUNGER

PAUL AUSTER is the author of *Mr. Vertigo, Leviathan, The Music of Chance* (nominated for the 1991 PEN/Faulkner Award), *Moon Palace, In the Country of Last Things,* and the three novels known as "The New York Trilogy": *City of Glass, Ghosts,* and *The Locked Room.* He has also written a memoir, *The Invention of Solitude,* and a volume of poems, *Disappearances.* He has won literary fellowships from the National Endowment for the Arts in both poetry and prose, and in 1990 received the Morton Dauwen Zabel Award from the American Academy and Institute of Arts and Letters. His work has been translated into nineteen languages. He lives in Brooklyn, New York, with his wife and two children.

OTHER BOOKS BY PAUL AUSTER

Novels

Nonfiction

Poetry

Editor

Translations

THE ART OF HUNGER

ESSAYS, PREFACES, INTERVIEWS

AND
THE RED NOTEBOOK

PAUL AUSTER

PENGUIN BOOKS

PENGUIN BOOKS
Published by the Penguin Group
Penguin Books USA Inc., 375 Hudson Street,
New York, New York 10014, U.S.A.
Penguin Books Ltd, 27 Wrights Lane, London W8 5TZ, England
Penguin Books Australia Ltd, Ringwood, Victoria, Australia
Penguin Books Canada Ltd, 10 Alcorn Avenue,
Toronto, Ontario, Canada M4V 3B2
Penguin Books (N.Z.) Ltd, 182–190 Wairau Road,
Auckland 10, New Zealand

Penguin Books Ltd, Registered Offices:
Harmondsworth, Middlesex, England

First published in the United States of America by
Sun & Moon Press 1992
This edition with the selections "The Death of Sir Walter Raleigh"
and "The Red Notebook" published in Penguin Books 1993

3 5 7 9 10 8 6 4 2

This book was made possible, in part, through a grant from the
California Arts Council and through contributions to
The Contemporary Arts Educational Project, Inc.,
a non-profit corporation.

A shorter edition of this book, containing eleven of the pieces herein,
was published by Menard Press (London) in 1982. Some sections of this
work have previously appeared in the magazines *The Archive Newsletter*
(University of California, San Diego), *American Letters & Commentary*,
Bomb, *Commentary*, *Contemporary Literature*, *Chelsea*, *Derriere le miroir*, *Eu-
ropean Judaism*, *Granta*, *Harper's*, *Harper's Bookletter*, *The Mississippi Review*,
Modern Poetry in Translation, *Montemora*, *Mulch*, *The New York Review of
Books*, *The New York Times Book Review*, *Parnassus*, *San Francisco Review of
Books*, and *Saturday Review*; and in the following books: *Fits and Starts:
Selected Poems of Jacques Dupin* (New York: Living Hand, 1974); *The Un-
inhabited: Selected Poems of Andre du Bouchet* (New York: Living Hand,
1976); *A Tomb for Anatole* by Stephane Mallarmé (San Francisco: North
Point Press, 1983); and *The Random House Book of Twentieth-Century French
Poetry* (New York: Random House, 1982). The essay "Black and White"
was distributed as a leaflet at an exhibition of David Reed's paintings at
the Susan Cauldwell Gallery (New York, March 1975). The author wishes
to thank the publishers and presenters of these books and events.

ISBN: 0 14 01.7168 1
(CIP data available)

Printed in the United States of America
Set in New Baskerville

Contents

I / Essays

II / Prefaces

III / Interviews

IV / The Red Notebook *321*

I

— — —

Essays

The Art of Hunger

*What is important, it seems to me, is not so much to defend
a culture whose existence has never kept a man from going
hungry, as to extract, from what is called culture, ideas whose
compelling force is identical with that of hunger.*

—Antonin Artaud

A young man comes to a city. He has no name, no home, no
work: he has come to the city to write. He writes. Or, more
exactly, he does not write. He starves to the point of death.

The city is Christiania (Oslo); the year is 1890. The young
man wanders through the streets: the city is a labyrinth of
hunger, and all his days are the same. He writes unsolicited
articles for a local paper. He worries about his rent, his
disintegrating clothes, the difficulty of finding his next
meal. He suffers. He nearly goes mad. He is never more than
one step from collapse.

Still, he writes. Now and then he manages to sell an article,
to find a temporary reprieve from his misery. But he is too
weak to write steadily and can rarely finish the pieces he
has begun. Among his abortive works are an essay entitled
"Crimes of the Future," a philosophical tract on the freedom
of the will, an allegory about a bookstore fire (the books
are brains), and a play set in the Middle Ages, "The Sign
of the Cross." The process is inescapable: he must eat in
order to write. But if he does not write, he will not eat. And
if he cannot eat, he cannot write. He cannot write.

He writes. He does not write. He wanders through the streets of the city. He talks to himself in public. He frightens people away from him. When, by chance, he comes into some money, he gives it away. He is evicted from his room. He eats, and then throws everything up. At one point, he has a brief flirtation with a girl, but nothing comes of it except humiliation. He hungers. He curses the world. He does not die. In the end, for no apparent reason, he signs on board a ship and leaves the city.

These are the bare bones of Knut Hamsun's first novel, *Hunger*. It is a work devoid of plot, action, and — but for the narrator — character. By nineteenth-century standards, it is a work in which nothing happens. The radical subjectivity of the narrator effectively eliminates the basic concerns of the traditional novel. Similar to the hero's plan to make an "invisible detour" when he came to the problem of space and time in one of his essays, Hamsun manages to dispense with historical time, the basic organizing principle of nineteenth-century fiction. He gives us an account only of the hero's worst struggles with hunger. Other, less difficult times, in which his hunger has been appeased — even though they might last as long as a week — are passed off in one or two sentences. Historical time is obliterated in favor of inner duration. With only an arbitrary beginning and an arbitrary ending, the novel faithfully records the vagaries of the narrator's mind, following each thought from its mysterious inception through all its meanderings, until it dissipates and the next thought begins. What happens is allowed to happen.

This novel cannot even claim to have a redeeming social

value. Although *Hunger* puts us in the jaws of misery, it offers
no analysis of that misery, contains no call to political
action. Hamsun, who turned fascist in his old age during
the Second World War, never concerned himself with the
problems of class injustice, and his narrator-hero, like
Dostoevsky's Raskolnikov, is not so much an underdog as
a monster of intellectual arrogance. Pity plays no part in
Hunger. The hero suffers, but only because he has chosen
to suffer. Hamsun's art is such that he rigorously prevents
us from feeling any compassion for his character. From the
very beginning, it is made clear that the hero need not
starve. Solutions exist, if not in the city, then at least in
departure. But buoyed by an obsessive, suicidal pride, the
young man's actions continually betray a scorn for his own
best interests.

> I began running so as to punish myself, left street
> after street behind me, pushed myself on with inward
> jeers, and screeched silently and furiously at myself
> whenever I felt like stopping. With the help of these
> exertions I ended up along Pile Street. When I finally
> did stop, almost weeping with anger that I couldn't
> run any farther, my whole body trembled, and I threw
> myself down on a house stoop. "Not so fast!" I said.
> And to torture myself right, I stood up again and
> forced myself to stand there, laughing at myself and
> gloating over my own fatigue. Finally, after a few
> minutes I nodded and so gave myself permission to
> sit down; however, I chose the most uncomfortable
> spot on the stoop. *

He seeks out what is most difficult in himself, courting
pain and adversity in the same way other men seek out
pleasure. He goes hungry, not because he has to, but from

---

*All quotations are from the Robert Bly translation, Farrar, Straus, and
Giroux, 1967.

some inner compulsion, as if to wage a hunger strike against himself. Before the book begins, before the reader has been made the privileged witness of his fate, the hero's course of action has been fixed. A process is already in motion, and although the hero cannot control it, that does not mean he is unaware of what he is doing.

> I was conscious all the time that I was following mad whims without being able to do anything about it ... Despite my alienation from myself at that moment, and even though I was nothing but a battleground for invisible forces, I was aware of every detail of what was going on around me.

Having withdrawn into a nearly perfect solitude, he has become both the subject and object of his own experiment. Hunger is the means by which this split takes place, the catalyst, so to speak, of altered consciousness.

> I had noticed very clearly that every time I went hungry a little too long it was as though my brains simply ran quietly out of my head and left me empty. My head became light and floating, I could no longer feel its weight upon my shoulders . . .

If it is an experiment, however, it has nothing to do with the scientific method. There are no controls, no stable points of reference — only variables. Nor can this separa-tion of mind and body be reduced to a philosophical abstraction. We are not in the realm of ideas here. It is a physical state, brought into being under conditions of extreme duress. Mind and body have been weakened; the hero has lost control over both his thoughts and actions. And yet he persists in trying to control his destiny. This is the paradox, the game of circular logic that is played out through the pages of the book. It is an impossible situation for the hero. For he has willfully brought himself to the brink of danger. To give up starving would not mean victory, it would simply mean that the game was over. He wants to survive, but only on his own terms: survival that will bring him face to face with death.

He fasts. But not in the way a Christian would fast. He is not denying earthly life in anticipation of heavenly life; he is simply refusing to live the life he has been given. And the longer he goes on with his fast, the more death intrudes itself upon his life. He approaches death, creeps toward the edge of the abyss, and once there, clings to it, unable to move either forward or backward. Hunger, which opens the void, does not have the power to seal it up. A brief moment of Pascalian terror has been transformed into a permanent condition.

His fast, then, is a contradiction. To persist in it would mean death, and with death the fast would end. He must therefore stay alive, but only to the extent that it keeps him on the point of death. The idea of ending is resisted in the interests of maintaining the constant possibility of the end. Because his fasting neither posits a goal nor offers a promise of redemption, its contradiction must remain unresolved. As such, it is an image of despair, generated by the same self-consuming passion as the sickness unto death. The soul, in its despair, seeks to devour itself, and because it cannot — precisely because it despairs — sinks further into despair.

Unlike a religious art, in which self-debasement can play an ultimately cleansing role (the meditative poetry of the seventeenth century, for example), hunger only simulates the dialectic of salvation. In Fulke Greville's poem, "Down in the depth of mine iniquity," the poet is able to look into a "fatal mirror of transgression" which "shows man as fruit of his degeneration," but he knows that this is only the first step in a two-fold process, for it is in this mirror that Christ is revealed "for the same sins dying / And from that hell I feared, to free me, come . . ." In Hamsun's novel, however, once the depths have been sounded, the mirror of meditation remains empty.

He remains at the bottom, and no God will come to rescue the young man. He cannot even depend on the props of social convention to keep him standing. He is rootless, without friends, denuded of objects. Order has disappeared for him; everything has become random. His actions are inspired by nothing but whim and ungovernable urge, the weary frustration of anarchic discontent. He pawns his waistcoat in order to give alms to a beggar, hires a carriage in search of a fictitious acquaintance, knocks on strangers' doors, and repeatedly asks the time of passing policemen, for the single reason that he fancies to do so. He does not revel in these actions, however. They remain profoundly disquieting for him. Furiously trying to stabilize his life, to put an end to his wanderings, find a room, and settle down to his writing, he is thwarted by the fast he has set in motion. Once it starts, hunger does not release its progenitor-victim until its lesson has been made unforgettable. The hero is seized against his will by a force of his own making and is compelled to respond to its demands.

He loses everything — even himself. Reach the bottom of a Godless hell, and identity disappears. It is no accident that Hamsun's hero has no name: as time goes on, he is truly shorn of his self. What names he chooses to give himself are all inventions, summoned forth on the spur of the moment. He cannot say who he is because he does not know. His name is a lie, and with this lie the reality of his world vanishes.

He peers into the darkness hunger has created for him, and what he finds is a void of language. Reality has become a confusion of thingless names and nameless things for him. The connection between self and world has been broken.

> I remained for a while looking into the dark — this dense substance of darkness that had no bottom, which I couldn't understand. My thoughts could not grasp such a thing. It seemed to be a dark beyond all measurement, and I felt its presence weigh me down. I closed my eyes and took to singing half aloud and rocking myself back and forth on the cot to amuse myself, but it did no good. The dark had captured my brain and gave me not an instant of peace. What if I myself became dissolved into the dark, turned into it?

At the precise moment that he is in the greatest fear of losing possession of himself, he suddenly imagines that he has invented a new word: *Kubooa* — a word in no language, a word with no meaning.

> I had arrived at the joyful insanity hunger was: I was empty and free of pain, and my thoughts no longer had any check.

He tries to think of a meaning for his word but can only come up with what it doesn't mean, which is neither "God," nor the "Tivoli Gardens," nor "cattle show," nor "padlock," nor "sunrise," nor "emigration," nor "tobacco factory," nor "yarn."

No, the word was actually intended to mean something spiritual, a feeling, a state of mind — if only
I could understand it? And I thought and thought to
find something spiritual.

But he does not succeed. Voices, not his own, begin to
intrude, to confuse him, and he sinks deeper into chaos.
After a violent fit, in which he imagines himself to be dying,
all goes still, with no sounds but those of his own voice,
rolling back from the wall.

This episode is perhaps the most painful in the book.
But it is only one of many examples of the hero's language
disease. Throughout the narrative, his pranks most often
take the form of lies. Retrieving his lost pencil from a pawn
shop (he had accidentally left it in the pocket of a vest he
had sold), he tells the proprietor that it was with this very
pencil that he had written his three-volume treatise on
Philosophical Consciousness. An insignificant pencil, he
admits, but he has a sentimental attachment to it. To an old
man on a park bench he recites the fantastic story of a
Mr. Happolati, the inventor of the electric prayer book.
Asking a store clerk to wrap his last possession, a tattered
green blanket that he is too ashamed to carry around
exposed to view, he explains that it is not really the blanket
he wants wrapped, but the pair of priceless vases he has
folded inside the blanket. Not even the girl he courts is
immune from this sort of fiction. He invents a name for
her, a name that pleases him for its beauty, and he refuses
to call her by anything else.

These lies have a meaning beyond the jests of the moment. In the realm of language the lie has the same relationship to truth that evil has to good in the realm of morals.

That is the convention, and it works if we believe in it. But Hamsun's hero no longer believes in anything. Lies and truths are as one to him. Hunger has led him into the darkness, and there is no turning back.

This equation of language and morals becomes the gist of the final episode in *Hunger*.

> My brain grew clearer, I understood that I was close to total collapse. I put my hands against the wall and shoved to push myself away from it. The street was still dancing around. I began to hiccup from fury, and struggled with every bit of energy against my collapse, fought a really stout battle not to fall down. I didn't want to fall, I wanted to die standing. A wholesale grocer's cart came by and I saw it was filled with potatoes, but out of fury, from sheer obstinacy, I decided that they were not potatoes at all, they were cabbages, and I swore violent oaths that they were cabbages. I heard my own words very well, and I took the oath again and again on this lie, and swore deliberately just to have the delightful satisfaction of committing such clear perjury. I became drunk over this superb sin, I lifted three fingers in the air and swore with trembling lips in the name of the Father, the Son, and the Holy Ghost that they were cabbages.

And that is the end of it. There are only two possibilities left for the hero now: live or die; and he chooses to live. He has said no to society, no to God, no to his own words. Later that same day he leaves the city. There is no longer any need to continue the fast. Its work has been done.

Hunger: or a portrait of the artist as a young man. But it is an apprenticeship that has little in common with the early

struggles of other writers. Hamsun's hero is no Stephen
Dedalus, and there is hardly a word in *Hunger* about
aesthetic theory. The world of art has been translated into
the world of the body — and the original text has been
abandoned. Hunger is not a metaphor; it is the very crux
of the problem itself. If others, such as Rimbaud, with his
program for the voluntary derangement of the senses, have
turned the body into an aesthetic principle in its own right,
Hamsun's hero steadfastly rejects the opportunity to use his
deficiencies to his own advantage. He is weak, he has lost
control over his thoughts, and yet he continues to strive for
lucidity in his writing. But hunger affects his prose in the
same way it affects his life. Although he is willing to sacrifice
everything for his art, even submit to the worst forms of
debasement and misery, all he has really done is make it
impossible for himself to write. You cannot write on an
empty stomach, no matter how hard you try. But it would
be wrong to dismiss the hero of *Hunger* as a fool or a
madman. In spite of the evidence, he knows what he is
doing. He does not want to succeed. He wants to fail.

Something new is happening here, some new thought
about the nature of art is being proposed in *Hunger*. It is first
of all an art that is indistinguishable from the life of the
artist who makes it. That is not to say an art of autobiographical excess, but rather, an art that is the direct expression
of the effort to express itself. In other words, an art of
hunger: an art of need, of necessity, of desire. Certainty
yields to doubt, form gives way to process. There can be no
arbitrary imposition of order, and yet, more than ever, there
is the obligation to achieve clarity. It is an art that begins
with the knowledge that there are no right answers. For that

reason, it becomes essential to ask the right questions. One finds them by living them. To quote Samuel Beckett:

> What I am saying does not mean that there will hence-forth be no form in art. It only means that there will be a new form, and that this form will be of such a type that it admits the chaos and does not try to say that the chaos is really something else . . . To find a form that accommodates the mess, that is the task of the artist now.*

Hamsun gives the portrait of this artist in the first stages of his development. But it is in Kafka's story, *A Hunger Artist*, that the aesthetics of hunger receives its most meticulous elaboration. Here the contradictions of the fast conducted by Hamsun's hero — and the artistic impasse it leads to — are joined in a parable that deals with an artist whose art consists in fasting. The hunger artist is at once an artist and not an artist. Though he wants his performances to be admired, he insists that they shouldn't be admired, because they have nothing to do with art. He has chosen to fast only because he could never find any food that he liked. His performances are therefore not spectacles for the amusement of others, but the unravelling of a private despair that he has permitted others to watch.

Like Hamsun's hero, the hunger artist has lost control over himself. Beyond the theatrical device of sitting in his cage, his art in no way differs from his life, even what his life would have been had he not become a performer. He is not trying to please anyone. In fact, his performances cannot even be understood or appreciated.

> No one could possibly watch the hunger artist contin-uously, day and night, and so no one could produce

---

*From an interview with Tom Driver, "Beckett at the Madeleine," in *The Columbia University Forum*, Summer 1961.

firsthand evidence that the fast had really been
rigorous and continuous; only the artist himself could
know that; he was therefore bound to be the sole
completely satisfied spectator of his own fast.

This is not the classic story of the misunderstood artist,
however. For the very nature of the fast resists comprehension. Knowing itself from the outset to be an impossibility,
and condemning itself to certain failure, it is a process
that moves asymptotically toward death, destined to reach
neither fruition nor destruction. In Kafka's story, the hunger
artist dies, but only because he forsakes his art, abandoning the restrictions that had been imposed on him by
his manager. The hunger artist goes too far. But that is the
risk, the danger inherent in any act of art: you must be
willing to give your life.

In the end, the art of hunger can be described as an
existential art. It is a way of looking death in the face, and
by death I mean death as we live it today: without God,
without hope of salvation. Death as the abrupt and absurd
end of life.

I do not believe that we have come any farther than this.
It is even possible that we have been here much longer
than we are willing to admit. In all this time, however,
only a few artists have been able to recognize it. It takes
courage, and not many of us would be willing to risk
everything for nothing. But that is what happens in *Hunger*,
a novel written in 1890. Hamsun's character systematically
unburdens himself of every belief in every system, and in
the end, by means of the hunger he has inflicted upon
himself, he arrives at nothing. There is nothing to keep him
going — and yet he keeps on going. He walks straight into
the twentieth century.

1970

Itinerary

No writer has asked more of words than Laura Riding. And no one has taken on their burden more bravely, has so clearly understood that to ask life of words is to run the risk of being crushed by them. If the poem finally is to become something we do not merely leave behind, but something we can take with us, something, at rare and fortuitous moments, that can even open the way for us, it is to her work that we must turn, and — most of all — to the long silence that grew from it, and which stands beside it, like an image of its source.

Laura Riding is the first American poet to have accorded the poem the value and the dignity of a struggle. Turned in upon itself, challenging its very right to exist, the poem, in her hands, becomes act rather than object, transparence rather than thing. There is nothing here, nothing in her work we could call a subject, if not the attempt to uncover the origin of the work itself. Everything takes place in absence, in the distance between word and utterance, and each poem emerges at the moment there is nothing left to say. The why of the poem usurps the how and becomes its generating principle, its will to seek its own annihilation, to render itself light. But the struggle is an impossible one: to win is to lose. And yet, it is the only struggle possible. For if words will not give way, they will become a wall.

The poem. And nevertheless: the poem. It is the power to burrow through walls. And nevertheless: it is what can become a wall. To be what it must, what it is capable of being — a going-toward, a moving toward the Other — it must begin in the knowledge of its otherness, acknowledge, once and for all, that it speaks from a place apart, and that it cannot impose itself on any other, but must merely offer itself, nakedly and unasked for, in the silence that surrounds it. No poem can be born from the belief that there is already a language that links other with other: it is a not-yet of a language we have still to discover and create: the hunger for utopia — for nowhere. As though, from this point of null, we could at last move on and find where we are.

That Laura Riding herself came to a wall that could not be breached is not so much a sign of failure as a recognition of the necessity to move on. Nothing less than this barrier, this silence, could have revealed to us the seriousness of the journey. And if she herself now looks upon her poetic work as having reached the end of poetic possibilities, it is in this end that we must look for a new beginning, and through her wall that we must pass.

1973

Pages for Kafka

on the fiftieth anniversary of his death

He wanders toward the promised land. That is to say: he moves from one place to another, and dreams continually of stopping. And because this desire to stop is what haunts him, is what counts most for him, he does not stop. He wanders. That is to say: without the slightest hope of ever going anywhere.

He is never going anywhere. And yet he is always going. Invisible to himself, he gives himself up to the drift of his own body, as if he could follow the trail of what refuses to lead him. And by the blindness of the way he has chosen, against himself, in spite of himself, with its veerings, detours, and circlings back, his step, always one step in front of nowhere, invents the road he has taken. It is his road, and his alone. And yet on this road he is never free. For all he has left behind still anchors him to his starting place, makes him regret ever having taken the first step, robs him of all assurance in the rightness of departure. And the farther he travels from his starting place, the greater his doubt grows. His doubt goes with him, like breath, like his breathing between each step — fitful, oppressive — so that no true rhythm, no one pace, can be held. And the farther his doubt goes with him, the nearer he feels to the source of that doubt, so that in the end it is the sheer distance between him and what he has left behind that allows him to see what is behind him: what he is not and might have been. But this thought brings him neither solace nor hope.

For the fact remains that he has left all this behind, and in all these things, now consigned to absence, to the longing born of absence, he might once have found himself, fulfilled himself, by following the one law given to him, to remain, and which he now transgresses, by leaving.

All this conspires against him, so that at each moment, even as he continues on his way, he feels he must turn his eyes from the distance that lies before him, like a lure, to the movement of his feet, appearing and disappearing below him, to the road itself, its dust, the stones that clutter its way, the sound of his feet clattering upon them, and he obeys this feeling, as though it were a penance, and he, who would have married the distance before him, becomes, against himself, in spite of himself, the intimate of all that is near. Whatever he can touch, he lingers over, examines, describes with a patience that at each moment exhausts him, overwhelms him, so that even as he goes on, he calls this going into question, and questions each step he is about to take. He who lives for an encounter with the unseen becomes the instrument of the seen: he who would quarry the earth becomes the spokesman of its surfaces, the surveyor of its shades.

Whatever he does, then, he does for the sole purpose of subverting himself, of undermining his strength. If it is a matter of going on, he will do everything in his power not to go on. And yet he will go on. For even though he lingers, he is incapable of rooting himself. No pause conjures a place. But this, too, he knows. For what he wants is what he does not want. And if his journey has any end, it will only be by finding himself, in the end, where he began.

He wanders. On a road that is not a road, on an earth

that is not his earth, an exile in his own body. Whatever
is given to him, he will refuse. Whatever is spread before
him, he will turn his back on. He will refuse, the better to
hunger for what he has denied himself. For to enter the
promised land is to despair of ever coming near it. Therefore, he holds everything away from him, at arm's length,
at life's length, and comes closest to arriving when farthest
from his destination. And yet he goes on. And from one step
to the next he finds nothing but himself. Not even himself,
but the shadow of what he will become. For in the least stone
touched, he recognizes a fragment of the promised land.
Not even the promised land, but its shadow. And between
shadow and shadow lives light. And not just any light, but
this light, the light that grows inside him, unendingly, as
he goes along his way.

                                                    1974

New York Babel

In the preface to his novel *Le Bleu du Ciel*, Georges Bataille makes an important distinction between books that are written for the sake of experiment and books that are born of necessity. Literature, Bataille argues, is an essentially disruptive force, a presence confronted in "fear and trembling" that is capable of revealing to us the truth of life and its *excessive* possibilities. Literature is not a continuum, but a series of dislocations, and the books that mean most to us in the end are usually those that ran counter to the idea of literature that prevailed at the time they were written. Bataille speaks of "a moment of rage" as the kindling spark of all great works: it cannot be summoned by an act of will, and its source is always extra-literary. "How can we linger," he says, "over books we feel the author was not compelled to write?" Self-conscious experimentation is generally the result of a real longing to break down the barriers of literary convention. But most avant-garde works do not survive; in spite of themselves, they remain prisoners of the very conventions they try to destroy. The poetry of Futurism, for example, which made such a commotion in its day, is hardly read by anyone now except scholars and historians of the period. On the other hand, certain writers who played little or no part in the literary life around them — Kafka, for example — have gradually come to be recognized as essential. The work that revives our sense of literature, that gives us a new feeling for what literature can be, is the work that changes our life. It often seems improbable, as if it had come from nowhere, and because it stands so ruthlessly outside the norm, we have no choice but to create a new place for it.

Le Schizo et les Langues by Louis Wolfson* is such a book. It is not only improbable, but totally unlike anything that has come before it. To say that it is a work written in the margins of literature in not enough: its place, properly speaking, is in the margins of language itself. Written in French by an American, it has little meaning unless it is considered an American book: and yet, for reasons that will be made clear, it is also a book that excludes all possibility of translation. It hovers somewhere in the limbo between the two languages, and nothing will ever be able to rescue it from this precarious existence. For what we are presented with here is not simply the case of a writer who has chosen to write in a foreign language. The author of this book has written in French precisely because he had no choice. It is the result of brute necessity, and the book itself is nothing less than an act of survival.

Louis Wolfson is a schizophrenic. He was born in 1931 and lives in New York. For want of a better description, I would call his book a kind of third-person autobiography, a memoir of the present, in which he records the facts of his disease and the utterly bizarre method he has devised for dealing with it. Referring to himself as "the schizophrenic student of languages," "the mentally ill student," "the demented student of idioms," Wolfson uses a narrative style that partakes of both the dryness of a clinical report and the inventiveness of fiction. Nowhere in the text is there even the slightest trace of delirium or "madness": every passage is lucid, forthright, objective. As we read along,

*Published by Editions Gallimard in 1971. Preface by Gilles Deleuze.

wandering through the labyrinth of the author's obsessions, we come to feel with him, to identify with him, in the same way we identify with the eccentricities and torments of Kirilov, or Molloy.

Wolfson's problem is the English language, which has become intolerably painful to him, and which he refuses either to speak or listen to. He has been in and out of mental institutions for over ten years, steadfastly resisting all cooperation with the doctors, and now, at the time he is writing the book (the late sixties), he is living in the cramped lower-middle-class apartment of his mother and stepfather. He spends his days sitting at his desk studying foreign languages — principally French, German, Russian, and Hebrew — and protecting himself against any possible assault of English by keeping his fingers stuck in his ears, or listening to foreign language broadcasts on his transistor radio with two earplugs, or keeping a finger in one ear and an earplug in the other. In spite of these precautions, however, there are times when he is not able to ward off the intrusion of English — when his mother, for example, bursts into his room shrieking something to him in her loud and high-pitched voice. It becomes clear to the student that he cannot drown out English by simply translating it into another language. Converting an English word into its foreign equivalent leaves the English word intact; it has not been destroyed, but only put to the side, and is still there waiting to menace him.

The system that he develops in answer to this problem is complex, but not difficult to follow once one has become familiar with it, since it is based on a consistent set of rules. Drawing on the several languages he has studied, he becomes able to transform English words and phrases into phonetic combinations of foreign letters, syllables, and words that form new linguistic entities, which not only resemble the English in meaning, but in sound as well. His descriptions of these verbal acrobatics are highly detailed, often taking up as many as ten pages, but perhaps the end result of one of the simpler examples will give some idea of the process. The sentence, "Don't trip over the wire!" is changed in the following manner: "Don't" becomes the German "Tu'nicht," "trip" becomes the first four letters of the French "trébucher," "over" becomes the German "über," "the" becomes the Hebrew "èth hé," and "wire" becomes the German "zwirn," the middle three letters of which correspond to the first three letters of the English word: "Tu'nicht tréb über èth hé zwirn." At the end of this passage, exhausted but gratified by his efforts, Wolfson writes: "If the schizophrenic did not experience a feeling of joy as a result of his having found, that day, these foreign words to annihilate yet another word of his mother tongue (for perhaps, in fact, he was incapable of this sentiment), he certainly felt much less miserable than usual, at least for a while."*

The book, however, is far more than just a catalogue of these transformations. They are at the core of the work, and in some sense define its purpose, but the real substance is elsewhere, in the human situation and the daily life that envelop Wolfson's preoccupation with language. There are few books that have given a more immediate feeling of what it is like to live in New York and to wander through the streets of the city. Wolfson's eye for detail is excruciatingly precise, and each nuance of his observations — whether

---

* My translation.

it be the prison-like atmosphere of the Forty-Second Street Public Library reading room, the anxieties of a high school dance, the Times Square prostitute scene, or a conversation with his father on a bench in a city park — is rendered with attentiveness and authority. A strange movement of objectification is continually at work, and much of the fascination of the prose is a result of this distancing, which acts as a kind of lure, always drawing us toward what is written. By treating himself in the third person, Wolfson is able to create a space between himself and himself, to prove to himself that he exists. The French language serves much the same function. By looking out on his world through a different lens, by punning his world — which is immured in English — into a different language, he is able to see it with new eyes, in a way that is less oppressive to him, as if, to some slight degree, he were able to have an effect upon it.

His powers of evocation are devastating, and in his toneless, deadpan style, he manages to present a portrait of life among the Jewish poor that is so horrendously comical and vivid that it stands comparison with the early passages of Celine's *Death on the Installment Plan*. There seems to be no question that Wolfson knows what he is doing. His aims are not aesthetic ones, but in his patient determination to record everything, to set down the facts as accurately as possible, he has exposed the true absurdity of his situation, which he is often able to respond to with an ironical sense of detachment and whimsy.

His parents were divorced when he was four or five years old. His father has spent most of his life on the periphery of the world, without work, living in cheap hotels, idling away his time in cafeterias smoking cigars. He claims that his marriage took place "with a cat in the bag," since it was not until later that he learned his wife had a glass eye. When she eventually remarried, her second husband disappeared after the wedding with her diamond ring — only to be tracked down by her and thrown into jail the moment he stepped off a plane a thousand miles away. His release was granted only on the condition that he go back to his wife.

The mother is the dominant, suffocating presence of the book, and when Wolfson speaks of his "langue maternelle," it is clear that his abhorrence of English is in direct relation to his abhorrence of his mother. She is a grotesque character, a monster of vulgarity, who ridicules her son's language studies, insists on speaking to him in English, and perseveres in doing exactly the opposite of what would make his life bearable. She spends much of her spare time playing popular songs on an electric organ, with the volume turned up full blast. Sitting over his books, his fingers stuck in his ears, the student sees the lampshade on his desk begin to rattle, to feel the whole room vibrate in rhythm to the piece, and as soon as the deafening music penetrates him, he automatically thinks of the English lyrics of the songs, which drives him into a fury of despair. (Half a chapter is devoted to his linguistic transformation of the words to *Good Night Ladies*). But Wolfson never really judges her. He only describes. And if he allows himself an occasional smirk of understatement, it would seem to be his right.

"Naturally, her optical weakness seemed in no way to interfere with the capacity of her speech organs (perhaps it was even the reverse), and she would speak, at least for the most part, in a very high and very shrill voice, even though she was positively able to whisper over the telephone

when she wanted to arrange secretly for her son's entrance
into the psychiatric hospital, that is to say, without his
knowledge."

Beyond the constant threat of English posed by his mother
(who is the very embodiment of the language for him),
the student suffers from her in her role as provider.
Throughout the book, his linguistic activities are counter-
pointed by his obsession with food, eating, and the possible
contamination of his food. He oscillates between a violent
disgust at the thought of eating, as if it were a basic contradiction of his language work, and terrifying orgies of
gluttony that leave him sick for hours afterward. Each time
he enters the kitchen, he arms himself with a foreign book,
repeats aloud certain foreign phrases he has been memo-
rizing, and forces himself to avoid reading the English labels
on the packages and cans of food. Reciting one of the
phrases over and over again, like a magical incantation to
keep away evil spirits, he tears open the first package that
comes to hand — containing the food that is easiest to eat,
which is usually the least nutritional — and begins to stuff
the food into his mouth, all the while making sure that it
does not touch his lips, which he feels must be infested with
the eggs and larvae of parasites. After such bouts, he is filled
with self-recriminations and guilt. As Gilles Deleuze sug-
gests in his preface to the book, "His guilt is no less great
when he has eaten than when he has heard his mother
speak. It is the same guilt."

This is the point, I feel, at which Wolfson's private
nightmare locks with certain universal questions about
language. There is a fundamental connection between
speaking and eating, and by the very excessiveness of

Wolfson's experience, we are able to see how profound this relationship is. Speech is a strangeness, an anomaly, a biologically secondary function of the mouth, and myths about language are often linked to the idea of food. Adam is granted the power of naming the creatures of Paradise and is later expelled for having eaten of the Tree of Knowledge. Mystics fast in order to prepare themselves to receive the word of God. The body of Christ, the word made flesh, is eaten in holy communion. It is as if the life-serving function of the mouth, its role in eating, had been transferred to speech, for it is language that creates us and defines us as human beings. Wolfson's fear of eating, the guilt he feels over his escapades of self-indulgence, are an acknowledgement of his betrayal of the task he has set for himself: that of discovering a language he can live with. To eat is a compromise, since it sustains him within the context of an already discredited and unacceptable world.

In the end, Wolfson's search is undertaken in the hope of one day being able to speak English again — a hope that flickers now and then through the pages of the book. The invention of his system of transformations, the writing of the book itself, are part of a slow progression beyond the hermetic agony of his disease. By refusing to allow anyone to impose a cure on him, by forcing himself to confront his own problems, to live through them alone, he senses in himself a dawning awareness of the possibility of living among others — of being able to break free from his one-man language and enter a language of men.

The book he has created from this struggle is difficult to define, but it should not be dismissed as a therapeutic exercise, as yet another document of mental illness to be

filed on the shelves of medical libraries. Gallimard, it seems
to me, has made a serious error in bringing out *Le Schizo
et les Langues* as part of a series on psychoanalysis. By giving
the book a label, they have somehow tried to tame the
rebellion that gives the book its extraordinary force, to
soften "the moment of rage" that everywhere informs
Wolfson's writing.

On the other hand, even if we avoid the trap of considering this work as nothing more than a case history,
we should still hesitate to judge it by established literary
standards and to look for parallels with other literary works.
Wolfson's method, in some sense, does resemble the elaborate word play in *Finnegans Wake* and in the novels of
Raymond Roussel, but to insist on this resemblance would
be to miss the point of the book. Louis Wolfson stands
outside literature as we know it, and to do him justice
we must read him on his own terms. For it is only in this
way that we will be able to discover his book for what it is:
one of those rare works that can change our perception of
the world.

1974

The Decisive Moment

Charles Reznikoff is a poet of the eye. To cross the threshold of his work is to penetrate the prehistory of matter, to find oneself exposed to a world in which language has not yet been invented. Seeing, in his poetry, always comes before speech. Each poetic utterance is an emanation of the eye, a transcription of the visible into the brute, undeciphered code of being. The act of writing, therefore, is not so much an ordering of the real as a discovery of it. It is a process by which one places oneself between things and the names of things, a way of standing watch in this interval of silence and allowing things to be seen — as if for the first time — and henceforth to be given their names. The poet, who is the first man to be born, is also the last. He is Adam, but he is also the end of all generations: the mute heir of the builders of Babel. For it is he who must learn to speak from his eye — and cure himself of seeing with his mouth.

The poem, then, not as a telling, but as a taking hold. The world can never be assumed to exist. It comes into being only in the act of moving towards it. *Esse est percipii*: no American poet has ever adhered so faithfully to the Berkeleyan formula as Reznikoff. It is more than just the guiding principle of his work — it is *embedded* in the work, and it contains all the force of a moral dogma. To read Reznikoff is to understand that nothing can be taken for granted: we do not find ourselves in the midst of an already established world, we do not, as if by preordained birthright, automatically take possession of our surroundings. Each moment, each thing, must be earned, wrested away from the confusion of inert matter by a steadiness of gaze, a purity of perception so intense that the effort, in itself, takes on the value of a religious act. The slate has been wiped clean. It is up to the poet to write his own book.

Tiny poems, many of them barely a sentence long, make up the core of Reznikoff's work. Although his total output includes fiction, biography, drama, long narrative poems, historical meditations, and book-length documentary poems, these short lyrics are the Ur-texts of Reznikoff's imagination: everything else follows from them. Notable for their precision and simplicity, they also run counter to normal assumptions about what a poem should aspire to be. Consider these three examples:

April

The stiff lines of the twigs
blurred by buds.

Moonlit Night

The trees' shadows lie in black pools in the lawns.

The Bridge

In a cloud bones of steel.

The point is that there is no point. At least not in any traditional sense. These poems are not trying to drum home universal truths, to impress the reader with the skill of their making, or to invoke the ambiguities of human experience. Their aim, quite simply, is clarity. Of seeing and of speaking. And yet, the unsettling modesty of these poems should not blind us to the boldness of their ambition. For even in these tiniest of poems, the gist of Reznikoff's poetics is there. It is as much an ethics of the poetic moment as it is a theory of writing, and its message never varies in any of Reznikoff's work: the poem is always more than just a construction of words. Art, then, for the sake of something — which means that art is almost an incidental by-product of the effort to make it. The poem, in all instances, must be an effort to perceive, must be a moving *outward*. It is less a mode of expressing the world than it is a way of being in the world. Merleau-Ponty's account of contemplation in *The Phenomenology of Perception* is a nearly exact description of the process that takes place in a Reznikoff poem:

> ... when I contemplate an object with the sole intention of watching it exist and unfold its riches before my eyes, then it ceases to be an allusion to a general type, and I become aware that each perception, and not merely that of sights which I am discovering for the first time, re-enacts on its own account the birth of intelligence and has some element of creative genius about it: in order that I may recognize the tree as a tree, it is necessary that, beneath this familiar meaning, the momentary arrangement of the visible scene should begin all over again, as on the very first day of the vegetable kingdom, to outline the individual idea of this tree.

Imagism, yes. But only as a source, not as a method. There is no desire on Reznikoff's part to use the image as a medium for transcendence, to make it quiver ineffably in some ethereal realm of the spirit. The progress from symbolism to imagism to objectivism is more a series of short-circuits than a direct lineage. What Reznikoff learned from the Imagists was the value — the force — of the image in itself, unadorned by the claims of the ego. The poem, in Reznikoff's hands, is an act of image-ing rather than of imagining. Its impulse is away from metaphor and into the tangible, a desire to take hold of what is rather than what is merely possible. A poem fit to the measure of the perceived world, neither larger than this world nor smaller than it. "I see something," Reznikoff stated in a 1968 interview with L. S. Dembo, "and I put it down as I see it. In the treatment of it, I abstain from comment. Now, if I've done something that moves me — if I've portrayed the object well — somebody will come along and also be moved, and somebody else will come along and say, 'What the devil is this?' And maybe they're both right."

If the poet's primary obligation is to see, there is a similar though less obvious injunction upon the poet — the duty of not being seen. The Reznikoff equation, which weds seeing to invisibility, cannot be made except by renunciation. In order to see, the poet must make himself invisible. He must disappear, efface himself in anonymity.

> I like the sound of the street —
> but I, apart and alone,
> beside an open window
> and behind a closed door.

*

> I am alone —
> and glad to be alone;
> I do not like people who walk about

so late; who walk slowly after midnight
through the leaves fallen on the sidewalks.
I do not like
my own face
in the little mirrors of the slot-machines
before the closed stores.

It seems no accident that most Reznikoff poems are
rooted in the city. For only in the modern city can the one
who sees remain unseen, take his stand in space and yet
remain transparent. Even as he becomes a part of the landscape he has entered, he continues to be an outsider.
Therefore, objectivist. That is to say — to create a world
around oneself by seeing as a stranger would. What counts
is the thing itself, and the thing that is seen can come to
life only when the one who sees it has disappeared. There
can never be any movement toward possession. Seeing is
the effort to create presence: to possess a thing would be
to make it vanish.

And yet, it is *as if* each act of seeing were an attempt to
establish a link between the one who sees and the thing
that is seen. *As if* the eye were the means by which the
stranger could find his place in the world he has been exiled
to. For the building of a world is above all the building and
recognition of relations. To discover a thing and isolate it
in its singularity is only a beginning, a first step. The world
is not merely an accumulation, it is a process — and each
time the eye enters this world, it partakes in the life of all
the disparate things that pass before it. While objectivity
is the premise, subjectivity is the tacit organizer. As soon
as there is more than one thing, there is memory, and
because of memory, there is language: what is born in the

eye, and nevertheless beyond it. In which, and out of which, the poem.

In his 1968 interview with Dembo, Reznikoff went on to say: "The world is very large, I think, and I certainly can't testify to the whole of it. I can only testify to my own feelings; I can only say what I saw and heard, and I try to say it as well as I can. And if your conclusion is that what I saw and heard makes you feel the way I did, then the poem is successful."

New York was Reznikoff's home. It was a city he knew as intimately as a woodcutter knows his forest, and in his prime he would walk between ten and twenty miles a day, from Brooklyn to Riverdale and back. Few poets have ever had such a deep feeling for city life, and in dozens of brief poems Reznikoff captures the strange and transitory beauties of the urban landscape.

> This smoky winter morning —
> do not despise the green jewel among the twigs
> because it is a traffic light.

                              *

> Feast, you who cross the bridge
> this cold twilight
> on these honeycombs of light, the buildings of
>   Manhattan.

                              *

> Rails in the subway,
> what did you know of happiness
> when you were ore in the earth;
> now the electric lights shine upon you.

But Reznikoff's attention is focused on more than just
the objects to be found in the city. He is equally interested
in the people who fill the streets of New York, and no
encounter, however brief, is too slight to escape his notice,
too banal to become a source of epiphany. These two examples, from among many possibilities:

> I was walking along Forty-Second Street as night was
> falling.
> On the other side of the street was Bryant Park.
> Walking behind me were two men
> and I could hear some of their conversation:
> "What you must do," one of them was saying to his
> companion,
> "is to decide on what you want to do
> and then stick to it. Stick to it!
> And you are sure to succeed finally."
>
> I turned to look at the speaker giving such good advice
> and was not surprised to see that he was old,
> But his companion
> to whom the advice was given so earnestly,
> was just as old;
> and just then the great clock on top of a building
> across he park
>
> began to shine.

*

> The tramp with torn shoes
> and clothing dirty and wrinkled —
> dirty hands and face —
> takes a comb out of his pocket
> and carefully combs his hair.

The feeling that emerges from these glimpses of city life is rough equivalent to what one feels when looking at a photograph. Cartier-Bresson's "decisive moment" is perhaps the crucial idea to remember in this context. The important thing is readiness: you cannot walk out into the street with the expectation of writing a poem or taking a picture, and yet you must be prepared to do so whenever the opportunity presents itself. Because the "work" can come into being only when it has been given to you by the world, you must be constantly looking at the world, constantly doing the work that will lead to a poem, even if no poem comes of it. Reznikoff walks through the city — not, as most poets do, with "his head in the clouds," but with his eyes open, his mind open, his energies concentrated on entering the life around him. Entering it precisely because he is apart from it. And therefore this paradox, lodged in the heart of the poem: to posit the reality of this world, and then to cross into it, even as you find yourself barred at all its gates. The poet as solitary wanderer, as man in the crowd, as faceless scribe. Poetry as an art of loneliness.

It is more than just loneliness, however. It is exile, and a way of coming to terms with exile that somehow, for better or worse, manages to leave the condition of exile intact. Reznikoff was not only an outsider by temperament, nurturing those aspects of himself that would tend to maintain his sense of isolation, he was also born into a state of *otherness*, and as a Jew, as the son of immigrant Jews in America, whatever idea of community he had was always ethnic rather than national (his dream as a poet was to go across the country on foot, stopping at synagogues along

the way to give readings of his work in exchange for food
and lodging). If his poems about the city — his American
poems, so to speak — dwell on the surfaces of things,
on the skin of everyday life, it is in his poems about Jewish
identity that he allows himself a certain measure of lyrical
freedom, allows himself to become a singer of songs.

> Let other people come as streams
> that overflow a valley
> and leave dead bodies, uprooted trees and fields
>   of sand:
> we Jews are as dew,
> on every blade of grass,
> trodden under foot today
> and here tomorrow morning.

And yet, in spite of this deep solidarity with the Jewish
past, Reznikoff never deludes himself into thinking that
he can overcome the essential solitude of his condition
simply by affirming his Jewishness. For not only has he been
exiled, he has been exiled twice — as a Jew, and from
Judaism as well.

> How difficult for me is Hebrew:
> even the Hebrew for *mother*, for *bread*, for *sun*
> is foreign. How far I have been exiled, Zion.

*

> The Hebrew of your poets, Zion,
> is like oil upon a burn,
> cool as oil;
> after work,
> the smell in the street at night
> of the hedge in flower.

> Like Solomon,
> I have married and married the speech of strangers;
> none are like you, Shulamite.

It is a precarious position, to say the least. Neither fully
assimilated nor fully unassimilated, Reznikoff occupies
the unstable middle ground between two worlds and is
never able to claim either one as his own. Nevertheless,
and no doubt precisely because of this ambiguity, it is
an extremely fertile ground — leading some to consider
him primarily as a Jewish poet (whatever that term might
mean) and others to look on him as quintessentially
American poet (whatever *that* term might mean). And yet
it is safe to say, I think, that in the end both statements
are true — or else that neither one is true, which probably
amounts to the same thing. Reznikoff's poems are what
Reznikoff is: the poems of an American Jew, or, if you will,
of a hyphenated American, a Jewish-American, with the
two terms standing not so much on equal footing as com-
bining to form a third and wholly different term: the condition of being in two places at the same time, or, quite
simply, the condition of being nowhere.

We have only to go on the evidence. In the two volumes
of *Complete Poems* (1918-75), recently published by Black
Sparrow Press, there are a surprising number of poems
on Jewish themes. Poems not only about Jewish immigrant
life in New York, but also long narratives on various
episodes from ancient and modern Jewish history. A list
of some of these titles will give a fair idea of some of
Reznikoff's concerns: "King David," "Jeremiah in the Stocks:
An Arrangement of the Prophecies," "The Synagogue
Defeated: Anno 1096," "Palestine under the Romans," "The

and I know that I never can.
Don't you think it best
to give me a divorce?
If you do,
I will not have to sell the house in Denver
that you gave me,
and I will give you back the ranch in Delta.
After we are divorced,
if you care for me and I care for you,
we will marry again. Polly."

*

Jessie was eleven years old, though some said fourteen,
and had the care of a child
just beginning to walk —
and suddenly pulled off the child's diaper
and sat the child in some hot ashes
where she had been cooking ash cakes;
the child screamed
and she smacked it on the jaw.

It would be difficult for a poet to make himself more invisible than Reznikoff does in this book. To find a comparable approach to the real, one would have to go back to the great prose writers of the turn of the century. As in Chekhov or in early Joyce, the desire is to allow events to speak for themselves, to choose the exact detail that will say everything and thereby allow as much as possible to remain unsaid. This kind of restraint paradoxically requires an openness of spirit that is available to very few: an ability to accept the given, to remain a witness of human behavior and not succumb to the temptation of becoming a judge.

The success of *Testimony* becomes all the more striking
when placed beside *Holocaust*, a far less satisfying work
that is based on many of the same techniques. Using as
his sources the US Government publication, *Trials of the
Criminals before the Nuremberg Tribunal*, and the records of
the Eichmann trial in Jerusalem, Reznikoff attempts to
deal with Germany's annihilation of the Jews in the same
dispassionate, documentary style with which he had explored the human dramas buried in American court
records. The problem, I think, is one of magnitude. Reznikoff is a master of the everyday; he understands the
seriousness of small events and has an uncanny sympathy
with the lives of ordinary people. In a work such as *Testimony*
he is able to present us with the facts in a way that
simultaneously makes us understand them; the two gestures
are inseparable. In the case of *Holocaust*, however, we all
know the facts in advance. The Holocaust, which is precisely
the unknowable, the unthinkable, requires a treatment
beyond the facts in order for us to be able to understand
it — assuming that such a thing is even possible. Similar
in approach to a 1960s play by Peter Weiss, *The Investigation*, Reznikoff's poem rigorously refuses to pass judgment
on any of the atrocities it describes. But this is nevertheless
a false objectivity, for the poem is not saying to the reader,
"decide for yourself," it is saying that the decision has
already been made and that the only way we can deal with
these things is to remove them from their inherently emotional setting. The problem is that we cannot remove them.
This setting is a necessary starting point.

Holocaust is instructive, however, in that it shows us the

limits of Reznikoff's work. I do not mean shortcomings —
but limits, those things that set off and describe a space,
that create a world. Reznikoff is essentially a poet of *naming*.
One does not have the sense of a poetry immersed in language but rather of something that takes place before
language and comes to fruition at the precise moment language has been discovered — and it yields a style that is
pristine, fastidious, almost stiff in its effort to say exactly
what it means to say. If any one word can be used to describe
Reznikoff's work, it would be humility — toward language
and also toward himself.

> I am afraid
> because of the foolishness
> I have spoken.
> I must diet
> on silence;
> strengthen myself
> with quiet.

It could not have been an easy life for Reznikoff.
Throughout the many years he devoted to writing poetry
(his first poems were published in 1918, when he was twenty-
four, and he went on publishing until his death in early
1976), he suffered from a neglect so total it was almost
scandalous. Forced to bring out most of his books in private
editions (many of them printed by himself), he also had to
fight the constant pressures of making a living.

> After I had worked all day at what I earn my living
> I was tired. Now my own work has lost another day,
> I thought, but began slowly,
> and slowly my strength came back to me.
> Surely, the tide comes in twice a day.

It was not until he was in his late sixties that Reznikoff began to receive some measure of recognition. New Directions published a book of his selected poems, *By The Waters of Manhattan*, which was followed a few years later by the first volume of *Testimony*. But in spite of the success of these two books — and a growing audience for his works — New Directions saw fit to drop Reznikoff from its list of authors. More years passed. Then, in 1974, Black Sparrow Press brought out *By The Well of Living & Seeing: New & Selected Poems 1918-1973*. More importantly, it committed itself to the long overdue project of putting all of Reznikoff's work back into print. Under the intelligent and sensitive editing of Seamus Cooney, the sequence so far includes the two volumes of *Complete Poems, Holocaust, The Manner Music* (a posthumous novel), the first two volumes of *Testimony*, and will go on to include more volumes of *Testimony* and a book of *Collected Plays*.

If Reznikoff lived his life in obscurity, there was never the slightest trace of resentment in his work. He was too proud for that, too busy with the work itself to be overly concerned with its fate in the world. Even if people are slow to listen to someone who speaks quietly, he knew that eventually he would be heard.

Te Deum

Not because of victories
I sing,
having none,
but for the common sunshine,
the breeze,
the largess of the spring.

Not for victory
but for the day's work done
as well as I was able;
not for a seat upon the dais
but at the common table.

(1974; 1976; 1978)

Dada Bones

Of all the movements of the early avant-garde, Dada is the one that continues to say the most to us. Although its life was short — beginning in 1916 with the nightly spectacles at the Cabaret Voltaire in Zurich, and ending effectively, if not officially, in 1922 with the riotous demonstrations in Paris against Tristan Tzara's play, *Le Coeur à gaz* — its spirit has not quite passed into the remoteness of history. Even now, more than fifty years later, not a season goes by without some new book or exhibition about Dada, and it is with more than academic interest that we continue to investigate the questions it raised. For Dada's questions remain our questions, and when we speak of the relationship between art and society, of art versus action and art as action, we cannot help but turn to Dada as a source and as an example. We want to know about it not only for itself, but because we feel that it will help us toward an understanding of our own, present moment.

The diaries of Hugo Ball are a good place to begin. Ball, a key figure in the founding of Dada, was also the first defector from the Dada movement, and his record of the years between 1914 and 1921 is an extremely valuable document.* *Flight Out of Time* was originally published in Germany in 1927, shortly before Ball's death from stomach cancer at the age of forty-one, and it consists of passages that Ball extracted from his journals and edited with clear and partisan hindsight. It is not so much a self-portrait as an account

---

*Flight Out of Time: A Dada Diary, edited by John Elderfield and translated by Ann Raimes (Viking Press, 1975).

of his inner progress, a spiritual and intellectual reckoning, and it moves from entry to entry in a rigorously dialectical manner. Although there are few biographical details, the sheer adventure of the thought is enough to hold us. For Ball was an incisive thinker; as a participant in early Dada, he is perhaps our finest witness to the Zurich group, and because Dada marked only one stage in his complex development, our view of it through his eyes gives us a kind of perspective we have not had before.

Hugo Ball was a man of his time, and to an extraordinary degree his life seems to embody the passions and contradictions of European society during the first quarter of this century. Student of Nietzsche's work; stage manager and playwright for the Expressionist theatre; left-wing journalist; vaudeville pianist; poet; novelist; author of works on Bakunin, the German Intelligentsia, early Christianity, and the writings of Hermann Hesse; convert to Catholicism: he seemed, at one moment or another, to have touched on nearly all the political and artistic preoccupations of the age. And yet, despite his many activities, Ball's attitudes and interests were remarkably consistent throughout his life, and in the end his entire career can be seen as a concerted, even feverish attempt to ground his existence in a fundamental truth, in a single, absolute reality. Too much an artist to be a philosopher, too much a philosopher to be an artist, too concerned with the fate of the world to think only in terms of personal salvation, and yet too inward to be an effective activist, Ball struggled toward solutions that could somehow answer both his inner and outer needs, and even in the deepest solitude he never saw himself as separate from the society around him. He was a man for whom

everything came with great difficulty, whose sense of himself
was never fixed, and whose moral integrity made him
capable of brashly idealistic gestures totally out of keeping
with his delicate nature. We have only to examine the
famous photograph of Ball reciting a sound poem at the
Cabaret Voltaire to understand this. He is dressed in an
absurd costume that makes him look like a cross between
the Tin Man and a demented bishop, and he stares out from
under a high witch doctor's hat with an expression on his
face of overwhelming terror. It is an unforgettable expression, and in this one image of him we have what amounts
to a parable of his character, a perfect rendering of inside
confronting outside, of darkness meeting darkness.

In the Prologue to *Flight Out of Time* Ball presents the
reader with a cultural autopsy that sets the tone for all that
follows: "The world and society in 1913 looked like this: life
is completely confined and shackled . . . The most burning
question day and night is this: is there anywhere a force that
is strong enough and above all vital enough to put an end
to this state of affairs?" Elsewhere, in his 1917 lecture on
Kandinsky, he states these ideas with even greater urgency:
"A thousand-year-old culture disintegrates. There are no
columns and no supports, no foundations anymore — they
have all been blown up . . . The meaning of the world
has disappeared." These feelings are not new to us. They
confirm our sense of the European intellectual climate
around the time of the First World War, and echo much
of what we now take for granted as having formed the
modern sensibility. What is unexpected, however, is what
Ball says a little further on in the Prologue: "It might seem
as if philosophy had been taken over by the artists; as if

the new impulses were coming from them; as if they were the prophets of rebirth. When we said Kandinsky and Picasso, we meant not painters, but priests; not craftsmen, but creators of new worlds and new paradises." Dreams of total regeneration could not exist side by side with the blackest pessimism, and for Ball there was no contradiction in this: both attitudes were part of a single approach. Art was not a way of turning from the problems of the world, it was a way of directly solving these problems. During his most difficult years, it was this faith that sustained Ball, from his early work in the theater — "Only the theater is capable of creating the new society" — to his Kandinsky-influenced formulation of "the union of all artistic mediums and forces," and beyond, to his Dada activities in Zurich.

The seriousness of these considerations, as elaborated in the diaries, helps to dispel several myths about the beginnings of Dada, above all the idea of Dada as little more than the sophomoric rantings of a group of young draft-dodgers, a kind of willful Marx Brothers zaniness. There was, of course, much that was plainly silly in the Cabaret performances, but for Ball this buffoonery was a means to an end, a necessary catharsis: "Perfect skepticism makes perfect freedom possible . . . One can almost say that when belief in an object or a cause comes to an end, this object or cause returns to chaos and becomes common property. But perhaps it is necessary to have resolutely, forcibly produced chaos and thus a complete withdrawal of faith before an entirely new edifice can be built up on a changed basis of belief." To understand Dada, then, at least in this early phase, we must see it as a vestige of old humanistic ideals, a reassertion of individual dignity in a mechanical age of standardization, as a simultaneous expression of despair and hope. Ball's particular contribution to the Cabaret performances, his sound poems, or "poems without words," bears this out. Although he cast aside ordinary language, he had no intention of destroying language itself. In his almost mystical desire to recover what he felt to be a prelapsarian speech, Ball saw in this new, purely emotive form of poetry a way of capturing the magical essences of words. "In these phonetic poems we totally renounce the language that journalism has abused and corrupted. We must return to the innermost alchemy of the word . . . ."

Ball retreated from Zurich only seven months after the opening of the Cabaret Voltaire, partly from exhaustion, and partly from disenchantment with the way Dada was developing. His conflict was principally with Tzara, whose ambition was to turn Dada into one of the many movements of the international avant-garde. As John Elderfield summarizes in his introduction to Ball's diary: "And once away he felt he discerned a certain 'Dada hubris' in what they had been doing. He had believed they were eschewing conventional morality to elevate themselves as new men, that they had welcomed irrationalism as a way toward the 'supernatural', that sensationalism was the best method of destroying the academic. He came to doubt all this — he had become ashamed of the confusion and eclecticism of the cabaret — and saw isolation from the age as a surer and more honest path toward these personal goals . . . ." Several months later, however, Ball returned to Zurich to take part in the events of the Galerie Dada and to deliver his important lecture on Kandinsky, but within a short while he was again feuding with Tzara, and this time the break was final.

In July 1917, under Tzara's direction, Dada was officially launched as a movement, complete with its own publication, manifestos, and promotion campaign. Tzara was a tireless organizer, a true avant-gardist in the style of Marinetti, and eventually, with the help of Picabia and Serner, he led Dada far from the original ideas of the Cabaret Voltaire, away from what Elderfield correctly calls "the earlier equilibrium of construction-negation" into the bravura of anti-art. A few years later there was a further split in the movement, and Dada divided itself into two factions: the German group, led by Huelsenbeck, George Grosz, and the Herzefelde brothers, which was predominantly political in approach, and Tzara's group, which moved to Paris in 1920, and which championed the aesthetic anarchism that ultimately developed into Surrealism.

If Tzara gave Dada its identity, he also robbed it of the moral purpose it had aspired to under Ball. By turning it into a doctrine, by garnishing it with a set of programmatic ideals, Tzara led Dada into self-contradiction and impotence. What for Ball had been a true cry from the heart against all systems of thought and action became one organization among others. The stance of anti-art, which opened the way for endless provocations and attacks, was essentially an inauthentic idea. For art opposed to art is nevertheless art; you can't have it both ways at once. As Tzara wrote in one of his manifestos: "The true Dadaists are against Dada." The impossibility of establishing this as dogma is obvious, and Ball, who had the foresight to realize this contradiction quite early, left as soon as he saw signs of Dada becoming a movement. For the others, however, Dada became a kind of bluff that was pushed to further and further extremes. But the real motivation was gone, and when Dada finally died, it was not so much from the battle it had fought as from its own inertia.

Ball's position, on the other hand, seems no less valid today than it did in 1917. Of what we have come to realize were several different periods and divergent tendencies in Dada, the moment of Ball's participation, as I see it, remains the moment of Dada's greatest strength, the period that speaks most persuasively to us today. This is perhaps a heretical view. But when we consider how Dada exhausted itself under Tzara, how it succumbed to the decadent system of exchange in the bourgeois art world, provoking the very audience whose favor it was courting, this branch of Dada must be seen as a symptom of art's essential weakness under modern capitalism — locked in the invisible cage of what Marcuse has called "repressive tolerance." But because Ball never treated Dada as an end in itself, he remained flexible, and was able to use Dada as an instrument for reaching higher goals, for producing a genuine critique of the age. Dada, for Ball, was merely the name for a kind of radical doubt, a way of sweeping aside all existing ideologies and moving on to an examination of the world around him. As such, the energy of Dada can never be used up: it is an idea whose time is always the present.

Ball's eventual return to the Catholicism of his childhood in 1921 is not really as strange as it may seem. It represents no true shift in his thinking, and in many ways can be seen as simply a further step in his development. Had he lived longer, there is no reason to believe that he would not have undergone further metamorphosis. As it is, we discover in his diaries a continual overlapping of ideas and concerns, so that even during the Dada period, for example, there are repeated references to Christianity ("I do not know if we will go beyond Wilde and Baudelaire in spite of all our efforts; or if we will not just remain romantics. There are probably other ways of achieving the miracle and other ways of opposition too — asceticism, for example, the church") and during the time of his most serious Catholicism there is a preoccupation with mystical language that clearly resembles the sound poem theories of his Dada period. As he remarks in one of his last entries, in 1921: "The socialist, the aesthete, the monk: all three agree that modern bourgeois education must be destroyed. The new ideal will take its new elements from all three." Ball's short life was a constant straining toward a synthesis of these different points of view. If we regard him today as an important figure, it is not because he managed to discover a solution, but because he was able to state the problems with such clarity. In his intellectual courage, in the fervor of his confrontation with the world, Hugo Ball stands out as one of the exemplary spirits of the age.

1975

Truth, Beauty, Silence

Laura Riding was still in her thirties when she published her 477- page *Collected Poems* in 1938. At an age when most poets are just beginning to come into their own, she had already reached full maturity, and the list of her accomplishments in literature up to that time is impressive: nine volumes of poetry, several collections of critical essays and fiction, a long novel, and the founding of a small publishing house, the Seizin Press. As early as 1924, soon after her graduation from Cornell, *The Fugitive* had called her "the discovery of the year, a new figure in American poetry," and later, in Europe, during the period of her intimate and stormy relationship with Robert Graves, she became an important force of the international avant-garde. Young Auden was apparently so influenced by her poems that Graves felt obliged to write him a letter reprimanding him for his blatant Laura Riding imitations, and the method of close textual criticism developed in *A Survey of Modernist Poetry* (written in collaboration with Graves) directly inspired Empson's *Seven Types of Ambiguity*. Then, after 1938, nothing. No more poems, no more stories, no more essays. As time went on, Laura Riding's name was almost totally forgotten, and to a new generation of poets and writers it was as if she had never existed.

She was not heard from again until 1962, when she agreed to give a reading of some of her poems for a BBC broadcast and to deliver a few remarks about the philosophical and linguistic reasons for her break with poetry. Since then, there have been several appearances in print, and now, most recently, the publication of two books: a selection of her poems, which is prefaced by a further discussion of her attitude toward poetry, and *The Telling*, a prose work which she has described as a "personal evangel." Clearly, Laura Riding is back. Although she has written no poems since 1938, her new work in *The Telling* is intimately connected with her earlier writings, and in spite of her long public silence, her career is of a single piece. Laura Riding and Laura (Riding) Jackson — the married name she now uses — are in many ways mirror images of one another. Each has attempted to realize a kind of universal truth in language, a way of speaking that would somehow reveal to us our essential humanness — "a linguistically ordained ideal, every degree of fulfillment of which is a degree of express fulfillment of the hope comprehended in being, in its comprehending us within it, as human" — and if this ambition seems at times to be rather grandiosely stated, it has nevertheless been constant. The only thing that has changed is the method. Up to 1938, Laura Riding was convinced that poetry was the best way to achieve this goal. Since then, she has revised her opinion, and has not only given up poetry, but now sees it as one of the prime obstacles on this path toward linguistic truth.

When we turn to her own poetry, what is above all striking is its consistency of purpose and manner. From the very beginning, it seems, Laura Riding knew where she was going, and her poems ask to be read not as isolated lyrics, but as interconnecting parts of an enormous poetic project.

We must learn better
What we are and are not.
We are not the wind.
We are not every vagrant mood that tempts
Our minds to giddy homelessness.
We must distinguish better
Between ourselves and strangers.
There is much that we are not.
There is much that is not.
There is much that we have not to be.

(from "The Why of the Wind")

This is essential Riding: the abstract level of discourse, the insistence upon confronting ultimate questions, the tendency toward moral exhortation, the quickness and cleanness of thought, the unexpected juxtapositions of words, as in the phrase "giddy homelessness." The physical world is hardly present here, and when it is mentioned, it appears only as metaphor, as a kind of linguistic shorthand for indicating ideas and mental processes. The wind, for example, is not a real wind, but a way of expressing what is changeable, a reference to the idea of flux, and we feel its impact only as an idea. The poem itself proceeds as an argument rather than as a statement of feeling or an evocation of personal experience, and its movement is toward generalization, toward the utterance of what the poet takes to be a fundamental truth.

"We are not the wind." In other words, we are what does not change. For Laura Riding, this is the given of her project; it cannot be proved, but nevertheless operates as the informing principle of her work as a whole. In poem after poem we witness her trying somehow to peel back the

skin of the world in order to find some absolute and
unassailable place of permanence, and because the poems
are rarely grounded in a physical perception of that world,
they tend, strangely, to exist in an almost purely emotional
climate, created by the fervor of this metaphysical quest.
And yet, in spite of the high seriousness of the poems,
there are moments of sharp wit that remind us of Emily
Dickinson:

> Then follows a description
> Of an interval called death
> By the living.
> But I shall speak of it
> As of a brief illness.
> For it lasted only
> From being not ill
> To being not ill.
> It came about by chance —
> I met God.
> "What," he said, "you already?"
> "What," I said, "you still?"

(from "Then Follows," in Collected Poems)

In the beginning, it is difficult to take the full measure
of these poems, to understand the particular kinds of problems they are trying to deal with. Laura Riding gives us
almost nothing to see, and this absence of imagery and
sensuous detail, of any true *surface*, is at first baffling. We
feel as though we had been blinded. But this is intentional
on her part, and it plays an important role in the themes
she develops. She does not so much want to see as to consider the notion of what is seeable.

You have pretended to be seeing.
I have pretended that you saw.
So came we by such eyes —
And within mystery to have language.

                              *

There was no sight to see.
That which is to be seen is no sight.
You made it a sight to see.
It is no sight, and this was the cause.

Now, having seen, let our eyes close
And a dark blessing pass among us —
A quick-slow blessing to have seen
And said and done no worse or better.

                              (from "Benedictory")

The only thing that seems to be present here is the poet's
voice, and it is only gradually, as we "let our eyes close,"
that we begin to listen to this voice with special care, to
become extremely sensitive to its nuances. Malebranche said
that attention is the natural prayer of the soul. In her
best poems, I think, Laura Riding coaxes us into a state of
rapt listening, *into* a voice to which we give our complete
attention, so that we, as readers, become participants in the
unfolding of the poem. The voice is not so much speaking
out loud as thinking, following the complex process of
thought, and in such a way that it is almost immediately
internalized by us. Few poets have ever been able to manipulate abstractions so persuasively. Having been stripped
of ornament, reduced to their bare essentials, the poems

emerge as a kind of rhetoric, a system of pure argument that works in the manner of music, generating an interaction of themes and counter-themes, and giving the same formal pleasure that music gives.

> And talk in talk like time in time vanishes.
> Ringing changes on dumb supposition,
> Conversation succeeds conversation,
> Until there's nothing left to talk about
> Except truth, the perennial monologue,
> And no talker to dispute it but itself.

(from "The Talking World")

These strengths, however, can also be weaknesses. For in order to sustain the high degree of intellectual precision necessary to the success of the poems, Laura Riding has been forced to engage in a kind of poetic brinkmanship, and she has often lost more than she has won. Eventually, we come to realize that the reasons for her break with poetry are implicit in the poems themselves. No matter how much we might admire her work, we sense that there is something missing in it, that it is not really capable of expressing the full range of experience it claims to be expressing. The source of this lack, paradoxically, lies in her conception of language, which in many ways is at odds with the very idea of poetry:

> Come, words, away from mouths,
> Away from tongues in mouths
> And reckless hearts in tongues
> And mouths in cautious heads —

> Come, words, away to where
> The meaning is not thickened
> With the voice's fretting substance . . .

(from "Come, Words, Away")

This is a self-defeating desire. If anything, poetry is precisely that way of using language which forces words to remain *in* the mouth, the way by which we can most fully experience and understand "the voice's fretting substance." There is something too glacial in Laura Riding's approach to gain our sympathy. If the truth in language she is seeking is a human truth, it would seem to be contradictory to want this truth at the expense of what is human. But in trying to deny speech its physical properties — in refusing to acknowledge that speech is an imperfect tool of imperfect creatures — this seems to be exactly what she is doing.

In the 1938 preface to the *Collected Poems*, at the moment of her most passionate adherence to poetry, we can see this desire for transcendence as the motivating force behind her work. "I am going to give you," she writes, "poems written for all the reasons of poetry — poems which are also a record of how, by gradual integration of the reasons of poetry, existence in poetry becomes more real than existence in time — more real because more good, more good because more true." Thirty years later, she uses almost the same terms to justify her equally passionate opposition to poetry: "To a poet the mere making of a poem can seem to solve the problem of truth . . . But only a problem of art is solved in poetry. Art, whose honesty must work through artifice, cannot avoid cheating truth. Poetic art cheats truth to further and finer degrees than art of any other kind because the spoken word is its exclusive medium . . . ."

For all their loftiness and intensity, these statements remain curiously vague. For the truth that is referred to is never really defined, except as something beyond time, beyond art, beyond the senses. Such talk seems to set us afloat in a vast realm of Platonic idealism, and it is difficult for us to know where we are. At the same time, we are unconvinced. Neither statement is very believable to us as a statement about poetry, because, at heart, neither one *is* about poetry. Laura Riding is clearly interested in problems that extend beyond the scope of poetry, and by dwelling on these problems *as if* they were poetry's exclusive concerns, she only confuses the issue. She did not renounce poetry because of any objective inadequacy in poetry itself — for it is no more or less adequate than any other human activity — but because poetry as she conceived of it was no longer capable of saying what she wanted to say. She now feels that she had "reached poetry's limit." But what really happened, it would seem, is that she had reached her own limit in poetry.

It is appropriate, then, that her work since 1938 has been largely devoted to a more general investigation of language, and when we come to *The Telling* we find a deeper discussion of many of the same questions she had tried to formulate in her poetry. The book, which fits into no established literary category, is positively Talmudic in structure. "The Telling" itself is a short text of less than fifty pages, divided into numbered paragraphs, originally written for an issue of the magazine *Chelsea* in 1967. To this "core-text" which is written in a dense, highly abstract prose almost totally devoid of outside references, she has added a series of commentaries, commentaries on commentaries, notes, and addenda, which flesh out many of the earlier conclusions and treat of various literary, political, and philosophical matters. It is an astonishing display of a consciousness confronting and examining itself. Based on the idea that "the human utmost is marked out in a linguistic utmost," she pursues an ideal of "humanly perfect word-use" (as opposed to "artistically perfect word-use"), by which she aims to uncover the essential nature of being. Again, or rather still, she is straining toward absolutes, toward an unshakable and unified vision of the world: ". . . the nature of our being is not to be known as we know the weather, which is by the sense of the momentary. Weather is all change, while our being, in its human nature, is all constancy . . . it is to be known only by the sense of the constant." Although Laura (Riding) Jackson has put her former poet self in parentheses, she looks upon *The Telling* as the successful continuation of her efforts as a poet: "To speak as I speak in it, say such things as I say in it, was part of my hope as a poet."

The first paragraph of *The Telling* sets forth the substance of the problem that she confronts in the rest of the book:

> There is something to be told about us for the telling of which we all wait. In our unwilling ignorance we hurry to listen to stories of old human life, new human life, fancied human life, avid of something to while away the time of unanswered curiosity. We know we are explainable, and not explained. Many of the lesser things concerning us have been told but the greater things have not been told; and nothing can fill their

> place. Whatever we learn of what is not ourselves, but
> ours to know, being of our universal world, will
> likewise leave the emptiness an emptiness. Until the
> missing story of ourselves is told, nothing besides told
> can suffice us: we shall go on quietly craving it.

What immediately strikes us here is the brilliance of the
writing itself. The quiet urgency and strong, cadenced
phrasing entice us to go on listening. It seems that we
are about to be told something radically different from
anything we have ever been told before, and of such fundamental importance that it would be in our best interests
to pay careful attention to what follows. "We know we are
explainable, and not explained." In the subsequent paragraphs we are shown why the various human disciplines
— science, religion, philosophy, history, poetry — have not
and cannot explain us. Suddenly, everything has been swept
aside; the way seems to have been cleared for a totally
fresh approach to things. And yet, when she reaches the
point of offering her own explanations, we are once again
presented with the mysterious and unbelievable Platonism
we had encountered before. It seems, finally, as if she were
rejecting the myth-making tendencies of previous thought
only in order to present another myth of her own devising
— a myth of memory, a faith in the capacity of human
beings to remember a time of wholeness that preceded the
existence of individual selves. "May our Manyness become
All-embracing. May we see in one another the All that
was once All-One re-become One." And elsewhere: "Yes,
I think we remember our creation! — have the memory
of it in us, to know. Through the memory of it we apprehend
that there was a Before-time of being from which being

passed into what would be us." The problem is not that
we doubt this belief of hers. We feel, in fact, that she is
trying to report back to us about a genuine mystical experience; what is hard for us to accept is that she assumes
this experience to be accessible to everyone. Perhaps it is.
But we have no way of knowing — and would have no way
of proving it even if we did. Laura (Riding) Jackson speaks
of this purely personal experience in rigorous and objective
terms, and as a result mingles two kinds of incompatible
discourse. Her private perceptions have been projected
on to the world at large, so that when she looks out on that
world she thinks she sees a confirmation of her findings.
But there is no distinction made between what is asserted
as fact and what is verifiable as fact. As a consequence,
there is no common ground established with us, and we
find no place where we would want to stand with her in
her beliefs.

In spite of this, however, it would be wrong simply to
dismiss the book. If *The Telling* ultimately fails to carry out
its promises, it is still valuable to us for the exceptional
quality of its prose and the innovations of its form. The
sheer immensity of its ambitions makes it an exciting work,
even when it is most irritating. More importantly, it is
crucial to us for what it reveals — retroactively — about
Laura Riding's earlier work as a poet. For, in the end, it is
as a poet that she will be read and remembered. Whatever
objections we might want to raise about her approach to
poetry in general, it would be difficult not to recognize her
as a poet of importance. We need not be in agreement with
her to admire her.

Roses are buds, and beautiful,
One petal leaning toward adventure.
Roses are full, all petals forward,
Beauty and power indistinguishable.
Roses are blown, startled with life,
Death young in their faces.
Then comes the halt, and recumbence, and failing.
But none says, "A rose is dead."
But men die: it is said, it is seen.
For a man is a long, late adventure;
His budding is a purpose,
His fullness more purpose,
His blowing a renewal,
His death a cramped spilling
Of rash measure and miles.
To the roses no tears:
Which flee before the race is called.
And to man no mercy but his will:
That he has had his will, and is done.
The mercy of truth — it is to be truth.

(from "The Last Covenant")

In one of the supplementary chapters of *The Telling*, "Extracts From Communications," she speaks of the relationship between the writer and his work in a way that seems to express her aspirations as a poet. "If what you write is true, it will not be so because of what you are as a writer but because of what you are as a being. There can be no literary equivalent to truth. If, in writing, truth is the quality of what is said, told, this is not a literary achievement: it is a simple human achievement." This is not very far from the spirit of Ben Jonson's assertion that only a good man is capable of writing a good poem. It is an idea that stands at one extreme of our literary consciousness, and it places poetry within an essentially moral framework. As a poet, Laura Riding followed this principle until she reached what she felt to be "a crisis-point at which division between craft and creed reveals itself to be absolute." In the making of poems, she concluded, the demands of art would always outweigh the demands of truth.

Beauty and truth. It is the old question, come back to haunt us. Laura Riding sacrificed her poetic career in a choice between the two. But whether she has really answered the question, as she appears to think she has, is open to debate. What we do have are the poems she left behind her, and it is not surprising, perhaps, that we are drawn to them most of all for their beauty. We cannot call Laura Riding a neglected poet, since she was the cause of her own neglect. But after more than thirty years of absence, these poems strike us with all the force of a rediscovery.

1975

The Death of Sir Walter Raleigh

The Tower is stone and the solitude of stone. It is the skull of a man around the body of a man—and its quick is thought. But no thought will ever reach the other side of the wall. And the wall will not crumble, even against the hammer of a man's eye. For the eyes are blind, and if they see, it is only because they have learned to see where no light is. There is nothing here but thought, and there is nothing. The man is a stone that breathes, and he will die. The only thing that waits for him is death.

The subject is therefore life and death. And the subject is death. Whether the man who lives will have truly lived until the moment of his death, or whether death is no more than the moment at which life stops. This is an argument of act, and therefore an act which rebuts the argument of any word. For we will never manage to say what we want to say, and whatever is said will be said in the knowledge of this failure. All this is speculation.

One thing is sure: this man will die. The Tower is impervious, and the depth of stone has no limit. But thought nevertheless determines its own boundaries, and the man who thinks can now and then surpass himself, even when there is nowhere to go. He can reduce himself to a stone, or he can write the history of the world. Where no possibility exists, everything becomes possible again.

Therefore Raleigh. Or life lived as a suicide pact with oneself. And whether or not there is an art—if one can call it art—of living. Take everything away from a man, and this man will continue to exist. If he has been able to live, he will be able to die. And when there is nothing left, he will know how to face the wall.

It is death. And we say "death," as if we meant to say the thing we cannot know. And yet we know, and we know that we know. For we hold this knowledge to be irrefutable. It is a question for which no answer comes, and it will lead us to many questions that in their turn will lead us back to the thing we cannot know. We may well ask, then, what we will ask. For the subject is not only life and death. It is death, and it is life.

At each moment there is the possibility of what is not. And from each thought, an opposite thought is born. From death, he will see an image of life. And from one place, there will be the boon of another place. America. And at the limit of thought, where the new world nullifies the old, a place is invented to take the place of death. He has already touched its shores, and its image will haunt him to the very end. It is Paradise, it is the Garden before the Fall, and it gives birth to a thought that ranges farther than the grasp of any man. And this man will die. And not only will he die—he will be murdered. An axe will cut off his head.

This is how it begins. And this is how it ends. We all know that we will die. And if there is any truth we live with, it is that we die. But we may well ask the question of how and when, and we may well begin to ask ourselves if chance is not the only god. The Christian says not, and the suicide says not. Each of them says he can choose, and each of them does choose, by faith, or the lack of it. But

what of the man who neither believes nor does not believe?
He will throw himself into life, live life to the fullest of
life, and then come to his end. For death is a very wall,
and beyond this wall no one can pass. We will not ask,
therefore, whether or not one can choose. One can choose
and one cannot. It depends on whom and on why. To
begin, then, we must find a place where we are alone and
nevertheless together, that is to say, the place where we
end. There is the wall, and there is the truth we confront.
The question is: at what moment does one begin to see
the wall?

  Consider the facts. Thirteen years in the Tower, and
then the final voyage to the West. Whether or not he was
guilty (and he was not) has no bearing on the facts. Thirteen years in the Tower, and a man will begin to learn
what solitude is. He will learn that he is nothing more
than a body, and he will learn that he is nothing more
than a mind, and he will learn that he is nothing. He can
breathe, he can walk, he can speak, he can read, he can
write, he can sleep. He can count the stones. He can be
a stone that breathes, or he can write the history of the
world. But at each moment he is the captive of others,
and his will is no longer his own. Only his thoughts belong
to him, and he is as alone with them as he is alone with
the shadow he has become. But he lives. And not only
does he live—he lives to the fullest that his confines will
permit. And beyond them. For an image of death will
nevertheless goad him into finding life. And yet, nothing
has changed. For the only thing that waits for him is death.

  But this is not all. And the facts must be considered still
further. For the day comes when he is allowed to leave

the Tower. He has been freed, but he is nevertheless not free. A full pardon will be granted only on the condition that he accomplish something that is flatly impossible to accomplish. Already the victim of the basest political intrigue, the butt of justice gone berserk, he will have his last fling and create his most magnificent failure as a sadistic entertainment for his captors. Once called the Fox, he is now like a mouse in the jaws of a cat. The King instructs him: go where the Spanish have rightful claim, rob them of their gold, and do not antagonize them or incite them to retaliation. Any other man would have laughed. Accused of having conspired with the Spanish thirteen years ago and put into the Tower as a result, he is now told to do a thing in such terms that they invalidate the very charge for which he was found guilty in the first place. But he does not laugh.

One must assume that he knew what he was doing. Either he thought that he could do what he set out to do, or the lure of the new world was so strong that he simply could not resist. In any case, it hardly matters now. Everything that could go wrong for him did go wrong, and from the very beginning the voyage was a disaster. After thirteen years of solitude, it is not easy to return to the world of men, and even less so when one is old. And he is an old man now, more than sixty, and the prison reveries in which he had seen his thoughts turn into the most glorious deeds now turn to dust before his eyes. The crew rebels against him, no gold can be found, the Spanish are hostile. Worst of all: his son is killed.

Take everything away from a man, and that man will continue to exist. But the everything of one man is not that of another, and even the strongest of men will have within himself a place of supreme vulnerability. For Raleigh, this place is occupied by his son, who is at once the emblem of his greatest strength and the seed of his undoing. To all things outward, the boy will bring doom, and though he is a child of love, he remains the living proof of lust—the wild heat of a man willing to risk everything to answer the call of his body. But this lust is nevertheless love, and such a love as seldom speaks more purely of a man's worth. For one does not cavort with a lady of the Queen unless one is ready to destroy one's position, one's honor, one's name. These women are the Queen's person, and no man, not even the most favored man, can approach or possess without royal consent. And yet, he shows no signs of contrition; he makes good on all he has done. For disgrace need not bring shame. He loves the woman, he will continue to love her, she will become the very substance of his life. And in this first, prophetic exile, his son is born.

The boy grows. And he grows wild. The father can do no more than dote and fret, prescribe warnings, be warmed by the fire of his flesh and blood. He writes an extraordinary poem of admonition to the boy, at once an ode to chance and a raging against the inevitable, telling him that if he does not mend his ways he will wind up at the end of a rope, and the boy sallies off to Paris with Ben Jonson on a colossal binge. There is nothing the father can do. It is all a question of waiting. When he is at last allowed to leave the Tower, he takes the boy along with him. He needs the comfort of his son, and he needs to feel himself the father. But the boy is murdered in the jungle. Not only does he come to the end his father had predicted for him, but the father himself has become the unwitting executioner of his own son.

And the death of the son is the death of the father. For this man will die. The journey has failed, the thought of grace does not even enter his head. England means the axe—and the gloating triumph of the King. The very wall has been reached. And yet, he goes back. To a place where the only thing that waits for him is death. He goes back when everything tells him to run for life—or to die by his own hand. For if nothing else, one can always choose one's moment. But he goes back. And the question therefore is: why cross an entire ocean only to keep an appointment with death?

We may well speak of madness, as others have. Or we may well speak of courage. But it hardly matters what we speak. For it is here that words begin to fail. And if we ever manage to say what we want to say, it will nevertheless be said in the knowledge of this failure. All this, therefore, is speculation.

If there is such a thing as an art of living, then the man who lives life as an art will have a sense of his own beginning and his own end. And beyond that, he will know that his end is in his beginning, and that each breath he draws can only bring him nearer to that end. He will live, but he will also die. For no work remains unfinished, even the one that has been abandoned.

Most men abandon their lives. They live until they do not live, and we call this death. For death is a very wall. A man dies, and therefore he no longer lives. But this does not mean it is death. For death is only in the seeing

of death, and in the living of death. And we may truly say
that only the man who lives his life to the fullest of life
will be able to see his own death. And we may truly say
what we will say. For it is here that words begin to fail.

Each man approaches the wall. One man turns his back,
and in the end he is struck from behind. Another goes
blind at the very thought of it and spends his life groping
ahead in fear. And another sees it from the very beginning, and though his fear is no less, he will teach himself
to face it, and go through life with open eyes. Every act
will count, even to the last act, because nothing will matter
to him anymore. He will live because he is able to die.
And he will touch the very wall.

Therefore Raleigh. Or the art of living as the art of
death. Therefore England—and therefore the axe. For
the subject is not only life and death. It is death. And it
is life. And we may truly say what we will say.

                                                      1975

From Cakes to Stones

A note on Beckett's French

Mercier and Camier was the first of Samuel Beckett's novels to be written in French. Completed in 1946, and withheld from publication until 1970, it is also the last of his longer works to have been translated into English. Such a long delay would seem to indicate that Beckett is not overly fond of the work. Had he not been given the Nobel prize in 1969, in fact, it seems likely that *Mercier and Camier* would not have been published at all. This reluctance on Beckett's part is somewhat puzzling, for if *Mercier and Camier* is clearly a transitional work, at once harking back to *Murphy* and *Watt* and looking forward to the masterpieces of the early fifties, it is nevertheless a brilliant work, with its own particular strengths and charms, unduplicated in any of Beckett's six other novels. Even at his not quite best, Beckett remains Beckett, and reading him is like reading no one else.

Mercier and Camier are two men of indeterminate middle age who decide to leave everything behind them and set off on a journey. Like Flaubert's Bouvard and Pécuchet, like Laurel and Hardy, like the other "pseudo couples" in Beckett's work, they are not so much separate characters as two elements of a tandem reality, and neither one could exist without the other. The purpose of their journey is never stated, nor is their destination ever made clear. "They had consulted together at length, before embarking on this journey, weighing with all the calm at their command what benefits they might hope from it, what ills apprehend, maintaining turn about the dark side and the rosy. The only certitude they gained from these debates was that of not lightly launching out, into the unknown." Beckett, the master of the comma, manages in these few sentences to cancel out any possibility of a goal. Quite simply, Mercier and Camier agree to meet, they meet (after painful confusion), and set off. That they never really get anywhere, only twice, in fact, cross the town limits, in no way impedes the progress of the book. For the book is not about what Mercier and Camier do; it is about what they are.

Nothing happens. Or, more precisely, what happens is what does not happen. Armed with the vaudeville props of umbrella, sack, and raincoat, the two heroes meander through the town and the surrounding countryside, encountering various objects and personages: they pause frequently and at length in an assortment of bars and public places; they consort with a warm-hearted prostitute named Helen; they kill a policeman; they gradually lose their few possessions and drift apart. These are the outward events, all precisely told, with wit, elegance, and pathos, and interspersed with some beautiful descriptive passages ("The sea is not far, just visible beyond the valleys disappearing eastward, pale plinth as pale as the pale wall of sky"). But the real substance of the book lies in the conversations between Mercier and Camier:

> If we have nothing to say, said Camier, let us say nothing.
> We have things to say, said Mercier.
> Then why can't we say them? said Camier.
> We can't, said Mercier.
> Then let us be silent, said Camier.
> But we try, said Mercier.

In a celebrated passage of *Talking about Dante*, Mandelstam wrote: "The *Inferno* and especially the *Purgatorio* glorify the human gait, the measure and rhythm of walking, the foot and its shape . . . In Dante philosophy and poetry are forever on the move, forever on their feet. Even standing still is a variety of accumulated motion; making a place for people to stand and talk takes as much trouble as scaling an Alp." Beckett, who is one of the finest readers of Dante, has learned these lessons with utter thoroughness. Almost uncannily, the prose of *Mercier and Camier* moves along at a walking pace, and after a while one begins to have the distinct impression that somewhere, buried deep within the words, a silent metronome is beating out the rhythms of Mercier and Camier's perambulations. The pauses, the hiatuses, the sudden shifts of conversation and description do not break this rhythm, but rather take place under its influence (which has already been firmly established), so that their effect is not one of disruption but of counter-point and fulfillment. A mysterious stillness seems to envelop each sentence in the book, a kind of gravity, or calm, so that between each sentence the reader feels the passing of time, the footsteps that continue to move, even when nothing is said. "Sitting at the bar they discoursed of this and that, brokenly, as was their custom. They spoke, fell silent, listened to each other, stopped listening, each as he fancied or as bidden from within."

This notion of time, of course, is directly related to the notion of *timing*, and it seems no accident that *Mercier and Camier* immediately precedes *Waiting for Godot* in Beckett's oeuvre. In some sense, it can be seen as a warm-up for the play. The music-hall banter, which was perfected in the dramatic works, is already present in the novel:

What will it be? said the barman.
When we need you we'll tell you, said Camier.
What will it be? said the barman.
The same as before, said Mercier.
You haven't been served, said the barman.
The same as this gentleman, said Mercier.
The barman looked at Camier's empty glass.
I forget what it was, he said.
I too, said Camier.
I never knew, said Mercier.

But whereas *Waiting for Godot* is sustained by the implicit drama of Godot's absence — an absence that commands the scene as powerfully as any presence — *Mercier and Camier* progresses in a void. From one moment to the next, it is impossible to foresee what will happen. The action, which is not buoyed by any tension or intrigue, seems to take place against a background of nearly total silence, and whatever is said is said at the very moment there is nothing left to say. Rain dominates the book, from the first paragraph to the last sentence ("And in the dark he could hear better too, he could hear the sounds the long day had kept from him, human murmurs for example, and the rain on the water") — an endless Irish rain, which is accorded the status of a metaphysical idea, and which creates an atmosphere that hovers between boredom and anguish, between bitterness and jocularity. As in the play, tears are shed, but more from a knowledge of the futility of tears than from any need to purge oneself of grief. Likewise, laughter is merely what happens when tears have been spent. All goes on, slowly waning in the hush of time, and unlike Vladimir and Estragon, Mercier and Camier must endure without any hope of redemption.

The key word in all this, I feel, is dispossession. Beckett, who begins with little, ends with even less. The movement in each of his works is toward a kind of unburdening, by which he leads us to the limits of experience — to a place where aesthetic and moral judgments become inseparable. This is the itinerary of the characters in his books, and it has also been his own progress as a writer. From the lush, convoluted, and jaunty prose of *More Pricks than Kicks* (1934) to the desolate spareness of *The Lost Ones* (1970), he has gradually cut closer and closer to the bone. His decision thirty years ago to write in French was undoubtedly the crucial event in this progress. This was an almost inconceivable act. But again, Beckett is not like other writers. Before truly coming into his own, he had to leave behind what came most easily to him, struggle against his own facility as a stylist. Beyond Dickens and Joyce, there is perhaps no English writer of the past hundred years who has equalled Beckett's early prose for vigor and intelligence; the language of *Murphy*, for example, is so packed that the novel has the density of a short lyric poem. By switching to French (a language, as Beckett has remarked, that "has no style"), he willingly began all over again. *Mercier and Camier* stands at the very beginning of this new life, and it is interesting to note that in this English translation Beckett has cut out nearly a fifth of the original text. Phrases, sentences, entire passages have been discarded, and what we have been given is really an editing job as well as a translation. This tampering, however, is not difficult to understand. Too many echoes, too many ornate and clever flourishes from the past remain, and though a considerable amount of superb

material has been lost, Beckett apparently did not think it
good enough to keep.

In spite of this, or perhaps because of this, *Mercier and
Camier* comes close to being a flawless work. As with all of
Beckett's self-translations, this version is not so much a
literal translation of the original as a re-creation, a "repatria-
tion" of the book into English. However stripped his style
in French may be, there is always a little extra something
added to the English renderings, some slight twist of diction
or nuance, some unexpected word falling at just the right
moment, that reminds us that English is nevertheless
Beckett's home.

> George, said Camier, five sandwiches, four wrapped
> and one on the side. You see, he said, turning gra-
> ciously to Mr Conaire, I think of everything. For the
> one I eat here will give me the strength to get back
> with the four others.
>
> Sophistry, said Mr Conaire. You set off with your
> five, wrapped, feel faint, open up, take one out, eat,
> recuperate, push on with the others.
>
> For all response Camier began to eat.
>
> You'll spoil him, said Mr Conaire. Yesterday cakes,
> today sandwiches, tomorrow crusts, and Thursday
> stones.
>
> Mustard, said Camier.

There is a crispness to this that outdoes the French.
"Sophistry" for "raisonnement du clerc," "crusts" for "pain
sec," and the assonance with 'mustard' in the next sentence give a neatness and economy to the exchange that
is even more satisfying than the original. Everything has
been pared down to a minimum; not a syllable is out
of place.

We move from cakes to stones, and from page to page
Beckett builds a world out of almost nothing. Mercier and
Camier set out on a journey and do not go anywhere. But
at each step of the way, we want to be exactly where they
are. How Beckett manages this is something of a mystery.
But as in all his work, less is more.

1975

The Poetry of Exile

A Jew, born in Romania, who wrote in German and lived in France. Victim of the Second World War, survivor of the death camps, suicide before he was fifty. Paul Celan was a poet of exile, an outsider even to the language of his own poems, and if his life was exemplary in its pain, a paradigm of the destruction and dislocation of midcentury Europe, his poetry is defiantly idiosyncratic, always and absolutely his own. In Germany, he is considered the equal of Rilke and Trakl, the heir to Hölderlin's metaphysical lyricism, and elsewhere his work is held in similar esteem, prompting statements such as George Steiner's recent remark that Celan is "almost certainly the major European poet of the period after 1945." At the same time, Celan is an exceedingly difficult poet, both dense and obscure. He demands so much of a reader, and in his later work his utterances are so gnomic, that it is nearly impossible to make full sense of him, even after many readings. Fiercely intelligent, propelled by a dizzying linguistic force, Celan's poems seem to explode on the page, and encountering them for the first time is a memorable event. It is to feel the same strangeness and excitement that one feels in discovering the work of Hopkins, or Emily Dickinson.

Czernovitz, Bukovina, where Celan was born as Paul Anczel in 1920, was a multilingual area that had once been part of the Habsburg Empire. In 1940, after the Hitler-Stalin pact, it was annexed by the Soviet Union, in the following year occupied by Nazi troops, and in 1943 retaken by the Russians. Celan's parents were deported to a concentration camp in 1942 and did not return; Celan, who managed to escape, was put in a labor camp until December 1943. In 1945 he went to Bucharest, where he worked as a translator and publisher's reader, then moved to Vienna in 1947, and finally, in 1948, settled permanently in Paris, where he married and became a teacher of German literature at the Ecole Normale Supérieure. His output comprises seven books of poetry and translations of more than two dozen foreign poets, including Mandelstam, Ungaretti, Pessoa, Rimbaud, Valéry, Char, du Bouchet, and Dupin.

Celan came to poetry rather late, and his first poems were not published until he was almost thirty. All his work, therefore, was written after the Holocaust, and his poems are everywhere informed by its memory. The unspeakable yields a poetry that continually threatens to overwhelm the limits of what can be spoken. For Celan forgot nothing, forgave nothing. The death of his parents and his own experiences during the war are recurrent and obsessive themes that run through all his work.

> With names, watered
> by every exile.
> With names and seeds,
> with names dipped
> into all
> the calyxes that are full of your
> regal blood, man, — into all
> the calyxes of the great
> ghetto-rose, from which

you look at us, immortal with so many
deaths died on morning errands.

> (from "Crowned Out . . .", 1963,
> trans. by Michael Hamburger)

Even after the war, Celan's life remained an unstable one.
He suffered acutely from feelings of persecution, which led
to repeated breakdowns in his later years — and eventually
to his suicide in 1970, when he drowned himself in the
Seine. An incessant writer who produced hundreds of
poems during his relatively short writing life, Celan poured
all his grief and anger into his work. There is no poetry
more furious than his, no poetry so purely inspired by
bitterness. Celan never stopped confronting the dragon of
the past, and in the end it swallowed him up.

"Todesfugue" (Death Fugue) is not Celan's best poem, but
it is unquestionably his most famous poem — the work that
made his reputation. Coming as it did in the late forties,
only a few years after the end of the war — and in striking
contrast to Adorno's rather fatuous remark about the "bar-
barity" of writing poems after Auschwitz — "Todesfugue"
had a considerable impact among German readers, both
for its direct mention of the concentration camps and for
the terrible beauty of its form. The poem is literally a
fugue composed of words, and its pounding, rhythmical
repetitions and variations mark off a terrain no less circum-
scribed, no less closed in on itself than a prison surrounded
by barbed wire. Covering slightly less than two pages, it
begins and ends with the following stanzas:

Black milk of dawn we drink it at dusk
we drink it at noon and at daybreak we drink it at night
we drink and drink
we are digging a grave in the air there's room for us all
A man lives in the house he plays with the serpents he
   writes
he writes when it darkens to Germany your golden hair
   Margarete
he writes it and steps outside and the stars all aglisten he
   whistles for his hounds
he whistles for his Jews he has them dig a grave in the
   earth
he commands us to play for the dance

                          *

Black milk of dawn we drink you at night
we drink you at noon death is a master from Germany
we drink you at dusk and at daybreak we drink and we
   drink you
death is a master from Germany his eye is blue
he shoots you with bullets of lead his aim is true
a man lives in the house your golden hair Margarete
he sets his hounds on us he gives us a grave in the air
he plays with the serpents and dreams death is a master
   from Germany
your golden hair Margarete
your ashen hair Shulamite

                    (trans. by Joachim Neugroschel)

In spite of the poem's great control and the formal
sublimation of an impossibly emotional theme, "Todesfugue" is one of Celan's most explicit works. In the sixties,

he even turned against it, refusing permission to have it
reprinted in more anthologies because he felt that his
poetry had progressed to a stage where "Todesfugue" was
too obvious and superficially realistic. With this in mind,
however, one does discover in this poem elements common
to much of Celan's work: the taut energy of the language,
the objectification of private anguish, the unusual distancing effected between feeling and image. As Celan
himself expressed it in an early commentary on his poems:
"What matters for this language . . . is precision. It does
not transfigure, does not 'poetize', it names and composes,
it tries to measure out the sphere of the given and the
possible."

This notion of the possible is central to Celan. It is the
way by which one can begin to enter his conception of the
poem, his vision of reality. For the seeming paradox of
another of his statements — "Reality is not. It must be
searched for and won" — can lead to confusion unless one
has already understood the aspiration for the real that
informs Celan's poetry. Celan is not advocating a retreat
into subjectivity or the construction of an imaginary
universe. Rather, he is staking out the distance over which
the poem must travel and defining the ambiguity of a world
in which all the values have been subverted.

> Speak —
> But keep yes and no unsplit,
> And give your say this meaning:
> give it the shade.

Give it shade enough,
give it as much
as you know has been dealt out between
midday and midday and midnight.

Look around:
look how it all leaps alive —
where death is! Alive!
He speaks truly who speaks the shade.

(from "Speak, You Also," trans. by Michael Hamburger)

In a public address delivered in the city of Bremen in
1958 after being awarded an important literary prize, Celan
spoke of language as the one thing that had remained intact
for him after the war, even though it had to pass through
"the thousand darknesses of death-bringing speech." "In
this language," Celan said — and by this he meant German,
the language of the Nazis and the language of his poems
— "I have tried to write poetry, in order to acquire a
perspective of reality for myself." He then compared the
poem to a message in a bottle — thrown out to sea in the
hope that it will one day wash up to land, "perhaps on the
shore of the heart." "Poems," he continued, "even in this
sense are under way: they are heading toward something.
Toward what? Toward some open place that can be inhabited, toward a thou which can be addressed, perhaps
toward a reality which can be addressed."

The poem, then, is not a transcription of an already
known world, but a process of discovery, and the act of
writing for Celan is one that demands personal risks. Celan
did not write solely in order to express himself, but to orient

himself within his own life and take his stand in the world, and it is this feeling of necessity that communicates itself to a reader. These poems are more than literary artifacts. They are a means of staying alive.

In a 1946 essay on Van Gogh, Meyer Schapiro refers to the notion of realism in a way that could also apply to Celan. "I do not mean realism in the repugnant, narrow sense that it has acquired today," Professor Schapiro writes, ". . . but rather the sentiment that external reality is an object of strong desire or need, as a possession and potential means of fulfillment of the striving human being, and is therefore the necessary ground of art." Then, quoting a phrase from one of Van Gogh's letters – "I'm terrified of getting away from the possible. . ." — he observes: "Struggling against the perspective that diminishes an individual object before his eyes, he renders it larger than life. The loading of the pigment is in part a reflex of this attitude, a frantic effort to preserve in the image of things their tangible matter and to create something equally solid and concrete on the canvas."

Celan, whose life and attitude toward his art closely parallel Van Gogh's, used language in a way that is not unlike the way Van Gogh used paints, and their work is surprisingly similar in spirit.* Neither Van Gogh's stroke nor Celan's syntax is strictly representational, for in the eyes of each the "objective" world is interlocked with his perception of it. There is no reality that can be posited without

---

*Celan makes reference to Van Gogh in several of his poems, and the kinship between the poet and painter is indeed quite strong: both began as artists in their late twenties after having lived through experiences that marked them deeply for the rest of their lives; both produced work prolifically, at a furious pace, as if depending on the work for their very survival; both underwent debilitating mental crises that led to confinement; both committed suicide, foreigners in France.

the simultaneous effort to penetrate it, and the work of art
as an ongoing process bears witness to this desire. Just as
Van Gogh's painted objects acquire a concreteness "as real
as reality," Celan handles words as if they had the density
of objects, and he endows them with a substantiality that
enables them to become a part of the world, his world —
and not simply its mirror.

Celan's poems resist straightforward exegesis. They are
not linear progressions, moving from word to word, from
point A to point B. Rather, they present themselves to a
reader as intricate networks of semantic densities. Inter-
lingual puns, oblique personal references, intentional mis-
quotations, bizarre neologisms: these are the sinews that
bind Celan's poems together. It is not possible to keep up
with him, to follow his drift at every step along the way. One
is guided more by a sense of tone and intention than by
textual scrutiny. Celan does not speak explicitly, but he
never fails to make himself clear. There is nothing random
in his work, no gratuitous elements to obscure the perception of the poem. One reads with one's skin, as if by osmosis,
unconsciously absorbing nuances, overtones, syntactical
twists, which in themselves are as much the meaning of
poem as its analytic content. Celan's method of composition
is not unlike that of Joyce in *Finnegans Wake*. But if Joyce's
art was one of accumulation and expansion — a spiral
whirling into infinity — Celan's poetry is continually col-
lapsing into itself, negating its very premises, again and
again arriving at zero. We are in the world of the absurd, but
we have been led there by a mind that refuses to acquiesce
to it.

Consider the following poem, "Largo," one of Celan's later

poems — and a typical example of the difficulty a reader
faces in tackling Celan.* In Michael Hamburger's translation it reads:

> You of the same mind, moor-wandering near one:
>
> more-than-
> death-
> sized we lie
> together, autumn
> crocuses, the timeless, teems
> under our breathing eyelids,
> the pair of blackbirds hangs
> beside us, under
> our whitely drifting
> companions up there, our
>
> meta-
> stases.

The German text, however, reveals things that necessarily
elude the grasp of translation:

> Gleichsinnige du, heidegängerisch Nahe:
>
> über-
> sterbens-
> gross liegen
> wir beieinander, die Zeit-
> lose wimmelt
> dir unter den atmenden Lidern,

---

*I am grateful to Katharine Washburn, a scrupulous reader and translator
of Celan, for help in deciphering the German text of this poem and
suggesting possible references.

Das Amselpaar hängt
neben uns, unter
unsern gemeinsam droben mit-
ziehenden weissen

Meta-
stasen.

In the first line, *heidegängerisch* is an inescapable allusion to Heidegger — whose thinking was in many ways close to Celan's, but who, as a pro-Nazi, stood on the side of the murderers. Celan visited Heidegger in the sixties, and although it is not known what they said to each other, one can assume that they discussed Heidegger's position during the war. The reference to Heidegger in the poem is underscored by the use of some of the central words from his philosophical writings: *Nahe, Zeit,* etc. This is Celan's way: he does not mention anything directly, but weaves his meanings into the fabric of the language, creating a space for the invisible, in the same way that thought accompanies us as we move through a landscape.

Further along, in the third stanza, there are the two blackbirds (stock figures in fairy tales, who speak in riddles and bring bad tidings). In the German one reads *Amsel* — which echoes the sound of Celan's own name, Anczel. At the same time, there is an evocation of Günter Grass's novel, *Dog Years,* which chronicles the love-hate relationship between A Jew and a Nazi during the war. The Jewish character in the story is named Amsel, and throughout the book — to quote George Steiner again — "there is a deadly pastiche of the metaphysical jargon of Heidegger."

Toward the end of the poem, the presence of "our whitely

drifting / companions up there" is a reference to the Jewish victims of the Holocaust: the smoke of the bodies burned in crematoria. From early poems such as "Todesfugue" ("he gives us a grave in the air") to later poems such as "Largo," the Jewish dead in Celan's work inhabit the air, are the very substance we are condemned to breathe: souls turned into smoke, into dust, into nothing at all — "our / meta- / stases."

Celan's preoccupation with the Holocaust goes beyond mere history, however. It is the primal moment, the first cause and last effect of an entire cosmology. Celan is essentially a religious poet, and although he speaks with the voice of one forsaken by God, he never abandons the struggle to make sense of what has no sense, to come to grips with his own Jewishness. Negation, blasphemy, and irony take the place of devotion; the forms of righteousness are mimicked; Biblical phrases are turned around, subverted, made to speak against themselves. But in so doing, Celan draws nearer to the source of his despair, the absence that lives in the heart of all things. Much has been said about Celan's "negative theology." It is most fully expressed in the opening stanzas of "Psalm":

> No One kneads us anew from earth and clay,
> no one addresses our dust.
> No One.
>
> Laudeamus te, No One.
> For your sake would we
> bloom forth:
> unto
> You.

Nothing
were we, and are we and
will be, all abloom:
this Nothing's-, this
no-man's-rose.

(trans. by Katharine Washburn)

In the last decade of his life, Celan gradually refined his work to a point where he began to enter new and uncharted territory. The long lines and ample breath of the early poems give way to an elliptical, almost panting style in which words are broken up into their component syllables, unorthodox word-clusters are invented, and the reductionist natural vocabulary of the first books is inundated by references to science, technology, and political events. These short, usually untitled poems move along by lightning-quick flashes of intuition, and their message, as Michael Hamburger aptly puts it, "is at once more urgent and more reticent." One feels both a shrinking and an expansion in them, as if, by traveling to the inmost recesses of himself, Celan had somehow vanished, joining with the greater forces beyond him — and at the same time sinking more deeply into his isolation.

Thread-suns
over the gray-black wasteland.
A tree-
high thought
strikes the note of light: there are
still songs to sing beyond
mankind.

(trans. by Joachim Neugroschel)

In poems such as this one, Celan has set the stakes so high that he must surpass himself in order to keep even with himself — and push his life into the void in order to cling to his identity. It is an impossible struggle, doomed from the start to disaster. For poetry cannot save the soul or retrieve a lost world. It simply asserts the given. In the end, it seems, Celan's desolation became too great to be borne, as if, in some sense, the world were no longer there for him. And when nothing was left, there could be no more words.

> You were my death:
> you I could hold
> when all fell away from me.

(trans. by Michael Hamburger)

1975

Ideas and Things

John Ashbery is a poet who speaks to us intimately, from an almost suffocating nearness; we recognize his world as ours, and his language is that of our everyday experience. Yet few poets writing today have such an uncanny ability to undermine our certainties, to articulate so fully the ambiguous zones of our consciousness. We are constantly thrown off guard as we read his work, and because we are lulled by the flatness and familiarity of his tone, our sense of dislocation is all the more troubling. The ordinary becomes strange, and things that a moment ago seemed clear are suddenly cast into doubt. Everything remains in place, and yet nothing is the same.

> The whole is stable within
> Instability, a globe like ours, resting
> On a pedestal of vacuum, a ping-pong ball
> Secure on its jet of water.

Ashbery stands to the side of most recent American poetry, and because of this many critics have seen his work as willfully obscure or abstract. But it is simply that his work is conceived within a different frame of reference from that of most other poets. In general, American poetry continues to be written from the bias of an undaunted empirical faith, and it embodies what can be called a "common sense" view of the world. No matter what the range of possibilities within this scheme — and it is vast — the starting point is the world of things. William Carlos Williams's famous phrase, "no ideas but in things," was not a solitary call for a new kind of poetry but a manifestation of a widespread tendency in twentieth-century American thought and liter-ature. In Ashbery's work, however, the emphasis shifts. Although he, too, begins with the world of perceived objects, perception itself is problematical for him, and he is never able to rely on the empirical certitudes that nearly all our poets seem to take for granted. At times, in fact, it is as if he has set out to reverse the Williams formula.

> What is writing?
> Well, in my case, it's getting down on paper
> Not thoughts, exactly, but ideas, maybe:
> Ideas about thoughts.

Reality for Ashbery is elusive, and things are never what they seem to be. They cannot be separated from one another, isolated into component parts, but overlap, inter-sect, and finally merge into an enormous and constantly changing whole. "All things seem mention of themselves / And the names which stem from them branch out to other referents." Ashbery's manner of dealing with this flux is associative rather than logical, and his pessimism about our ever really being able to know anything results, paradox-ically, in a poetry that is open to everything. "For where a mirage has once been, life must be." Things lead to other things and disappear into each other, and from moment to moment our sense of the whole is altered. Ashbery main-tains coherence in all this possible confusion by keeping an extremely close watch on himself, and his greatest talent, it seems to me, is his utter faithfulness to his own subjectivity.

I know that I braid too much my own
Snapped-off perceptions of things as they come to me.
They are private and always will be.

There is something in this that is reminiscent of the French symbolists of the late nineteenth century. We are made to think of Baudelaire's notion of synesthesia, Rimbaud's systematic derangement of the senses, and an important sentence in a letter written by Mallarmé at the age of twenty-two: "Paint, not the thing, but the effect that it produces." But there are, nevertheless, certain instructive differences between Ashbery and these earlier writers. Whereas the symbolists sought escape from the drabness of the quotidian and strained toward an evocation of the mysterious essences of things by means of a highly distilled language, it is the quotidian itself that Ashbery is after, happiness in the heart of banality, and his language is discursive, rhetorical, and even long-winded, a kind of obsessive talking *around* things, suggesting a reality that refuses to come forth and let itself be known.

Now approaching fifty, Ashbery has become a poet of loss and nostalgia, and in his best work he displays signs of a new maturity and a deepening awareness of his own direction as an artist.

But it is certain that
What is beautiful seems so only in relation to a specific
Life, experienced or not, channeled into some form
Steeped in the nostalgia of a collective past.

The collective past has evaporated in the dispersal of the present. Ashbery laments this lack of any unified vision of the world, and his work is an elegy to this absence. At the deepest level, we can see this in the relativism of his perceptions, in the way common sense is denied and replaced by private sense. Ashbery writes as an outsider, as one cut off from the possibility of a sustained interaction with the world, and no matter how sly or humorous he becomes, the essential feeling in his poems is one of homesickness.

If there is any flaw in this, it is perhaps that Ashbery seems too intent on maintaining this distance between himself and the world. His dealings with reality are essentially passive, almost dandyish, and his poems, in spite of their great richness, often come across as a kind of posing, a standing still rather than a moving toward. It is as if defeat had been declared before the struggle had even begun.

But Ashbery knows where he stands. He makes no claims for himself, and he never presents his poetry as more than it is. The failures of the world are also his failures. This awareness has yielded a style devoid of pretension and a beautiful ease of manner that is rarely less than enchanting. There is no one who writes quite like Ashbery, and the poetic territory he inhabits is very much his own. In the end, it is not the dexterity of his invention that is most admirable about him, but this peerless gift for always and resolutely remaining himself.

                                                                    1975

Book of the Dead

During the past few years, no French writer has received more serious critical attention and praise than Edmond Jabès. Maurice Blanchot, Emmanuel Levinas, and Jean Starobinski have all written extensively and enthusiastically about his work, and Jacques Derrida has remarked, flatly and without self-consciousness, that "in the last ten years nothing has been written in France that does not have its precedent somewhere in the texts of Jabès." Beginning with the first volume of *Le Livre des Questions*, which was published in 1963, and continuing on through the other volumes in the series,* Jabès has created a new and mysterious kind of literary work — as dazzling as it is difficult to define. Neither novel nor poem, neither essay nor play, *The Book of Questions* is a combination of all these forms, a mosaic of fragments, aphorisms, dialogues, songs, and commentaries that endlessly move around the central question of the book: how to speak what cannot be spoken. The question is the Jewish Holocaust, but it is also the question of literature itself. By a startling leap of the imagination, Jabès treats them as one and the same:

> I talked to you about the difficulty of being Jewish, which is the same as the difficulty of writing. For Judaism and writing are but the same waiting, the same hope, the same wearing out.

*Le Livre de Yukel (1964), *Le Retour au Livre* (1965), *Yaël* (1967), *Elya* (1969), *Aély* (1972), *El, ou le dernier livre* (1973), which are followed by three volumes of *Le Livre des Resemblances*. Four books are available in English, all of them admirably translated by Rosmarie Waldrop: *The Book of Questions, The Book of Yukel, Return to the Book* (Wesleyan University Press), and *Elya* (Tree Books).

The son of wealthy Egyptian Jews, Jabès was born in 1912 and grew up in the French-speaking community of Cairo. His earliest literary friendships were with Max Jacob, Paul Eluard, and René Char, and in the forties and fifties he published several small books of poetry which were later collected in *Je bâtis ma demeure* (1959). Up to that point, his reputation as a poet was solid, but because he lived outside France, he was not very well known.

The Suez Crisis of 1956 changed everything for Jabès, both in his life and in his work. Forced by Nasser's regime to leave Egypt and resettle in France — consequently losing his home and all his possessions — he experienced for the first time the burden of being Jewish. Until then, his Jewishness had been nothing more than a cultural fact, a contingent element of his life. But now that he had been made to suffer for no other reason than that he was a Jew, he had become the Other, and this sudden sense of exile was transformed into a basic, metaphysical self-description.

Difficult years followed. Jabès took a job in Paris and was forced to do most of his writing on the Metro to and from work. When, not long after his arrival, his collected poems were published by Gallimard, the book was not so much an announcement of things to come as a way of marking the boundaries between his new life and what was now an irretrievable past. Jabès began studying Jewish texts — the Talmud, the Kabbala —and though this reading did not initiate a return to the religious precepts of Judaism, it did provide a way for Jabès to affirm his ties with Jewish history and thought. More than the primary source of the Torah, it was the writings and rabbinical commentaries of the Diaspora that moved Jabès, and he began to see in these

books a strength particular to the Jews, one that translated
itself, almost literally, into a mode of survival. In the long
interval between exile and the coming of the Messiah, the
people of God had become the people of the Book. For
Jabès, this meant that the Book had taken on all the weight
and importance of a homeland.

> The Jewish world is based on written law, on a logic
> of words one cannot deny.
> So the country of the Jews is on the scale of their
> world, because it is a book . . .
> The Jew's fatherland is a sacred text amid the
> commentaries it has given rise to . . .

At the core of *The Book of Questions* there is a story — the
separation of two young lovers, Sarah and Yukel, during
the time of the Nazi deportations. Yukel is a writer —
described as the "witness" — who serves as Jabès's alter ego
and whose words are often indistinguishable from his;
Sarah is a young woman who is shipped to a concentration
camp and who returns insane. But the story is never really
told, and it in no way resembles a traditional narrative.
Rather, it is alluded to, commented on, and now and then
allowed to burst forth in the passionate and obsessive love
letters exchanged between Sarah and Yukel — which seem
to come from nowhere, like disembodied voices, articulating
what Jabès calls "the collective scream . . . the everlasting
scream."

> *Sarah:* I wrote you. I write you. I wrote you. I write
> you. I take refuge in my words, the words my pen
> weeps. As long as I am speaking, as long as I am
> writing, my pain is less keen. I join with each syllable
> to the point of being but a body of consonants, a soul

> of vowels. Is is magic? I write his name, and it becomes
> the man I love . . .

And Yukel, toward the end of the book:

> And I read in you, through your dress and your skin,
> through your flesh and your blood. I read, Sarah, that
> you were mine through every word of our language,
> through all the wounds of our race. I read, as one reads
> the Bible, our history and the story which could only
> be yours and mine.

This story, which is the "central text" of the book, is submitted to extensive and elusive commentaries in Talmudic fashion. One of Jabès's most original strokes is the invention of the imaginary rabbis who engage in those conversations and interpret the text with their sayings and poems. Their remarks, which most often refer to the problem of writing the book and the nature of the Word, are elliptical, metaphorical, and set in motion a beautiful and elaborate counterpoint with the rest of the work.

> "He is a Jew," said Reb Tolba. "He is leaning against
> a wall, watching the clouds go by."
> "The Jew has no use for clouds," replied Reb Jale.
> "He is counting the steps between him and his life."

Because the story of Sarah and Yukel is not fully told, because, as Jabès implies, it *cannot* be told, the commentaries are in some sense an investigation of a text that has not been written. Like the hidden God of classic Jewish theology, the text exists only by virtue of its absence.

> "I know you, Lord, in the measure that I do not know
> you. For you are He who comes."
>   Reb Lod

What happens in *The Book of Questions*, then, is the writing of *The Book of Questions* — or rather, the attempt to write it, a process that the reader is allowed to witness in all its gropings and hesitations. Like the narrator in Beckett's *The Unnamable*, who is cursed by "the inability to speak [and] the inability to be silent," Jabès's narrative goes nowhere but around and around itself. As Maurice Blanchot has observed in his excellent essay on Jabès: "The writing . . . must be accomplished in the act of interrupting itself." A typical page in *The Book of Questions* mirrors this sense of difficulty: isolated statements and paragraphs are separated by white spaces, then broken by parenthetical remarks, by italicized passages and italics within parentheses, so that the reader's eye can never grow accustomed to a single, unbroken visual field. One reads the book by fits and starts — just as it was written.

At the same time, the book is highly structured, almost architectural in its design. Carefully divided into four parts, "At the Threshold of the Book," "And You Shall Be in the Book," "The Book of the Absent," and "The Book of the Living," it is treated by Jabès as if it were a physical place, and once we cross its threshold we pass into a kind of enchanted realm, an imaginary world that has been held in suspended animation. As Sarah writes at one point: "I no longer know where I am. I know. I am nowhere. Here." Mythical in its dimensions, the book for Jabès is a place where the past and the present meet and dissolve into each other. There seems nothing strange about the fact that ancient rabbis can converse with a contemporary writer, that images of stunning beauty can stand beside descriptions of the greatest devastation, or that the visionary and the commonplace can coexist on the same page. From the very beginning, when the reader encounters the writer at the threshold of the book, we know that we are entering a space unlike any other.

> "What is going on behind this door?"
> "A book is shedding its leaves."
> "What is the story of the book?"
> "Becoming aware of a scream."
> "I saw rabbis go in."
> "They are privileged readers. They come in small groups to give us their comments."
> "Have they read the book?"
> "They are reading it."
> "Did they happen by for the fun of it?"
> "They foresaw the book. They are prepared to encounter it."
> "Do they know the characters?"
> "They know our martyrs."
> "Where is the book set?"
> "In the book."
> "What are you?"
> "I am the keeper of the house."
> "Where do you come from?"
> "I have wandered . . ."

The book "begins with difficulty — the difficulty of being and writing — and ends with difficulty." It gives no answers. Nor can any answers ever be given — for the precise reason that the "Jew," as one of the imaginary rabbis states, "answers every question with another question." Jabès conveys these ideas with a wit and eloquence that often evoke the logical hairsplitting — *pilpul* — of the Talmud. But he never deludes himself into believing that his words are anything more than "grains of sand" thrown to the wind. At the heart of the book there is nothingness.

> "Our hope is for knowledge," said Reb Mendel. But not all his disciples were of his opinion.
>
> "We have first to agree on the sense you give to the word 'knowledge'," said the oldest of them.
>
> "Knowledge means questioning," answered Reb Mendel.
>
> "What will we get out of these questions? What will we get out of all the answers which only lead to more questions, since questions are born of unsatisfactory answers?" asked the second disciple.
>
> "The promise of a new question," replied Reb Mendel.
>
> "There will be a moment," the oldest disciple continued, "when we will have to stop interrogating. Either because there will be no answer possible, or because we will not be able to formulate any further questions. So why should we begin?"
>
> "You see," said Reb Mendel, "at the end of an argument, there is always a decisive question unsettled."
>
> "Questioning means taking the road to despair," continued the second disciple. "We will never know what we are trying to learn."

Although Jabès's imagery and sources are for the most part derived from Judaism, *The Book of Questions* is not a Jewish work in the same way that one can speak of *Paradise Lost* as a Christian work. While Jabès is, to my knowledge, the first modern poet consciously to assimilate the forms and idiosyncrasies of Jewish thought, his relationship to Jewish teaching is emotional and metaphorical rather than one of strict adherence. The Book is his central image — but it is not only the Book of the Jews (the spirals of commentary around commentary in the Midrash), but an allusion to Mallarmé's ideal Book as well (the Book that contains the world, endlessly folding in upon itself). Finally, Jabès's work must be considered as part of the on-going French poetic tradition that began in the late nineteenth century. What Jabès had done is to fuse this tradition with a certain type of Jewish discourse, and he has done so with such conviction that the marriage between the two is almost imperceptible. *The Book of Questions* came into being because Jabès found himself as a writer in the act of discovering himself as a Jew. Similar in spirit to an idea expressed by Marina Tsvetaeva — "In this most Christian of worlds / all poets are Jews" — this equation is located at the exact center of Jabès's work, is the kernel from which everything else springs. To Jabès, nothing can be written about the Holocaust unless writing itself is first put into question. If language is to be pushed to the limit, then the writer must condemn himself to an exile of doubt, to a desert of uncertainty. What he must do, in effect, is create a poetics of absence. The dead cannot be brought back to life. But they can be heard, and their voices live in the Book.

1976

Private I, Public Eye

It is impossible to make a mistake without knowing it, impossible not to know that one has just smashed something. Unearned words are, in that context, simply ridiculous. . . . One's awareness of the world, one's concern for existence — they were not already in words — And the poem is NOT built out of words, one cannot make a poem by sticking words into it, it is the poem which makes the words and contains their meaning. . . . When the man is frightened by a word, he may have started . . . .

—George Oppen, from "Notes on Prosody?"

George Oppen is a deceptively simple poet. To read his work, in some sense, is to be forced to learn it. Throughout his writing life he has devoted himself to the investigation of a few central questions, and all his work is of a piece— interconnected, issuing from a single source, each poem strengthened by the presence of the others. The language is almost naked, and the syntax seems to derive its logic as much from the silences around words as from the words themselves. There is little ease in Oppen, little to reassure us in his surfaces. Constantly struggling against the lure of facility, he will never use a word that has not first been won and absorbed through experience. For style in his work is as much a question of moral concern as anything that might be said within the poem.

Oppen's work begins at a point beyond the certainty of

absolutes, beyond any pre-arranged or inherited system of values, and attempts to move toward some common ground of belief on which all men can stand. The locus is always the natural world, and the process is one that originates in the perception of objects, in the primal act of seeing:

> Impossible to doubt the world: it can be seen
> And because it is irrevocable

> It cannot be understood and I believe that fact is lethal

Oppen is a man who is able to *look*, wholeheartedly and without distraction. As Carl Rakosi has written, Oppen "has a great eye, precise and irreducible. If you've never seen what it sees, it's because you haven't sat still long enough and looked as hard as he has":

> There is no beauty in New England like the boats.
> Each itself, even the paint white
> Dipping to each wave each time
> At anchor, mast
> And rigging tightly part of it
> Fresh from the dry tools
> And the dry New England hands.

This notion of "each itself" — which is to say: "the thing in itself" — is central to Oppen's work. Again and again he poses awe of the physical world, a wonder in the sheer this-ness of things, against the confusion and brutality of the social world, as if seeking the basis for a new kind of language, a test, as he has said, of the word "humanity," in the simple fact of presence:

> . . . Nothing more

> But the sense
> Of where we are

Who are most northerly. The marvel of the wave
Even here is its noise seething
In the world; I thought that even if there were
      nothing

The possibility of being would exist;
I thought I had encountered

Permanence; thought leaped on us in that sea
For in that sea we breathe the open
Miracle

Of place, and speak
If we would rescue
Love to the ice-lit

Upper World a substantial language
Of clarity, and of respect.

As his work has developed over the years, Oppen's quest
for this "substantial language / Of clarity, and of respect"
has led him away from his early preoccupation with things
and individual perceptions to larger questions of society
and the possibility of community:

Obsessed, bewildered

By the shipwreck
Of the singular

We have chosen the meaning
Of being numerous.

Oppen offers no solutions to the problems he raises, and
his confrontation of the public and historical world seems

to spring more from a feeling of isolation and loss than from a naive hope in the future: ". . . because we find the others / Deserted like ourselves and therefore brothers." There is a deep sense of solidarity in this statement, but it offers very little on which to base a society. Oppen, however, can assert no more than this without abandoning his convictions, and his refusal to overstep the limit of his own beliefs is both ruthless and salutary. If his work holds no ultimate promise of redemption, there is nevertheless a redemptive quality in this work precisely because it does not offer false hopes. What emerges from Oppen's poetry is above all the decency of the man himself — a human voice speaking outward from the way deepest chasm of solitude. Oppen is a public poet, but in such a way that this term takes on a new definition, for his concern is less with the event than with feeling, with concern itself and the obligation to see "That which one cannot / Not see." His aim has never been to make pronouncements about the world, but, quite simply, to discover it. The sentence that occurs in one of his poems — "We want to be here" — is to be read, therefore, not as a desire to be in a particular place, but as a fundamental article of faith. It is an acceding to that which cannot be known, and for Oppen it carries all the power and mystery of a theological premise.

There is no rift between the epistemological foundations of Oppen's work and the broader metaphysical challenges that he presents. For seeing in his poetry is not simply a physical act; it implies an inner commitment as well. And the moment one posits the necessity of seeing the world — that is to say, of entering it — one must be prepared to take one's stand among other men. As a consequence, speech belongs to the realm of ethics.

Oppen's awareness of this consequence gives his work a lustre of maturity that few lyric poets ever achieve — a true seriousness that is never ponderous or burdensome. It is a rare and precious gift, and one that he seems to have sensed in himself from the very beginning. When he began writing again at the age of fifty — after writing nothing from the mid-thirties to the late-fifties — the first poem he completed foreshadowed everything he has written since, outlining, in direct and cryptic form, the entire poetic task he has set for himself. The poem was "Blood from the Stone," and it contains these lines:

> What do we believe
> To live with? Answer.
> Not invent — just answer — all
> That verse attempts.

1976

Innocence and Memory

From his earliest important poems, written in the trenches of the First World War, to the last poems of his old age, Giuseppe Ungaretti's work is a long record of confrontations with death. Cryptic in utterance, narrow in rage, and built on an imagery that is drawn exclusively from the natural world, Ungaretti's poetry nevertheless manages to avoid the predictable, and in spite of the limitations of his manner, he leaves an impression of almost boundless energy and invention. No word in Ungaretti's work is ever used lightly — "When I find / in this my silence / a word / it is dug into my life / like an abyss" — and the strength of his poetry comes precisely from this restraint. For a man who wrote for more than fifty years, Ungaretti published remarkably little before he died in 1970, and his collected poems amount to no more than a couple of hundred pages. Like Mallarmé before him (though in ways that are very different), Ungaretti's poetic source is silence, and in one form or another, all his work is an expression of the inexhaustible difficulty of expression itself. Reading him, one feels that he has only grudgingly allowed his words to appear on the page, that even the strongest words are in constant danger of annihilation.

Born in 1888, Ungaretti belonged to a celebrated generation of modern writers that included Pound, Joyce, Kafka, Trakl, and Pessoa. Like theirs, his importance is measured not only by his own achievement but by its effect on the history of the literature of his language. Before Ungaretti, there was no modern Italian poetry. When his first book, *Il Porto Sepolto (The Buried Port)*, appeared in 1916 in an edition of eighty copies, it seemed to have dropped from the sky, to be without precedent. These short, fragmented poems, at times hardly more ample than notes or inscriptions, announced a definitive break with the late-nineteenth-century conventions that still dominated Italian poetry. The horrible realities of the war demanded a new kind of expression, and for Ungaretti, who at that time was just finishing his poetic apprenticeship, the front was a training ground that taught the futility of all compromise.

Watch
Cima Quattro, December 23, 1915

One whole night
thrust down beside
a slaughtered comrade
his snarling
mouth
turned to the full moon
the bloating
of his hands
entering
my silence
I have written
letters full of love

Never have I held
so
fast to life*

---

*All quotations are translated by Allen Mandelbaum and appear in his *Selected Poems of Giuseppe Ungaretti*, published by Cornell University Press in 1975.

If the brevity and hardness of his first poems seemed violent in comparison to most Italian poetry of the period, Ungaretti was no poetic rebel, and his work showed none of the spirit of self-conscious sabotage that characterized the Futurists and other avant-garde groups. His break with the past was not a renunciation of literary tradition, but a way of affirming his connection with a more distant and vital past than the one represented by his immediate predecessors. He simply cleared the ground that lay between him and what he felt to be his true sources, and like all original artists, he created his own tradition. In later years, this lead him to extensive critical work, as well as translations of numerous foreign poets, including Gongora, Shakespeare, Racine, Blake, and Mallarmé.

Ungaretti's need to invent this poetic past for himself can perhaps be attributed to the unusual circumstances of his early life. By the twin accidents of his birthplace and the nature of his education, he was freed from many of the constraints of a pure Italian upbringing, and though he came from old Tuscan peasant stock, he did not set foot in Italy until he was twenty-four. His father, originally from Lucca, had emigrated to Egypt to work on the construction of the Suez Canal, and by the time of Ungaretti's birth he had become the proprietor of a bakery in the Arab quarter of Moharrem Bay in Alexandria. Ungaretti attended French schools, and his first real encounter with Europe took place a year before the war, in Paris, where he met Picasso, Braque, De Chirico, Max Jacob, and became close friends with Apollinaire. (In 1918, transferred to Paris at the time of the Armistice, he arrived at Apollinaire's house with the latter's favorite Italian cigars just moments after his death.)

Apart from serving in the Italian army, Ungaretti did not live in Italy until 1921 — long after he had found his direction as a poet. Ungaretti was a cultural hybrid, and elements of his varied past are continually mixed into his work. Nowhere is this more concisely expressed than in "I fiumi" ("The Rivers")(1916), a long poem that concludes:

> I have gone over
> the seasons
> of my life
>
> These are
> my rivers
>
> This is the Serchio
> from whose waters have drawn
> perhaps two thousand years
> of my farming people
> and my father and my mother
>
> This is the Nile
> that saw me
> born and growing
> burning with unknowing
> on its broad plains
>
> This is the Seine
> and in its troubled flow
> I was remingled and remade
> and came to know myself
>
> These are my rivers
> counted in the Isonzo

> This is my nostalgia
> as it appears
> in each river
> now it is night
> now my life seems to me
> a corolla
> of shadows

In early poems such as this one, Ungaretti manages to capture the past in the shape of an eternal present. Time exists, not as duration so much as accumulation, a gathering of discrete moments that can be revived and made to emerge in the nearness of the present. *Innocence and Memory* — the title given to the French edition of Ungaretti's essays — are the two contradictory aspirations embedded in his poetry, and all his work can be seen as a constant effort to renew the self without destroying its past. What concerns Ungaretti most is the search for spiritual self-definition, a way of discovering his own essence beyond the grip of time. It is a drama played out between the forces of permanence and impermanence, and its basic fact is human mortality. As in the war poem, "Watch," the sense of life for Ungaretti is experienced most fully in confronting death, and in a commentary on another of his poems, he describes this process as ". . . the knowing of being out of non-being, being out of the null, Pascalian knowing of being out of the null. Horrid consciousness."

If this poetry can be described as basically religious in nature, the sensibility that informs the poems is never monkish, and denial of the flesh is never offered as a solution to spiritual problems. It is, in fact, the conflict between the spiritual and the physical that sustains the poems and gives them their life. Ungaretti is a man of contradictions, a "man of pain," as he calls himself in one of his poems, but also a man of great passions and desires, who at times seems locked in "the glare of promiscuity," and who is able to write of ". . . the mare of your loins / Plunging you in agony / Into my singing arms." His obsession with death, therefore, does not derive from morbid self-pity or a search for other-worldliness, but from an almost savage will to live, and Ungaretti's robust sensuality, his firm adherence to the world of physical things, makes his poems tense with conflict between the irreconcilable powers of love and vanity.

In his later work, beginning with the second major collection, *Sentimento del Tempo (Sentiment of Time)* (1919-35), the distance between the present and the past grows, in the end becoming a chasm that is almost impossible to cross, either by an act of will or an act of grace. As with Pascal, as with Leopardi, the perception of the void translates itself into the central metaphor of an unappeasable agony in the face of an indifferent universe, and if Ungaretti's conversion to Catholicism in the late twenties is to be understood, it must be seen in the light of this "horrid consciousness." "La Pietà" (1928), the long poem that most clearly marks Ungaretti's conversion, is also one of his bleakest works, and it contains these lines, which can be read as a gloss on the particular nature of Ungaretti's anguish:

You have banished me from life.

And will you banish me from death?

Perhaps man is unworthy even of hope.

Dry, too, the fountain of remorse?

What matters sin
If it no longer leads to purity?

The flesh can scarcely remember
That once it was strong.

Worn out and wild — the soul.

God, look upon our weakness.

We want a certainty.

Not satisfied to remain on safe ground, without the comfort of a "certainty," he continually goads himself to the edge of the abyss, threatening himself with the image of his own extinction. But rather than inducing him to succumb to despair, these acts of metaphysical risk seem to be the source of an enduring strength. In poems such as "The Premeditated Death," a sequence that serves as the hub to the whole of *Sentimento del Tempo*, and nearly all the poems in his following collection, *Il Dolore (The Grief)* (1936-47) — most notably the powerful poem written on the death of his young son, "You Shattered" — Ungaretti's determination to situate himself at the extremes of his own consciousness is paradoxically what allows him to cure himself of the fear of these limits.

By the force and precision of his meditative insight, Ungaretti manages to transcend what in a lesser poet would amount to little more than an inventory of private griefs and fears: the poems stand as objects beyond the self for the very reason that the self within them is not treated as

an example of all selves or the self in general. At all times
one feels the presence of the man himself in the work. As
Allen Mandelbaum notes in the preface to his translations:
"Ungaretti's I is grave and slow, intensive rather than far-
ranging; and his longing gains its drama precisely because
that I is not a random center of desperations, but a *soma*
bound by weight, by earthly measure, a hard, resisting,
substantial object, not wished but willed, not dreamt-upon
but 'excavated'."

In the poems of his later years, Ungaretti's work comes
to an astonishing culmination in the single image of the
promised land. It is the promised land of both Aeneas and
the Bible, of both Rome and the desert, and the personal
and historical overtones of these final major poems —
"Canzone," "Choruses Describing the States of Mind of
Dido," "Recitative of Palinurus," and "Final Choruses for
the Promised Land," — refer back to all of Ungaretti's
previous work, as if to give it its final meaning. The return to
a Virgilian setting represents a kind of poetic homecoming
for him at the end of his career, just as the desert revives
the landscape of his youth, only to leave him in a last and
permanent exile:

> We cross the desert with remnants
> Of some earlier image in mind,
>
> That is all a living man
> Knows of the promised land.

Written between 1952 and 1960, the "Final Choruses" were
published in *Il Taccuino del Vecchio (The Old Man's Notebook)*,
and they reformulate all the essential themes of his work.
Ungaretti's universe remains the same, and in a language

that differs very little from that of his earliest poems, he prepares himself for his death — his real death, the last death possible for him:

> The kite hawk grips me in his azure talons
> And, at the apex of the sun,
> Lets me fall on the sand
> As food for ravens.
>
> I shall no longer bear mud on my shoulders,
> The fire will find me clean,
> The cackling beaks
> The stinking jaws of jackals.
>
> Then as he searches with his stick
> Through the sand, the bedouin
> Will point out
> A white, white bone.

1976

Resurrection

There are few stories in contemporary literature stranger than Carl Rakosi's, and few stories that show more clearly the extent to which the poet is a prisoner of his calling. Born in Central Europe in 1903 and brought to America at the age of six, Rakosi began writing poetry in his early twenties and seemed destined to have a career as a man of letters. His early poems — compact, incisive, vividly sensual in their grasp of physical things — attained a degree of force and accomplishment not usually achieved by young writers.

> This is the raw data.
> A mystery translates it
> into feeling and perception;
> then imagination;
> finally the hard
> inevitable quartz,
> figure of will
>   and language.

In 1931, some of his work appeared in the famous "Objectivist" issue of *Poetry* edited by Louis Zukofsky, and thereafter Rakosi's name became linked with the Objectivist group — which, in addition to Zukofsky, included such outstanding poets as William Carlos Williams, Charles Reznikoff, and George Oppen. But when the Depression came, and with it the necessity of scrambling for a living, things began to change for Rakosi. More or less by chance, he drifted into social work, and little by little, although he did not abandon the idea of writing poetry, the idea of writing poetry seemed to abandon him. As he put it in an interview with L.S. Dembo in 1969, his interest in poetry was literally engulfed by the events of the time.

> During the thirties I was working in New York — this was during the very depth of the Depression — and any young person with any integrity or intelligence had to become associated with some left-wing organization. You just couldn't live with yourself if you didn't. So I got caught up very strongly in the whole Marxian business. I took very literally the basic Marxian ideas about literature having to be an instrument for social change, for expressing the needs and desires of large masses of people. And believing that, I couldn't write poetry, because the poetry that I could write could not achieve these ends.

In 1941, New Directions published a book of Rakosi's selected poems, but by then he had already stopped writing. He was devoting all his time to social work, a profession that involved him passionately, and there was simply no room in his life anymore for poetry. By all the laws of logic and precedent, this is where the story should have ended. The man was a poet in his youth and then gave it up for something else. It is a common story, and one that needs no elaboration.

But then, out of the blue, Rakosi received a letter in the early Sixties from a young English poet by the name of Andrew Crozier. Crozier had come across a reference to Rakosi in an article by Kenneth Rexroth, had looked up his poetry in old magazines, and had fallen in love with the work. He was planning to compile a bibliography and wondered if Rakosi had written anything else. The letter, which took many months to reach Rakosi (who had completely disappeared from the literary world — and was even thought by some people to be dead) struck home deeply. It triggered a reaction in Rakosi that finally led him to break his poetic silence of twenty-five years. In his own words: "The thought that somebody his age would care that much for my work really touched me; after all, there were two generations between us. And that's what started me."

It must have been an extraordinary moment for Rakosi, beginning to write again after so many years. The sense of finding himself again — or better, of tearing down the wall that stood between him and his past — must have brought a rare and magnificent sense of freedom. For if there is any word that describes Rakosi's work of the past dozen years, it is joy. It is as if each poem he now writes were a gift, something above and beyond the life he has already lived. He no longer has to prove himself. Nothing can be lost, and everything can be gained.

There have been three books from Rakosi since his return to poetry: *Amulet* (1967), *Ere-Voice* (1971) — both published by New Directions — and *Ex Cranium, Night*, recently published by Black Sparrow Press. As in his earliest work, Rakosi's chief preoccupation remains "the raw data" of the world:

> Sights
>
> I mean to penetrate the particular
> the way an owl waits
>   for a kangaroo rat
> and the photomicrograph
> beholds the hairy
>   pappus of a dandelion.

But his interest is not limited to physical things. With an irrepressible ebullience and wit, he penetrates the world of other people as well.

    The Street

    Like slag
             the face,
    old,
    one who knows he has been
        banished,
    knows the place,
    expects no sympathy or interest.

    At seeing me
             the face
    lit up at once
             and smiled,
    expecting a smile:
             You're one of us!

The exclamation mark is one of Rakosi's favored devices, and in cases such as this one it serves not only to inject the poem with a sudden and unexpected vitality, but also to undercut the seriousness of the line that has just been written. It is as if Rakosi were reminding us that life is always more important than poetry — and that the only poetry worth writing is one that remains steadfastly in the world. It is a lesson that he is particularly qualified to teach.

Not surprisingly, Rakosi's second phase as a poet has been marked by an interest in questions of aesthetics and the theoretical aspects of writing. In *Ex Cranium, Night*, which is his richest book so far, almost half the material consists of prose notations on the nature of poetry and the imagination. Rakosi's observations are simple, almost homely, but at the same time shrewd, and now and then brilliant: "He who reveals the consequences of society on himself leaps across the intervening distance." More than any other, this elliptical but precise statement seems to define the movement of Rakosi's poetry — the poem as an equalizing gesture between subject and object, or the recognition of the separateness of things — which must be established before there can be commerce between the poet and the world.

Rakosi is probably the most personal of all the poets once associated with the Objectivists, and his charm as a writer lies in his ability to maintain a strict formal discipline in the interests of creating an art that never has the effect of artifice. It is a work that glows with the light of the everyday and the fullness of common experience.

1976

Kafka's Letters

Little by little, we are beginning to know Kafka. Of all modern writers he has been the most private, the most difficult of access, and his life and art have frequently been misunderstood. It is well known that he published little during his lifetime; if it had not been for the devotion of his friend Max Brod, who ignored Kafka's request to destroy all his unpublished writing after his death, it is probable that Kafka's name would have died with him in 1924. The very appearance of his work, then, was surrounded by mystery and ambiguity. Why had the novels remained un-finished? And why, given their obvious brilliance and originality, had their author wanted to suppress them? An image grew up of Kafka as a cringing bureaucrat, a classic victim of modern society, a kind of shadow-man. In the public mind he was Gregor Samsa of *The Metamorphosis*.

Over the years, as more biographical facts have become available, this image has changed. Publication of *The Diaries*, the meditations and aphorisms, the passionate letters to Milena and Felice, as well as biographies and memoirs by Brod, Gustav Janouch, and others, have revealed a Kafka infinitely more complex, sophisticated, and appealing than would have been thought possible. As Milena Pollak suc-cinctly put it in a letter to Brod soon after her affair with Kafka had ended: "His books are amazing. He himself is far more amazing . . ."

Kafka's character was one of intense contradiction. To his

friends and acquaintances he was a man of remarkable wit and charm, incredibly generous, trenchant in conversation, unflagging in spirit. Reading the accounts of him one is struck above all by his ability to give of himself, by his purity and integrity, by his unforgettable presence. He was, quite simply, like no one else — to such an extent that in Janouch's *Conversations With Kafka*, for example, he is portrayed as a saint. On the other hand, the Kafka of *The Diaries*, the Kafka in confrontation with himself, was tortured with self-doubts, almost pathologically aware of his slightest shortcoming. Torn between the ideal of marriage, family, and community and the demands of his writing (which led to his two disastrous engagements), unable to break away from his own family and the suffocating influence of his overbearing father, obsessed by his efforts at self-improvement (gardening, vegetarianism, carpentry, Hebrew lessons), knowing his talent as a writer and yet unable to believe deeply in anything he had written (in spite of the enthusiasm of his publisher, reviewers, and friends), Kafka did not achieve any measure of happiness until the final years of his life when he fell in love with young Dora Dymant and moved with her to Berlin. He set such impossibly high standards for himself that in the end he was bound to fail. But it is precisely this striving, this insatiable hunger to surpass himself, that makes his work so important. Like the hunger artist in one of his finest stories, Kafka's life and art were inseparable: to succeed in his art meant to consume himself as a human being. He wrote, not for recognition, but because his very life depended on it. As he expressed it in his diary: "Writing is a form of prayer."

Reading a writer's letters can sometimes be embarrassing.

We feel we are intruding on a private realm, seeing things
that were never meant for our eyes, and more often than
not we are unable to find anything that helps to illuminate
the writer's work — the reason for seeking out letters in
the first place. With Kafka, however, the letters are fundamental. Occupying a middle ground between the inner
battles of the diaries and the objective accounts of the
biographer, they help us to understand his relations with
the world and give us a context in which we can penetrate
his character. One conclusion presents itself immediately:
Kafka was a born writer, incapable of writing a bad sentence
or expressing himself awkwardly. As early as 1902, at the
age of 19, he wrote to a fellow student, Oskar Pollak, with
the whimsy and imaginative flair that were to become his
trademark:

> I sat at my fine desk. You don't know it. How could
> you? You see, it's a respectably minded desk which is
> meant to educate. Where the writer's knees usually are,
> it has two horrible wooden spikes. And now pay
> attention. If you sit down quietly, cautiously at it, and
> write something respectable, all's well. But if you
> become excited, look out — if your body quivers ever
> so little, you inescapably feel the spikes in your knees,
> and how that hurts. I could show you the black-and-
> blue marks. And what that means is simply: "Don't
> write anything exciting and don't let your body quiver
> while you write."

Two years later he wrote to the same Oskar Pollak:

> I think we ought to read only the kind of books that
> wound and stab us. If the book we're reading doesn't
> wake us up with a blow on the head, what are we

reading it for? . . . But we need the books that affect
us like a disaster, that grieve us deeply, like the death
of someone we loved more than ourselves, like being
banished into forests far from everyone, like a suicide.
A book must be the axe for the frozen sea within us.
That is my belief.

Max Brod, of course, was Kafka's principal correspondent,
and over the 20 years of their friendship Kafka poured out
his soul to him. The letters to Brod are by far the most
intimate in the book, dealing in great detail with personal
and literary matters — all the myriad events of Kafka's daily
life — and containing superb descriptions of the people
and atmosphere at the various sanitoria Kafka visited during his last years. It is impossible to read these letters
without marvelling at the depth of the friendship between
these two men, the bond of absolute trust that existed
between them. This correspondence alone would have been
enough to form a stunning book. But there is far more:
Kafka's numerous letters to Kurt Wolff, his publisher, written
with such humility in regard to his own work that it almost
seems that Kafka felt Wolff was doing him a favor by publishing his stories; Kafka's long correspondence with Minze
Eisner, a young girl with emotional troubles whom he
befriended, encouraged, gave advice to, and helped through
the difficult years of adolescence; a dazzling disquisition
on the education of children to Brod's sister; his constant
efforts to promote the work of young friends to publishers
and magazine editors; as well as assorted letters to Martin
Buber, Robert Musil, Franz Werfel, and other important
writers of the period. We see Kafka from so many different
perspectives, encounter him in relation to so many different

kinds of people, that we are finally able to witness the evolution of his personality, to come face to face with him as a man. The value of this book cannot be minimized. Because of it, our reading of Kafka's work will never be quite the same again.

The last eight pages are made up of "Conversation Slips," the notes scribbled by Kafka on his deathbed to Dora Dymant and Robert Klopstock — the two friends who stayed with him until the end and whom he called his "little family." Kafka was suffering from tuberculosis of the larynx and was not allowed to speak; eating had become so painful that as the disease was doing its final work he actually starved to death. These notes, in all their elliptical brevity, are among the most shattering things Kafka ever wrote. Here was Kafka, confined to his bed, surrounded by flowers, attended by his two friends, correcting proofs of *A Hunger Artist*, waiting to die.

> To think that I once could simply venture a large swallow of water . . . I'd especially like to take care of the peonies because they are so fragile . . . And move the lilacs into the sun . . . I'll hold out another week, maybe, I hope; such are the nuances . . . Please be careful that I don't cough in your face . . . How trying I am to all of you; it's crazy . . . Fear again and again . . . If there were no main topic, there would be no subjects for conversation . . . The trouble is that I cannot drink a single glass of water, though the craving itself is some satisfaction . . . How wonderful that is, isn't it? The lilac — dying, it drinks, goes on swilling . . . Put your hand on my forehead a moment to give me courage.

And finally, after the doctor had been in to see him:

So the help goes away again without helping.

He was 41 years old, on the brink of a new life, filled with hope for the future. Even today, the sense of loss is almost unbearable.

1977

Native Son

America swallows up its poets, hides them away, forgets them. Except for the few who become famous (often those of meager talent), the poet with no axe to grind or vogue to follow can expect little but neglect — or, at best, the admiration of his peers. No one is to blame for this. We are simply too vast, too chaotic to notice everything that passes before our eyes. Much of the finest poetry written today is published by small presses and seen by no more than a few hundred readers. That American poetry has historically found the sources of its greatest strengths in the self-published (Whitman, Charles Reznikoff) and the obscurely published (early Pound, early Williams, Olson) is an old story. It would be foolish to insist that only the unrecognized are worth reading, but it would be just as wrong to assume that the work published each week in *The New Yorker* (not to speak of each month in *Poetry*) represents contemporary American poetry at its best.

Consider William Bronk. Now in his sixtieth year, with nine collections of poetry and one volume of essays behind him, he is thought by a handful of his fellow writers to be one of the purest and most challenging poets we have. And yet his work is hardly known. There are several reasons for this oversight. First of all, Bronk's poetry is difficult and demanding — severe enough to frighten off even the best-intentioned reader. Second, all but one of his books have been published in small, elegant, and relatively expensive editions by Elizabeth Press and are not easily found. And finally, Bronk himself is an intensely private person who does not lead a literary life. He does nothing to promote his work, writes no articles, and gives few readings. Nevertheless, public response to his work has been increasing. In the past few years, *The New York Times Book Review* has published two enthusiastic articles; a recent issue of *Parnassus* contains a long and appreciative essay; numerous little magazines have printed commentaries and homages; and in 1976 the poet Cid Corman, whose interest in Bronk goes back to the early Fifties, brought out a book-length study of Bronk's work (*William Bronk, An Essay*; Truck Press).

Bronk's is a poetry of extreme positions. Ruthlessly solipsistic in outlook, plain of speech, and ranging in tone from the most bitter irony to the most gentle lyricism, nearly all his work revolves around a few essential problems and themes: the rift between our image of the world and the reality of the world, the force of desire, the agony of human relationships, our perception of nature. Some readers complain that Bronk's vision is too bleak, that it leaves one destitute, without hope. But like Samuel Beckett (Bronk's closest spiritual brother among contemporary writers), Bronk has an uncompromising approach to the things that haunt and obsess him that is in the end more salutary than depressing; for by compelling us to stare ourselves in the face, he brings us closer to what we are. His is a philosophical poetry, defiantly taking risks, whispering and screaming against the silence that surrounds it. Bronk takes nothing for granted. He wants, quite simply, to come to grips with the given.

Bronk's basic premise is that there is no inherent order

or truth to the world, that whatever form or shape we feel it possesses is the one we ourselves have imposed on it. We can speak not of *the* world, but rather of *a* world, *our* world, and it is constantly changing as we change. We cling to a belief in our world because we need to give coherence to our lives; but for Bronk, these beliefs are merely sham, a way of trying to domesticate the unknowable, for the world in his view is essentially that which cannot be mastered. As he says in the concluding lines of a poem entitled "The Difference": "Some of the things we think and say of the world / are reasonable, but none of them is true." Or again, in another poem, "Conjectural Reading": "The trouble with rational is, it seems to make sense, / in the end it doesn't make any sense at all." Nevertheless, one is left with desire for the world, and this desire is real, as is the joy it can give birth to. "Of the Natural World" is a case in point.

> Of the natural world, nothing is possible
> but praise if we speak at all. We can be still.
> The steadiest speakers are quiet after a time.
> I could be quiet and not wait for the time
> when quiet comes except that so little sound
> is hardly to be heard in the loud joy of the world
> and I grow impatient and practice the world's song.

Bronk is a solitary poet, and his lonely voice speaks to us as if from great distances. And yet his work is intimate, familiar, soon made part of us. Although he sounds like no other poet writing today, his poetry is very much the continuation of a particular American tradition started by Thoreau and Emily Dickinson. Bronk's universe, like theirs, is a mixture of the homely and the sublime. He writes about things that are close to hand, things he encounters in his daily life: the abandoned canals near his home in upstate New York, the natural landscape around him, his garden, his house, his friends, the Latin American ruins he has visited several times in his travels. Rarely anything more. And yet he brings to these simple subjects a metaphysical hunger, a clarity of utterance, and a rage and a humor that continually carry us beyond the confines of those subjects. Bronk plays for high stakes, and in the more than four hundred poems he has published, there are undoubtedly many failures and excesses, but by and large he is a poet of great consistency. It is impossible to get an accurate sense of his work from isolated poems and quotations, for what is most important in him is the ongoing process of writing, the subtle variations in thought and imagery that evolve from one poem to the next and from one book to the next. Taken as a whole, William Bronk's poetry stands as an eloquent and often beautiful attack on all our assumptions, a provocation, a monument to the questioning mind. It is a work that will outlive us all.

                                                                    1978

Providence

A Conversation with Edmond Jabès*

PAUL AUSTER: In the United States you are known primarily as the author of *The Book of Questions*. Few people are aware of the fact that you have also written numerous books of poetry. Readers here tend to think of you as a French writer, but in point of fact this is not strictly the case. You were born in Egypt, and it wasn't until the Suez Crisis of 1956 — when you were forty-four years old — that you moved to France. It has often occurred to me that *The Book of Questions* never would have come into being if you had been able to remain in Egypt.

EDMOND JABÈS: Yes, I think it's important to mention all this. I was born in Cairo, and except for the few years I spent in France as a student, I always lived in Egypt. I grew up in Egypt, I was married in Egypt, and I wrote poems in Egypt. In 1959, a few years after my arrival in France, Gallimard published a large collection of my poetry, *Je bâtis ma demeure*, which brought together all the little books and pamphlets I had published in Cairo and France. You say that in the United States I am known only for *The Book of Questions* . . . In France, too, I was hardly known at all, and when this big book appeared it came as something of a surprise to most people. I have always lived in the margins, so to speak . . . even though my early poems were very close to Surrealism and I had many friends who were Surrealists. Eluard, for example, was very eager for me to join the group,

---

* Originally in French; translated by the author.

to participate actively in the movement. But I have always refused to join any kind of group. From the very beginning I have felt that the risks a writer takes must be taken alone. The idea of sharing these risks is upsetting to me. Something very important is taken away from you then, and as far as I'm concerned, if there is no risk, there is no writing.

PA: But as individuals the Surrealists were important to you, as individual writers.

EJ: Very important. And I felt my work was very close to theirs . . . I should say, however, that my first guide was Max Jacob. Max Jacob gave me extraordinary lessons in poetry. We met in 1935 and went on writing to each other until the war, until 1940. I really owe him a great deal. The Surrealists, as you know, were very unjust to Max because of his religious beliefs. But we are beginning to understand his importance now, to see his work as a turning-point in poetry. He was much more concerned with a questioning of language than the others in his circle. Apollinaire, for example, was a great lyric poet, a poet of pure singing, but Max was something else altogether, and there is a very moving quality in the way he questions language. Everyone thought of him as a clown, as someone who played with puns, jokes, and linguistic tricks, but that wasn't so. It only looked that way on the surface. Underneath, Max was an extremely tortured, anguished person . . . As for the Surrealists, of course, they had an enormous influence on my work. But even so, there were important differences. When I look back on my early poems now, I am struck by what they seem to foreshadow of *The Book of Questions*. In the

aphorisms, for example, although I had no idea at the time
. . . But, as you say, I don't think I would have written *The
Book of Questions* if I had remained in Egypt. It took this
break in my life for my experience of Egypt, my experience
of the desert, to enter my writing in the way it does. These
books came into being as a result of this break . . . as a result
of my having to leave this country because I was a Jew. One
day I was told, this is it, you have to leave. Fine. This was a
little drama for me and my family. On a personal level it
was quite serious, of course, but on the larger human scale,
as part of the history of Jewish suffering, it was nothing
more than a little drama. But there I was, neither a prac-
ticing Jew nor a Jewish believer, forced to leave because I
was Jewish.

PA: Were you brought up in a religious family?

EJ: No. Our family was very bourgeois. We always considered
ourselves Jews, but nothing more. My father did not really
believe in God, and he observed very few Jewish practices.
We were brought up in an atmosphere of total freedom.

PA: And you weren't given any kind of Jewish education?

EJ: No, none whatsoever. But the fact of suddenly having
to live a condition, the condition of being Jewish, changed
things for me. I was faced with new problems, and this led
to a completely new kind of questioning for me. In some
sense this was the origin of the series of books that followed.

PA: Long before the Suez Crisis, of course, there was the

the problem. It's not that I'm against Israel . . . quite the contrary. But I think it's wrong to consider it as the one and only answer . . . There is the Israel of Jewish history, the age-old dream of Israel, and there is the State of Israel, which is one country among all the other countries in the world today. They are not the same.

PA: France, then, became the inevitable choice.

EJ: It was inevitable because French is my language, the language of my books. I was very warmly welcomed in France by everyone. But it would be impossible for me to say that France is my country, that it is my landscape . . . I feel a little lost living in Paris, even though I am surrounded by friends and feel comfortable there. It is not my landscape, not my place, my true place. In a sense, I am now living out the historical Jewish condition. The book has become my true place . . . practically my only place. This idea has become very important to me, to such an extent, in fact, that the condition of being a writer has little by little become almost the same for me as the condition of being a Jew. I feel that every writer in some way experiences the Jewish condition, because every writer, every creator, lives in a kind of exile. And for the Jew himself, the Jew living out the Jewish condition, the book has become not only the place where he can most easily find himself, but also the place where he finds his truth. And the questioning of the book for the Jew, as you know, is a search for the truth. And this truth is also the writer's truth. When the writer questions the book, it is solely in order to enter the truth of the book, which is his truth.

PA: How exactly did these ideas take shape for you?

EJ: Actually, it's quite curious. When I came to France I had fourteen years of poetry behind me, and when the book came out I was naturally very happy about it. But at the same time, I felt that a part of my life was over, that a page had been turned. It was as if I were reliving the experience of the desert . . . as if I had suddenly come to a blank page . . . In Egypt I had written some pieces for the theater, and I thought to myself that perhaps this was the sort of writing I would do now. The work that I was later to call *The Book of Questions* came to me very slowly . . . at first in the form of a drama that took on more and more symbolic impor-tance, and then in the form of reflections that had no definite shape. It was all very vague. Eventually I realized that this had nothing to do with the theater. But if it wasn't theater, what was it? Little by little, as if in spite of me, this thing began to emerge, the book I had been pursuing in total darkness began to take shape . . . by means of ques-tioning, by means of a dramatic story I wanted to present in the same way I felt it inside me, a story I wanted to tell without ever really telling it. It was as if there were stories that didn't have to be told in order to be known and understood. And this was something quite new in a formal sense: that wasn't the way you were supposed to tell a story. But the idea of a story in itself didn't satisfy me . . . that really wasn't what I was after. But around the story I had in mind, there was a questioning, and more and more that became what haunted me about the book. It was as if the book would be something in which I could at last find myself, in which I would find my universe, as if the book were about to become some fantastic thing in which a whole adventure was going to begin.

PA: Were the rabbis already present when you were thinking of the work in terms of the theater?

EJ: No, there were characters. But they became rabbis for the book, because, as you know, rabbis are interpreters, the best interpreters of the book. And once the rabbis were there, I needed a whole crowd of them. The nature of the questioning demanded it. You can't say black and white at the same time; you need one to say white and another to say black . . . Perhaps it would be best to explain this in terms of overall structure.

PA: By all means.

EJ: In the first trilogy — *The Book of Questions, The Book of Yukel,* and *Return to the Book* — the references to Judaism are very marked. At the center of each of these books there is a story, the story of two adolescents . . . two lovers who are deported. They return from the camps: she has gone mad, and her cries become indistinguishable from the cries of a persecuted people, a people persecuted over the centuries; in the second volume he commits suicide, and everything takes place as if after his death. But this after-death is also a before-death . . . like memory, as if there were always something before. Then the rabbis come . . . to reflect, to question, and so on. But it's not exactly that. It is an immense dialogue in time and outside of time. And these people who are there, sometimes separated by many centuries, can speak to each other only in the form of questions.

PA: Why is that?

EJ: Because — and it was Blanchot who noticed this . . .
in an article for the *NRF* published in 1964 — because when
two people talk, one of them must always remain silent. We
are talking now, for example, and as I am saying these words
you are forced to remain silent. If we both spoke at the same
time, neither one of us could hear what the other was saying.
Now, during this silence that you impose on yourself, you
are all the while forming questions and answers in your
mind, since you can't keep interrupting me. And as I continue to speak, you are eliminating questions from your
mind: ah, you say to yourself, that's what he meant, all right.
But what if I went on speaking for a long time and we went
away before you had a chance to reply? When we met again,
you wouldn't come back with an answer, you would come
back with a question. This is the way the rabbis answer each
other. Each one has already eliminated the questions, and
so he is able to say: this is what I think. They are not always
asking questions, then, sometimes they give answers. But
this answer immediately provokes a question from someone
else. The whole book operates in this manner. A first
dialogue is interrupted, then a second dialogue, then a
third, a fourth . . . and suddenly, the first dialogue, which
seemed to have been lost, is picked up again fifty pages later
after a thousand other things have happened.

PA: It took you three or four years to write *The Book of
Questions*.

EJ: Yes. I worked on it from 1959 to 1962, and it was published in 1963. But, as I said before, I was working in total
darkness. And when the book appeared, no one really knew
what to make of it. The idea of the *récit éclaté* [fragmented
story] had never been discussed in France at that time, and
that was how the book demanded to be read . . . demands
to be read. There is a story, but it is given only in little
pieces, and there are the two characters, Sarah and Yukel
— but Yukel is double. He is both the narrator (the one
who makes the book) and the hero. But they are the same,
they have the same name. And then, there is no place, the
book isn't situated anywhere, since there are all these
characters who come from various times. The rabbis — they
are imaginary rabbis, or course . . . there are both ancient
and modern rabbis. The most ancient rabbis are the ones
who say the simplest things, and the rabbis closest to us
in time say the most complicated things . . . And then, too,
there are the different kinds of typography in the book
. . . the parentheses and italics, for example. In all my books
there is a book that exists inside the book. There is the
part that is before the book . . . it is in the book, but it is
also the book that has not yet been written. To be before
the book is to be in a state of potential, to have the possibility of creating a book. But then the book creates itself,
against all the other books we carry inside us. And it goes
on and on like that. It is a circular work. Each question leads
to another question.

PA: The typographical layout of your books is one of the
things that most immediately strikes the reader . . . It sets
the rhythm of the work and enhances the feeling of frag-

mentation you create in the text itself. Are these shifts done in a systematic way, or are they more or less unconscious?

EJ: Sometimes it just happens, but more often than not it requires real work. It's not premeditated in the begin-ning, but as the text advances, there are things that come from farther and farther away, as if from another book, or from the book within the book . . . and these are the things in italics. The longer passages generally belong to the book itself, to the book that is being written, and they are there to continue the story, or to continue the ques-tioning . . . But the material in italics is also a book being created at the same time the other book is being created. There is always a book carrying a book carrying a book carrying a book . . . As for this distribution of long and short passages, it's a question of rhythm. This is very important to me. A full phrase, a lyrical phrase, is something that has great breath, that allows you to breathe very deeply. They say that Nietzsche wrote aphorisms, for example, because he suffered from atrocious headaches that made it impos-sible for him to write very much at one sitting. Whether this is true or not, I do believe that a writer works with his body. You live with your body, and the book is above all the book of your body. In my case, the aphorism — what you might call the naked phrase — comes from a need to surround the words with whiteness in order to let them breathe. As you know, I suffer from asthma, and some-times breathing is very difficult for me. By giving breath to my words I often have the feeling that I am helping myself breathe. It's really quite incredible how you live with your writing . . . I remember something that happened a few

years ago. I had just finished the seven *Books of Questions*
. . . it was in April. May is usually the month when my asthma
is worst, but this time May came and went and I hardly had
any trouble at all. June came, and I still felt fine. My doctor,
who happens to be an old friend, was at my house one day,
and I told him what a curious thing it was that I should
be feeling so well at that time of year. He answered that
perhaps it was because I had finished the series and the
anguish of the work had temporarily lifted . . . A little later
I went off on vacation — to the sea, where I am always fine
— and returned to Paris in September, which is usually a
good month for me. At that point my publisher called me
and asked me to write a *prière d'insérer* [a note for the back
of the book]. This kind of note is usually a bother to do,
often quite difficult . . . but after two or three days I managed to get it done. The last sentence of the note was: "With
this book, the seventh in the series, *The Book of Questions*
comes to an end." That night I had one of my most violent
asthma attacks. And it was the phrase "comes to an end"
that brought it on. It had thrown me into a terrible panic.
The doctor had to come at three in the morning to give
me a shot. I almost literally couldn't breathe . . . If I say
all this, it is only to show that we work with our bodies, our
breathing, our rhythm, and that writing in some sense
mimes all this. Writing works in two directions. It is both
an expansion and a contraction. This is what I learned from
Max Jacob, and it took me a long time to understand it.
When I was very young, nineteen, twenty, I would send him
my poems, and he would write back saying they were too
broad, I should tighten them up. So I would tighten them
up, and he would write back saying they are too tight, I

should broaden them. I was totally confused. It took me a long time to understand that both were valid, but that this was what style was all about, that this was the essence of writing. You have to write in the same way you breathe.

PA: You once told me that as you were writing *The Book of Questions* you had the feeling that you were taking dictation.

EJ: Not quite . . . but almost. A great part of it, as you know, was written on the metro going to and from work, and of course there were a lot of people around. It was as if . . . as if something had imposed this book on me. But I do not believe in inspiration, or anything like it. The book emerged from something that was already deeply inside me.

PA: Were your early poems written in this way? Or did something truly different begin for you with *The Book of Questions?*

EJ: There is something that always intrigued me about writing poems . . . which is that I could always say how long a poem would be even before I wrote it. I knew if it was going to be three pages, or six pages, or a half a page . . . The only way this can be explained, I think, is by the fact that when you begin writing a poem it has already been written within you, even though you are not aware of it. It was all very curious for me. I could begin writing a poem, for example, put down a phrase or two, and then go out, say to the movies, anywhere, and know that when I returned home I would be able to continue writing. Without for one minute having been separated from the poem. As if it had continued working inside me. I remember a long poem of ten pages. One evening I came home and went to bed. In the middle of the night I got up. My wife said, what's going on, are you ill? I said no, I'm going to write. And I sat down at my desk and began to write this poem. After a while I went back to bed. The next day I picked it up as if I had never left it. Going back to bed, I said to my wife: this is a poem that will be ten pages long. And it turned out to be ten pages, exactly. How can you explain this? It's incomprehensible. Something is already at work inside us and then some little thing, an emotion, a chance encounter, sets it off . . . That's why the dry stretches in poetry are particularly painful, the times when you can't write anything. You're going along very well. You write ten poems, twenty poems in just a few months, and you feel wonderful. And then, suddenly, you can't do a thing. You can't even pick up your pen, you can't write a line. At those times you are filled with terrible doubt. You are afraid you might never be able to write again. This is something extraordinary, something most people don't understand. Whenever you write you are running the risk of never writing again . . . And then, sometimes, a new poem comes, and you feel completely liberated. You say to yourself, at last, it's come back. And you write and write, and in the end you discover that it doesn't amount to anything . . . Writing comes in its own time . . . you can never force it.

PA: Concerning the narrative element in *The Book of Questions* . . . the fragmentary nature of the telling. Is it a matter of choice, or do you somehow find it impossible to tell a story in the traditional way?

EJ: It is neither a choice nor an impossibility. To tell a story, in my opinion, is to lose it. If I tell you about my life in detail, for example, it escapes in the details I have chosen to recount. In life you have no choice. How do you know what is most important? A story limits the life of a person to the things someone else can say about him. He is big, he is small, he is this, he is that. Even if all this is true, there is still something else. But if I say: he was born here, he died here, a whole life begins to take shape, a life that you might be able to imagine . . .

PA: What you are saying, then, is that the traditional narrative doesn't interest you.

EJ: . . . *The Book of Questions* is based on the idea that we all live with words that obsess us. There is no question that highly emotional words such as "death" or "love," for example, do not have precisely the same meanings for everyone. Behind these words we see our own stories of death and love. As for the story in the book, I simply wanted to point out the life and drama of this couple. It was not a question of telling the story of their lives, because in the end it wasn't their lives that interested me . . . I am more concerned with interiority than description. It is the questioning around the story that gives the story its dimension. But the story is there only as a kind of basic pretext. For the Jews unfortunately, after all the camps and all the horrors, it is an all too banal story. It isn't necessary to go into details. When you say: they were deported, that is enough for a Jew to understand the *whole* story . . . I once met a man who had lost his whole family in the camps. Only he and his son had escaped. He told me this and then went on to talk about completely different kinds of things. I felt that he had told me his *whole* life, past, present, and even future by simply saying to me: "My whole family was deported. Only my son and I escaped." This conversation made a particularly deep impression on me because the man later went on to tell me about his son. During the blockade of Jerusalem, when the Syrians were firing on the supply trucks going to the city, his son, who was only fifteen or sixteen at the time, asked his father permission to become a driver of one of these condemned trucks. The father said yes. And the boy was killed. And after that the father took his son's name. His name was Ben Zvi, and it was because I asked him about his name that he told me the story. It is something I will never forget . . . And it shows, I think, that it is enough simply to state the thing in order to reveal the whole drama.

PA: You spoke of obsessive words. There are a dozen or so words and themes that are repeated constantly, on nearly every page of your work: desert, absence, silence, God, nothingness, the void, the book, the word, exile, life, death . . . and it strikes me that each of these words is in some sense a word on the other side of speech, a kind of limit, something almost impossible to express.

EJ: Exactly. But at the same time, if these are things that cannot be expressed, they are also things that cannot be emptied of meaning. We can't get rid of them. I find it impossible to rid myself of the word "Jew," for example, or the word "God." This created considerable misunder-standing in the beginning. Why God, people asked, when you don't believe in God? There are people in France, you know, people who call themselves materialists, who are afraid of saying words like "God." I find this idiotic. The word "God" is in the dictionary, it's a word like any other word. I am not afraid of the word "God," because I am not afraid of this God . . . What I mean by God in my work is something we come up against, an abyss, a void, something against which we are powerless. It is a distance . . . the distance that is always between things . . . We get to where we are going, and then there is still this distance to cover. And a moment comes when you can no longer cover the distance; you get there and you say to yourself, it's finished, there are no more words. God is perhaps a word without words. A word without meaning. And the extraordinary thing is that in the Jewish tradition God is invisible, and as a way of underscoring this invisibility, he has an unpro-nounceable name. What I find truly fantastic is that when you call something "invisible," you are naming something, which means that you are almost giving a representation of the invisible. In other words, when you say "invisible," you are pointing to the boundary between the visible and the invisible; there are words for that. But when you can't say the word, you are standing before nothing. And for me this is even more powerful because, finally, there is a visible in the invisible, just as there is an invisible in the visible. And this, this abolishes everything.

PA: In a sense, all these words become the same word, and

they end up destroying each other.

EJ: They destroy each other in the questioning of themselves, in the process of moving toward the void. At one
point I wrote: "the truth is perhaps this void," meaning
whatever it is that stands at the limit of truth. There is a
constant effacement, a constant peeling of layers, a stripping
away of the name until this name becomes an unpronoun-
ceable name . . . This has nothing to do with nihilism,
even though certain people have accused me of nihilism. It
is the very nature of my work . . . This constant questioning
of things in order to say, finally, what is identity? What are
we? What is the name? This name that we bear with us, what
is it? . . . I don't presume to have any answers, I ask questions.
If I give a special status to the question, that is because I
find something unsatisfactory about the nature of the
answer. It can never completely contain us. Also, and this
is quite important, I feel that answers embody a certain
form of power. Whereas the question is a form of non-
power. But a subversive kind of non-power, one . . . that will
be upsetting to power. Power does not like discussions.
Power affirms, and it has only friends or enemies. Whereas
the question is in between . . . A young student who was
writing a paper on my books once asked me if there was
any lesson to be drawn from my work. I answered: none
whatsoever. It seems to me that if these books tell the reader
anything, it is that he should take on the burden of what
troubles him, that he should carry on his questioning to
the very end. Which means putting oneself in question,
doesn't it? To the very end.

PA: Which means, in other words, that it is endless.

EJ: Yes, there is no end to it. There are some people, of course, who eventually find some kind of peace . . . But I have never found this peace. It seems that I am someone compelled to ask questions. And in my books, everything truly important or essential to me, I think, has been called into question. After the first trilogy of *The Book of Questions* — in which the references to Judaism are very marked — the next two books *Yaël* and *Elya* deal with the relationship between the writer and his words. It becomes more and more personal . . . The series, which continues on through *Aély*, ends with *El*, which is a point, *El, ou le dernier livre* [the last book]. The point, or the dot, is on the cover of the book and is actually the title. It is the smallest possible circle, the circle that has become a dot, or a period, the circle within the circle. In the Kabbala it says, "God reveals himself in a dot," and by making this reference, the whole work of deconstruction seems to uncover a totality. But this totality can never be shown. Totality is an idea . . . and it can be shown only through fragments . . . For example, we are in this room and cannot see the whole house. But we know that we are in the house. The same thing happens in the book. We know that we are in something immense, but at each moment we can only see what is in front of us . . . Totality is something we reconstitute for ourselves through all these fragments, because these fragments are what provides visibility. In the same way, a book can be read because of the words. It is the words which allows us to read the book, not the book which allows us to read the word. The book, of course, is the place in which the word evolves, but as we move on, it is the word, the word in this void, in this space between one word and the next, that makes it possible to read. Our reading takes place in the very whiteness between the words, for this whiteness reminds us of the much greater space in which the word evolves.

PA: In speaking of "the word," of course, we are running into something of a translation problem. In French there is a clear distinction between *parole* and *mot*, whereas in English we have only "word." It is the difference between speaking and writing.

EJ: That is why I always use the word *vocable*. In English it must be a little difficult. "Vocable"? That sounds a bit heavy. In French, too, however, it is not a common word . . . One of the fundamental differences between the written and spoken word is that the written word can be seen. Speaking is more limited. One cannot speak about what will happen, only about what has already happened. In writing, however, you find yourself before something that is about to begin. You enter into another time, another world . . . into something that will express us, although you don't know exactly what it is. This is the reason for all my reticence concerning literary theory. I discuss many theoretical questions in these books, of course, but I never begin with theory *a priori*. Literature for me is a real adventure, and if things are already mapped out for you in advance, how can there be an adventure? You are always at the beginning . . . and each of my books in some way is the beginning of another book that is never written. That is why when the second book prolongs the first, it also cancels out part of the reading you have already made.

PA: They cancel out, in the same way the words cancel each other out.

EJ: Yes. They cancel out the reading so that you can make another reading. And this process keeps repeating itself, endlessly . . . Someone was talking about Mallarmé's book the other day . . . but I think there is an enormous difference between what I call the book and Mallarmé's book. Mallarmé wanted to put all knowledge into a book. He wanted to make a great book, the book of books. But in my opinion this book would be very ephemeral, since knowledge in itself is ephemeral. The book that would have a chance to survive, I think, is the book that destroys itself. That destroys itself in favor of another book that will prolong it. This is the point, if you will, of my deconstruction of the book.

PA: It remains open, whereas Mallarmé's book folds in on itself and remains closed.

EJ: Exactly. It all takes place because of the nature of the questioning. It is a matter of saying at each moment, that isn't enough, I have to go farther. This leads to something else, which in turn must be questioned . . . The book carries all books within itself, and each fragment is the beginning of the book, the book that is created within the book and which at the same time is taken apart. It is lost at the same time it comes into being . . . just as we lose ourselves in the child we create, since the child will eventually replace us

. . . As you can see, this attitude is very different from one that says: we do not exist, I obliterate myself, thank you and goodbye. No. I efface myself in order to go even farther.

PA: You have written somewhere that writing has nothing to do with imagination. This is a rather provocative state-ment, and I wonder if you could elaborate on it.

EJ: I don't imagine anything. I am carried along by the word [*vocable*] itself, by the questioning of the word. The progress of the book is what allows me to move ahead. It has nothing to do with inventing, with saying that I am going to imagine such and such and question it in this way. No. It's similar to what we are doing now. We're speaking, and it's you who are giving me the questions. I'm not imagining anything at all . . . It has to do with experience, with having lived something, rather than imagination. In Boulder a girl came up to me and said she had been struck by the sentence, "When I was twelve years old, I lost the sky." Why not ten years old, she asked, or fifteen, or why not simply "When I was a child"? Why does it have to be twelve? This was an excellent question. Twelve, as it turns out, was a very impor-tant age for me. When I was twelve years old my sister died in my arms . . . and this was something that marked me for life. You can see, then, that behind each thing there is a background of experience, something that has been lived in the past and that touches me deeply.

PA: Another important element in your work, especially in the more recent books — I'm thinking of *Aély* and *El* — is an almost constant playing with words, sounds, letters, meanings . . . The word *sol* [land], for example, which you detach from the word *solitude*, which in turn summons the word *solacier* [to console] . . . as if the whole range of feelings and ideas could be evoked in the simple act of breaking up a word.

EJ: I have tried to question the book on all its levels . . . In *El*, the last book, there is a great deal of what I call an examination of the surface. All my books are about cutting, about disjunction. From one end to the other the book is fragmented, cut up constantly . . . and in the last book I also wanted to show how this works on the level of the word itself. I have nothing against word play. Quite the contrary. I consider it to be something very important. Only for me it is not just play. It is a way of getting from one place to another, a way of advancing by means of the word itself . . . In the very center of *El*, for example — on page 63 in a book of 126 pages, in other words, exactly in the middle — there is a chart with "nul" [nothing] on the top and "l'un" [one] on the bottom. The whole work, in effect, takes place in this "one" and is finally canceled out to become this "nothing." This reveals the essence of the fragmentation, and in some way this chart is an image of all my books . . . This work of cutting is at the very heart of the writing, at the very heart of writing itself. Why? Because in words there are things that attract and repel each other . . . Tensions and relationships arise from the fact that they have the same letters, or because there is some kind of sonority or assonance . . . And this working of word with word can only be explored by means of the word itself, not by means of anything else . . . This is the way everything in my book

functions. One passage of particular importance to me, as
you know, is where I say that the Hebrew people gave Moses
a crucial lesson in reading when they forced him to break
the tablets of the law. Because they were not able to accept
a word without origins, the word of God. It was necessary
for Moses to break the book in order for the book to
become human . . . This gesture on the part of the Hebrew
people was necessary before they could accept the book.
This is exactly what we do as well. We destroy the book when
we read it in order to make it into another book. The book
is always born from a broken book. And the word, too, is
born from a broken word.

PA: What you are saying is that this metamorphosing of
words has nothing to do with playing or with magic. It is
a completely conscious act.

EJ: Absolutely. If there is anything conscious about what
I do, it is in this work with words.

PA: Is it a method?

EJ: No, I'm not suggesting a method . . .

PA: I mean a personal method, a means of arriving at a
certain kind of reflection.

EJ: Yes. But I'm not proposing it to others. It works for me,
but it might not be valid for someone else . . . I have always
worked on this principle . . . which is something one of the
rabbis in my next book says: do not hesitate to question the

book, even those things about it which might seem absurd
to others. Because everything can hide within itself a certain
truth . . . What I try to do is to show that behind each word
other words are hiding. And each time you change a word
or make a word emerge from another word, you change the
whole book. When I say there are many books in the book,
it is because there are many words in the word. Obviously,
if you change the word, the context of the sentence changes
completely. In this way another sentence is born from this
word, and a completely different book begins . . . I think
of this in terms of the sea, in the image of the sea as it breaks
upon the shore. It is not the wave that comes, it is the whole
sea that comes each time and the whole sea that draws back.
It is never just a wave, it is always everything that comes and
everything that goes. This is really the fundamental movement in all my books. Everything is connected to everything
else. There is the whole questioning of the ocean, in its
depths, in its movement, in the foam it leaves behind, in
the delicate lace it leaves upon the shore . . . At each moment, in the least question, it is the *whole* book which
returns and the *whole* book which draws back.

PA: In a sense, the project is inexhaustible by definition.
Each book gives birth to the next.

EJ: Yes . . . Or at least, I am incapable of abandoning it.
Because the book I am going to do is never the book I want
to do. If I could do the book I carry inside me, it would
be the last book. And this book is impossible. If I write, it
is because there is always this book I want to do over again.

PA: Earlier, we were talking about Beckett, and I'm reminded now of something he wrote in the late forties: "To
be an artist is to fail, as no other dares fail . . . ."

EJ: That's a very beautiful statement. It's very beautiful . . .
and that's it, exactly.

PA: It seems to me that you have been saying more or
less the same thing.

EJ: Absolutely. That's it, exactly.

                                                          1978

The Bartlebooth Follies

Georges Perec died in 1982 at the age of forty-six, leaving behind a dozen books and a brilliant reputation. In the words of Italo Calvino, he was "one of the most singular literary personalities in the world, a writer who resembled absolutely no one else." It has taken a while for us to catch on, but now that his major work has at last been translated into English — *Life: A User's Manual* (1978) — it will be impossible for us to think of contemporary French writing in the same way again.

Born into a Jewish family from Poland that emigrated to France in the 1920's, Perec lost his father in the German invasion of 1940 and his mother to the concentration camps in 1943. "I have no memories of childhood," he would later write. His literary career began early, and by the age of nineteen he was already publishing critical notes in the *NRF* and *Les Lettres Nouvelles*. His first novel, *Les Choses*, was awarded the Prix Renadot for 1965, and from then until his death he published approximately one book a year.

Given his tragic family history, it is perhaps surprising to learn that Perec was essentially a comic writer. For the last fifteen years of his life, in fact, he was an active member of Oulipo, a strange literary society founded by Raymond Queneau and the mathematician Francois le Lionnais. This Workshop for Potential Literature (*Ouvoir de Littérature Potentielle*) proposes all kinds of madcap operations to writers: the S-7 method (rewriting famous poems by re-

placing each word with the seventh word that follows it in
the dictionary), the Lipogram (eliminating the use of one
or more letters in a text), acrostics, palindromes, permutations, anagrams, and numerous other "literary constraints."
As one of the leading lights of this group, Perec once wrote
an entire novel of more than 200 pages without using the
letter "e"; this novel was followed by another in which "e"
is the only vowel that appears. Verbal gymnastics of this sort
seemed to come naturally to him. In addition to his literary
work, he produced a notoriously difficult weekly crossword
puzzle for the news magazine *Le Point*.

To read Georges Perec one must be ready to abandon
oneself to a spirit of play. His books are studded with
intellectual traps, allusions and secret systems, and if they
are not necessarily profound (in the sense that Tolstoy and
Mann are profound), they are prodigiously entertaining (in
the sense that Lewis Carroll and Laurence Sterne are entertaining). In Chapter Two of "Life," for example, Perec refers
to "the score of a famous American melody, 'Gertrude of
Wyoming,' by Arthur Stanley Jefferson." By pure chance, I
happened to know that Arthur Stanley Jefferson was the
real name of the comedian Stan Laurel, but just because
I caught this allusion does not mean there weren't a thousand others that escaped me.

For the mathematically inclined, there are magic squares
and chess moves to be discovered in this novel, but the fact
that I was unable to find them did not diminish my enjoy-
ment of the book. Those who have read a great deal will
no doubt recognize passages that quote directly or indi-
rectly from other writers — Kafka, Agatha Christie, Melville,
Freud, Rabelais, Nabokov, Jules Verne and a host of others

— but failure to recognize them should not be considered a handicap. Like Jorge Luis Borges, Georges Perec had a mind that was a storehouse of curious bits of knowledge and awesome erudition, and half the time the reader can't be sure if he is being conned or enlightened. In the long run, it probably doesn't matter. What draws one into this book is not Perec's cleverness, but the deftness and clarity of his style, a flow of language that manages to sustain one's interest through endless lists, catalogues, and descriptions. Perec had an uncanny gift for articulating the nuances of the material world, and in his hands even a worm-eaten table can become an object of fascination. "It was after he had done this that he thought of dissolving what was left of the original wood so as to disclose the fabulous aborescence within, this exact record of the worms' life inside the wooden mass: a static, mineral accumulation of all the movements that had constituted their blind existence, their undeviating single-mindedness, their obstinate itineraries; the faithful materialisation of all they had eaten and digested as they forced from their dense surroundings the invisible elements needed for their survival, the explicit, visible, immeasurably disturbing image of the endless progressions that had reduced the hardest of woods to an impalpable network of crumbling galleries."

Life: A User's Manual is constructed in the manner of a vast jigsaw puzzle. Perec takes a single apartment building in Paris, and in ninety-nine short chapters (along with a Preamble and an Epilogue) proceeds to give a meticulous description of each and every room as well as the life stories of all the inhabitants, both past and present. Ostensibly, we are watching the creation of a painting by Serge Valène, an old artist who has lived in the building for fifty-five years. "It was in the final months of his life that the artist Serge Valène conceived the idea of a painting that would reassemble his entire existence: everything his memory had recorded, all the sensations that had swept over him, all his fantasies, his passions, his hates would be recorded on canvas, a compendium of minute parts of which the sum would be his life."

What emerges is a series of self-contained but interconnecting stories. They are all briskly told, and they run the gamut from the bizarre to the realistic. There are tales of murder and revenge, tales of intellectual obsessions, humorous tales of social satire, and (almost unexpectedly) a number of stories of great psychological penetration. For the most part, Perec's microcosm is peopled with a motley assortment of oddballs, impassioned collectors, antiquarians, miniaturists, and half-baked scholars. If anyone can be called the central character in this shifting, kaleidoscopic work, it would have to be Percival Bartlebooth, an eccentric English millionaire whose insane and useless fifty-year project serves as an emblem for the book as a whole. Realizing as a young man that his wealth has doomed him to a life of boredom, he undertakes to study the art of watercolor from Serge Valène for a period of ten years. Although he has no aptitude whatsoever for painting, he eventually reaches a satisfactory level of competence. Then, in the company of a servant, he sets out on a twenty-year voyage around the world with the sole intention of painting watercolors of five hundred different harbors and seaports. As soon as one of these pictures is finished, he sends it to a man in Paris by the name of Gaspard Winckler, who also lives in the building. Winckler is an expert puzzle-maker whom Bartlebooth has hired to turn the watercolors into 750-piece jigsaw puzzles. One by one, the puzzles are made over the twenty-year period and stored in wooden boxes. Bartlebooth returns from his travels, settles back into his apartment, and methodically goes about putting the puzzles together in chronological order. By means of an elaborate chemical process that has been designed for the purpose at hand, the borders of the puzzle pieces are glued together in such a way that the seams are no longer visible, thus restoring the watercolor to its original integrity. The watercolor, good as new, is then removed from its wooden backing and sent back to the place where it was executed twenty years earlier. There, by prearrangement, it is dipped into a detergent solution that eliminates all traces of the painting, leaving Bartlebooth with a clean and unmarked sheet of paper. In other words, he is left with nothing, the same thing he started with. The project, however does not quite go according to plan. Winckler has made the puzzles too difficult, and Bartlebooth does not live long enough to finish all five hundred of them. As Perec writes in the last paragraph of the ninety-ninth chapter: "It is the twenty-third of June nineteen hundred and seventy-five, and it is eight o'clock in the evening. Seated at his jigsaw puzzle, Bartlebooth has just died. On the tablecloth, somewhere in the crepuscular sky of the four hundred and thirty-ninth puzzle, the black hole of the sole piece not yet filled in has the almost perfect shape of an X. But the ironical thing, which could have been foreseen long ago, is that the piece the dead man holds between his fingers is shaped like a W."

Like many of the other stores in *Life* Bartlebooth's weird

saga can be read as a parable (of sorts) about the efforts of
the human mind to impose an arbitrary order on the world.
Again and again, Perec's characters are swindled, hoaxed,
and thwarted in their schemes, and if there is a darker side
to this book, it is perhaps to be found in this emphasis on
the inevitability of failure. Even a self-annihilating project
such as Bartlebooth's cannot be completed, and when we
learn in the Epilogue that Valène's enormous painting
(which for all intents and purposes is the book we have just
been reading) has come no farther than a preliminary
sketch, we realize that Perec does not exempt himself from
the follies of his characters. It is this sense of self-mockery
that turns a potentially daunting novel into a hospitable
work, a book that for all its high-jinx and japery finally wins
us over with the warmth of its human understanding.

1987

II

— — —

Prefaces

Jacques Dupin

It is not easy to come to terms with Jacques Dupin's poetry. Uncompromisingly hermetic in attitude and rigorously concise in utterance, it does not demand of us a reading so much as an absorption. For the nature of the poem has undergone a metamorphosis, and in order to meet it on its own ground, we must change the nature of our expectations. The poem is no longer a record of feelings, a song, or a meditation. Rather, it is the field in mental space in which a struggle is permitted to unfold: between the destruction of the poem and the quest for the possible poem — for the poem can be born only when all chances for its life have been destroyed. Dupin's work is the progeny of this contradiction, existing within the narrowest of confines, like an invisible seed lodged in the core of stone. The struggle is not a simple either/or conflict between this and that, either destroy or create, either speak or be silent — it is a matter of destroying in order to create, and of maintaining a silent vigil within the word until the last living moment, when the word begins to crumble from the pressure that has been placed upon it.

That which I see, and do not speak of, frightens me. What I speak of, and do not know, delivers me. Do not deliver me.

Dupin has accepted these difficulties deliberately, choosing poverty and the astringencies of denial in place of facility. Because his purpose is not to subjugate his surroundings by means of some vain notion of mastery, but to harmonize

with them, to enter into relation with them, and finally, to
live within them, the poetic operation becomes a process
whereby he unburdens himself of his garments, his tools,
and his possessions, in order to assume, in nakedness,
the fullness of being. In this sense, the poem is a kind of
spiritual purification. But if a monk can fashion a worldly
poverty for himself in the knowledge that it will draw him
nearer to his God, Dupin is not able to give himself such
assurances. He takes on the distress of what is around him
as a way of ending his separation from it, but there is no
sign to lead him, and nothing to guarantee him salvation.
Yet, in spite of this austerity, or perhaps because of it, his
work holds an uncommon richness. This stems at least in
part from the fact that all his poems are grounded in a
landscape, firmly rooted in the palpability of the real. The
problems he confronts are never posed as abstractions, but
present themselves in and through this landscape, and in
the end cannot be separated from it. The universe he brings
forth is an alchemical itinerary through the elements, the
transfiguration of the seemingly indivisible by means of
the word. Similar in spirit to the cosmic correspondences
revealed in the pre-Socratic fragments, it is a universe in
which speech and metaphor are synonymous. Dupin has
not made nature his object, he carries it within him, and
when he finally speaks, it is with the force of what he already
contains. Like Rilke, he finds himself in what is around him.
His voice does more than conjure the presences of things,
it gives them the power of speech as well. But whereas Rilke
is usually passive in his relation to things — attempting to
isolate the thing and penetrate its essence in transcendent
stillness — Dupin is active, seeing things in their intercon-

nectedness, as perpetually changing.

To shatter, to retake, and thus, to rebuild. In the forest we are closer to the woodcutter than to the solitary wanderer. No innocent contemplation. No high forests crossed by sunlight and the songs of birds, but their hidden future: cords of wood. Everything is given to us, but for violence, to be forced open, to be almost destroyed — to destroy us.

The solitary wanderer is Dupin himself, and each poem emerges as an account of his movements through the terrain he has staked out for himself. Dominated by stone, mountain, farm implements, and fire, the geography is cruel, built of the barest materials, and human presence can never be taken for granted in it. It must be won. Generated by a desire to join what forbids him a place and to find a dwelling within it, the Dupin poem is always on the other side: the limit of the human step, the fruit of a terrestrial harrowing. Above all, it is trial. Where all is silence, where all seems to exclude him, he can never be sure where his steps are taking him, and the poem can never be hunted systematically. It comes to life suddenly and without warning, in unexpected places and by unknown means. Between each flash there is patience, and in the end it is this that quickens the landscape — the tenacity to endure in it — even if it offers us nothing. *At the limit of strength a naked word.*

The poem is created only in choosing the most difficult path. Every advantage must be suppressed and every ruse discarded in the interests of reaching this limit — an endless series of destructions, in order to come to a point at which the poem can no longer be destroyed. For the poetic word is essentially the creative word, and yet, nevertheless, a word among others, burdened by the weight of habit and layers of dead skin that must be stripped away before it can regain its true function. Violence is demanded, and Dupin is equal to it. But the struggle is pursued for an end beyond violence — that of finding a habitable space. As often as not, he will fail, and even if he does not, success will bear its own disquiet. *The torch which lights the abyss, which seals it up, is itself an abyss.*

The strength that Dupin speaks of is not the strength of transcendence, but of immanence and realization. The gods have vanished, and there can be no question of pretending to recover the divine *logos.* Faced with an unknowable world, poetry can do no more than create what already exists. But that is already saying a great deal. For if things can be recovered from the edge of absence, there is the chance, in so doing, of giving them back to men.

1971

André du Bouchet

. . . this irreducible sign — deutungslos — *. . . a word beyond
grasping, Cassandra's word, a word from which no lesson is to be
drawn, a word, each time, and every time, spoken to say nothing . . .*

> Hölderlin aujourd'hui (*lecture delivered March 1970
> in Stuttgart to commemorate the 200th anniversary of
> Hölderlin's birth*)

(*this joy . . . that is born of nothing . . .*)
Qui n'est pas tourné vers nous (1972)

Born of the deepest silences, and condemned to life
without hope of life (*I found myself / free / and without hope*),
the poetry of André du Bouchet stands, in the end, as an
act of survival. Beginning with nothing, and ending with
nothing but the truth of its own struggle, du Bouchet's work
is the record of an obsessive, wholly ruthless attempt to gain
access to the self. It is a project filled with uncertainty,
silence, and resistance, and there is no contemporary poetry,
perhaps, that lends itself more reluctantly to gloss. To read
du Bouchet is to undergo a process of dislocation: here, we
discover, is not here, and the body, even the physical
presence within the poems, is no longer in possession of
itself — but moving, as if into the distance, where it seeks
to find itself against the inevitability of its own disappearance (*. . . and the silence that claims us, like a vast field.*)
"Here" is the limit we come to. To be in the poem, from

this moment on, is to be nowhere.

A body in space. And the poem, as self-evident as this body. In space: that is to say, this void, this nowhere between sky and earth, rediscovered with each step that is taken. For wherever we are, the world is not. And wherever we go, we find ourselves moving in advance of ourselves — as if where the world would be. The distance, which allows the world to appear, is also that which separates us from the world, and though the body will endlessly move through this space, as if in the hope of abolishing it, the process begins again with each step taken. We move toward an infinitely receding point, a destination that can never be reached, and in the end, this going, in itself, will become a goal, so that the mere fact of moving onward will be a way of being in the world, even as the world remains beyond us. There is no hope in this, but neither is there despair. For what du Bouchet manages to maintain, almost uncannily, is a nostalgia for a possible future, even as he knows it will never come to pass. And from this dreadful knowledge, there is never-theless a kind of joy, a joy . . . that is born of nothing.

Du Bouchet's work, however, will seem difficult to many readers approaching it for the first time. Stripped of meta-phor, almost devoid of imagery, and generated by a syntax of abrupt, paratactic brevity, his poems have done away with nearly all the props that students of poetry are taught to look for — the very difficulties that poetry has always seemed to rely on — and this sudden opening of distances, in spite of the lessons buried in such earlier poets as Hölderlin, Leopardi, and Mallarmé, will seem baffling, even frightening. In the world of French poetry, however, du Bouchet has performed an act of linguistic surgery no less important than the one performed by William Carlos Williams in America, and against the rhetorical inflation that is the curse of French writing, his intensely understated poems have all the freshness of natural objects. His work, which was first published in the early fifties, became a model for a whole generation of postwar poets, and there are few young poets in France today who do not show the mark of his influence. What on first or second reading might seem to be an almost fragile sensibility gradually emerges as a vision of the greatest force and purity. For the poems themselves cannot be truly felt until one has penetrated the strength of the silence that lies at their source. It is a silence equal to the strength of any word.

1973

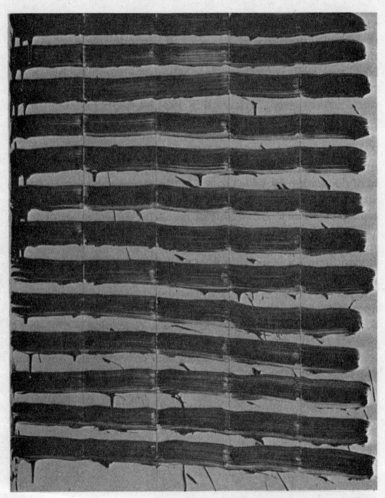

1975, Oil on Canvas (5 canvases bolted together), 76" x 44"

Black on White

Recent paintings by David Reed

The hand of the painter has rarely instructed us in the ways of the hand. When we look at a painting, we see an accumulation of gestures, the layering and shaping of materials, the longing of the inanimate to take on life. But we do not see the hand itself. Like the God of the deists, it seems to have withdrawn from its own creation, or vanished into the density of the world it has made. It does not matter whether the painting is figurative or abstract: we confront the work as an object, and, as such, the surface remains independent of the will behind it.

In David Reed's new paintings, this has been reversed. Suddenly, the hand has been made visible to us, and in each horizontal stroke applied to the canvas, we are able to see that hand with such precision that it actually seems to be *moving*. Faithful only to itself, to the demands of the movement it brings forth, the hand is no longer a means to an end, but the substance of the object it creates. For each stroke we are given here is unique: there is no backtracking, no modeling, no pause. The hand moves across the surface in a single, unbroken gesture, and once this gesture has been completed, is it inviolate. The finished work is not a representation of this process — it is the process itself, and it asks to be *read* rather than simply observed. Composed of a series of rung-like strokes that descend the length of the canvas, each of these painting resembles a vast poem without words. Our eyes follow its movement in the same way we follow a poem down a page, and just as the line in a poem is a unit of breath, so the line in the painting is a unit of gesture. The language of these works is the language of the body.

Some people will probably try to see them as examples of minimal art. But that would be a mistake. Minimal art is an art of control, aiming at the rigorous ordering of visual information, while Reed's paintings are conceived in a way that sabotages the idea of a preordained result. It is this high degree of spontaneity within a consciously limited framework that produces such a harmonious coupling of intellectual and physical energies in his work. No two paintings are or can be exactly alike, even though each painting begins at the same point, with the same fundamental premises. For no matter how regular or controlled the gesture may be, its field of action is unstable, and in the end it is chance that governs the result. Because the white background is still wet when the horizontal strokes are applied, the painting can never be fully calculated in advance, and the image is always at the mercy of gravity. In some sense, then, each painting is born from a conflict between opposing forces. The horizontal stroke tries to impose an order upon the chaos of the background, and is deformed by it as the white paint settles. It would surely be stretching matters to interpret this as a parable of man against nature. And yet, because these paintings evolve in time, and because our reading of them necessarily leads us back through their whole history, we are able to re-enact this conflict whenever we come into their presence. What remains is the drama: and we begin to understand that, fundamentally, these works are the statement of that drama.

In the last sentence of Maurice Blanchot's novel, *Death Sentence*, the nameless narrator writes: "And even more, let him try to imagine the hand that has written these pages: and if he is able to see it, then perhaps reading will become a serious task for him." David Reed's new work is an expression of this same desire in the realm of painting. By allowing us to imagine his hand, by allowing us to *see* his hand, he has exposed us to the serious task of seeing: how we see and what we see, and how what we see in a painting is different from what we see anywhere else. It has taken considerable courage to do this. For it pushes the artist out from the shadows, leaving him with nowhere to stand but in the painting itself. And in order for us to look at one of these works, we have no choice but to go in there with him.

1975

Northern Lights

The paintings by Jean-Paul Riopelle

PROGRESS OF THE SOUL

At the limit of a man, the earth will disappear. And each thing seen of earth will be lost in the man who comes to this place. His eyes will open on earth, and whiteness will engulf the man. For this is the limit of earth — and therefore a place where no man can be.

Nowhere. As if this were a beginning. For even here, where the land escapes all witness, a landscape will emerge. That is to say, there is never nothing where a man has come, even in a place where all has disappeared. For he cannot be anywhere until he is nowhere, and from the moment he begins to lose his bearings, he will find where he is.

Therefore, he goes to the limit of earth, even as he stands in the midst of life. And if he stands in this place, it is only by virtue of a desire to be here, at the limit of himself, as if this limit were the core of another, more secret beginning of the world. He will meet himself in his own disappearance, and in this absence he will discover the earth — even at the limit of earth.

THE BODY'S SPACE

There is no need, then, except the need to be here. As if he, too, could cross into life and take his stand among the things that stand among him: a single thing, even the least

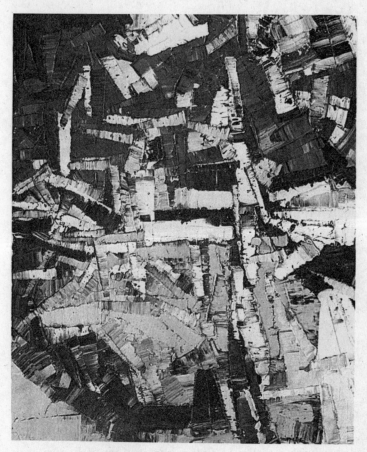

JEAN-PAUL RIOPELLE *Encounter* 1956

thing, of all the things he is not. There is this desire, and it is inalienable. As if, by opening his eyes, he might find himself in the world.

A forest. And within that forest, a tree. And upon that tree, a leaf. A single leaf, turning in the wind. This leaf, and nothing else. The thing to be seen.

To be seen: as if he could be here. But the eye has never been enough. It cannot merely see, nor can it tell him how to see. For when a single leaf turns, it is the entire forest that turns around it. And he who turns around himself.

He wants to see what is. But no thing, not even the least thing, has ever stood still for him. For a leaf is not only a leaf: it is the earth, it is the sky, it is the tree it hangs from in the light of any given hour. But it is also a leaf. That is to say, it is what moves.

It is not enough, then, simply for him to open his eyes. If he is to see, he must begin by moving toward the thing that moves. For seeing is a process that engages the entire body. And though he begins as a witness of the thing he is not, once the first step has been taken, he becomes a participant in a motion that knows no boundaries between self and object.

Distances: what the quickness of the eye discovers, the body must then follow into experience. There is this distance to be crossed, and each time it is a new distance, a different space that opens before the eye. For no two leaves are alike. Therefore, he must feel his feet on the earth: and learn, with a patience that is the instinct of breath and blood, that this same earth is the destiny of the leaf as well.

DISAPPEARANCE

He begins at the beginning. And each time he begins, it is as if he had never lived before. Painting: or the desire to vanish in the act of seeing. That is to say, to see the thing that is, and each time to see it for the first time, as if it were the last time that he would ever see.

At the limit of himself: the pursuit of the nearly-nothing. To breathe in the whiteness of the farthest north. And all that is lost, to be born again from this emptiness in the place where desire carries him, and dismembers him, and scatters him back into earth.

For when he is here, he is nowhere. And time does not exist for him. He will suffer no duration, no continuity, no history: time is merely an alternation between being and not being, and at the moment he begins to feel time passing within him, he knows that he is no longer alive. The self flares up in an image of itself, and the body traces a move-ment it has traced a thousand times before. This is the curse of memory, or the separation of the body from the world.

If he is to begin, then, he must carry himself to a place beyond memory. Once a gesture has been repeated, once a road has been discovered, the act of living becomes a kind of death. The body must empty itself of the world in order to find the world, and each thing must be made to disap-pear before it can be seen. The impossible is that which allows him to breathe, and if there is life in him, it is only because he is willing to risk his life.

Therefore, he goes to the limit of himself. And at the moment he no longer knows where he is, the world can begin for him again. But there is no way of knowing this

in advance, no way of predicting this miracle, and between
each lapse, in each void of waiting, there is terror. And not
only terror, but the death of the world in himself.

THE ENDS OF THE EARTH

Lassitude and fear. The endless beginning of time in the
body of a man. Blindness, in the midst of life; blindness,
in the solitude of a single body. Nothing happens. Or rather,
everything begins to be nothing. And the world is so far
from him that in each thing he sees of the world, he finds
nothing but himself.

Emptiness and immobility, for as long as it takes to kill
him. Here, in the midst of life, where the very density of
things seems to suffocate the possibility of life, or here, in
the place where memory inhabits him. There is no choice
but to leave. To lock his door behind him and set out from
himself, even to the ends of the earth.

The forest. Or a lapse in the heart of time, as if there were
a place where a man could stand. Whiteness opens before
him, and if he sees it, it will not be with the eye of a painter,
but with the body of a man struggling for life. Gradually,
all is forgotten, but not through any act of will: a man can
discover the world only because he must — and for the
simple reason that his life depends on it.

Seeing, therefore, as a way of being in the world. And
knowledge as a force that rises from within. For after being
nowhere at all, he will eventually find himself so near to
the things he is not that he will almost be within them.

Relations. That is to say, the forest. He begins with a single
leaf: the thing to be seen. And because there is one thing,

there can be everything. But before there is anything at all, there must be desire, and the joy of a desire that propels him toward his very limit. For in this place, everything connects; and he, too, is part of this process. Therefore, he must move. And as he moves, he will begin to discover where he is.

NATURE

No painting captures the spirit of natural plentitude more truly than this one. Because this painter understands that the body is what sees, that there can be no seeing without motion, he is able to carry himself across the greatest distances — and come to a place of nearness and intimacy, where each thing can be set free to be what it is.

To look at one of these paintings is to enter it: to be whirled into a field of forces that is composed not only of things, but of the motion of things — of their dislocation and their harmony. For this is a man who knows the forest, and the almost inhuman energy to be found in these canvases does not speak of an abstract program to become one-with-nature, but rather, more basically, of a tangible need to be present, as if life could be lived only in the fullness of this desire. As a consequence, this work does not merely re-present the natural landscape. It is a record of an encounter, a process of penetration and mutual dependence, and, as such, a portrait of a man at the limit of himself.

This is a painter who paints in the same way that he breathes. He has never sought merely to create beautiful objects, but rather, in the act of painting, to make life possible for himself. For this reason, he has always avoided facile solutions, and whenever he has found his work bec' ming automatic, he has stopped work altogether — for as long as it takes for him to unmemorize his work, to block his means of access to the canvas. In effect, each burst of activity is a new beginning, the fruit of a period of unlearning the art of painting — during which time he has allowed himself to discover the world once again. His is an art of both knowledge and innocence, and the perpetual freshness of his work derives from the fact that painting is not something that he does and then divorces from himself, but a necessary struggle to gain hold of his own life and place himself in the world. It is the very substance of the man.

1976

Twentieth-Century French Poetry

French and English constitute a single language.
— *Wallace Stevens*

This much is certain: If not for the arrival of William and his armies on English soil in 1066, the English language as we know it would never have come into being. For the next three hundred years French was the language spoken at the English court, and it was not until the end of the Hundred Years' War that it became clear, once and for all, that France and England were not to become a single country. Even John Gower, one of the first to write in the English vernacular, composed a large portion of his work in French, and Chaucer, the greatest of the early English poets, devoted much of his creative energy to a translation of *Le Roman de la rose* and found his first models in the work of the Frenchman Guillaume de Machaut. It is not simply that French must be considered an "influence" on the development of English language and literature; French is a part of English, an irreducible element of its genetic make-up.

Early English literature is replete with evidence of this symbiosis, and it would not be difficult to compile a lengthy catalogue of borrowings, homages and thefts. William Caxton, for instance, who introduced the printing press in England in 1477, was an amateur translator of medieval French works, and many of the first books printed in Britain

were English versions of French romances and tales of
chivalry. For the printers who worked under Caxton, translation was a normal and accepted part of their duties, and
even the most popular English work to be published by Caxton, Thomas Malory's *Morte d'Arthur*, was itself a ransacking
of Arthurian legends from French sources: Malory warns
the reader no less than fifty-six times during the course of
his narrative that the "French book" is his guide.

In the next century, when English came fully into its own
as a language and a literature, both Wyatt and Surrey —
two of the most brilliant pioneers of English verse — found
inspiration in the work of Clément Marot, and Spenser, the
major poet of the next generation, not only took the title
of his *Shepheardes Calender* from Marot, but two sections of
the work are direct imitations of that same poet. More
importantly, Spenser's attempt at the age of seventeen to
translate Joachim du Bellay (*The Visions of Bellay*) is the first
sonnet sequence to be produced in English. His later revi-
sion of that work and translation of another du Bellay
sequence, *Ruines of Rome*, were published in 1591 and stand
among the great works of the period. Spenser, however, is
not alone in showing the mark of the French. Nearly all
the Elizabethan sonnet writers took sustenance from the
Pléiade poets, and some of them — Daniel, Lodge, Chap-
man — went so far as to pass off translations of French
poets as their own work. Outside the realm of poetry, the
impact of Florio's translation of Montaigne's essays on
Shakespeare has been well documented, and a good case
could be made for establishing the link between Rabelais
and Thomas Nashe, whose 1594 prose narrative, *The Unfor-
tunate Traveler*, is generally considered to be the first novel

written in the English language.

On the more familiar terrain of modern literature, French has continued to exert a powerful influence on English. In spite of the wonderfully ludicrous remark by Southey that poetry is as impossible in French as it is in Chinese, English and American poetry of the past hundred years would be inconceivable without the French. Beginning with Swinburne's 1862 article in *The Spectator* on Baudelaire's *Les Fleurs du Mal* and the first translations of Baudelaire's poetry into English in 1869 and 1870, modern British and American poets have continued to look to France for new ideas. Saintsbury's article in an 1875 issue of *The Fortnightly Review* is exemplary. "It was not merely admiration of Baudelaire which was to be persuaded to English readers," he wrote, "but also imitation of him which, at least with equal earnestness, was to be urged on English writers."

Throughout the 1870's and 1880's, largely inspired by Theodore de Banville, many English poets began experimenting with French verse forms (ballades, lays, virelays and rondeaux), and the "art for art's sake" ideas propounded by Gautier were an important source for the Pre-Raphaelite movement in England. By the 1890's, with the advent of *The Yellow Book* and the Decadents, the influence of the French Symbolists became widespread. In 1893, for example, Mallarmé was invited to lecture at Oxford, a sign of the esteem he commanded in English eyes.

It is also true that little of substance was produced in English as a result of French influences during this period, but the way was prepared for the discoveries of two young American poets, Pound and Eliot, in the first decade of the new century. Each came upon the French independently,

and each was inspired to write a kind of poetry that had
not been seen before in English. Eliot would later write that
". . . the kind of poetry I needed, to teach me the use of
my own voice, did not exist in England at all, and was only
to be found in France." As for Pound, he stated flatly that
"practically the whole development of the English verse-
art has been achieved by steals from the French."

The English and American poets who formed the Imagist
group in the years just prior to World War I were the first
to engage in a *critical* reading of French poetry, with the
aim not so much of imitating the French as of rejuvenating
poetry in English. More or less neglected poets in France,
such as Corbière and Laforgue, were accorded major status.
F. S. Flint's 1912 article in *The Poetry Review* (London) and
Ezra Pound's 1913 article in *Poetry* (Chicago) did much to
promote this new reading of the French. Independent of
the Imagists, Wilfred Owen spent several years in France
before the war and was in close contact with Laurent
Tailhade, a poet admired by Pound and his circle. Eliot's
reading of the French poets began as early as 1908, while
he was still a student at Harvard. Just two years later he was
in Paris, reading Claudel and Gide and attending Bergson's
lectures at the Collège de France.

By the time of the Armory show in 1913, the most radical
tendencies in French art and writing had made their way
to New York, finding a home with Alfred Stieglitz and his
gallery at 291 Fifth Avenue. Many of the names associated
with American and European modernism became part of
this Paris-New York connection: Joseph Stella, Marsden
Hartley, Arthur Dove, Charles Demuth, William Carlos
Williams, Man Ray, Alfred Kreymborg, Marius de Zayas,

Walter C. Arensberg, Mina Loy, Francis Picabia and Marcel Duchamp. Under the influence of Cubism and Dada, of Apollinaire and the Futurism of Marinetti, numerous magazines carried the message of modernism to American readers: *291, The Blind Man, Rongwrong, Broom, New York Dada,* and *The Little Review,* which was born in Chicago in 1914, lived in New York from 1917 to 1927 and died in Paris in 1929. To read the list of *The Little Review*'s contributors is to understand the degree to which French poetry had permeated the American scene. In addition to work by Pound, Eliot, Yeats and Ford Madox Ford, as well as its most celebrated contribution, James Joyce's *Ulysses,* the magazine published Breton, Eluard, Tzara, Péret, Reverdy, Crevel, Aragon and Soupault.

Beginning with Gertrude Stein, who arrived in Paris well before World War I, the story of American writers in Paris during the twenties and thirties is almost identical to the story of American writing itself. Hemingway, Fitzgerald, Faulkner, Sherwood Anderson, Djuna Barnes, Kay Boyle, e e cummings, Hart Crane, Archibald MacLeish, Malcolm Cowley, John Dos Passos, Katherine Anne Porter, Laura Riding, Thornton Wilder, Williams, Pound, Eliot, Glenway Wescott, Henry Miller, Harry Crosby, Langston Hughes, James T. Farrell, Anaïs Nin, Nathanael West, George Oppen — all of these and others either visited or lived in Paris. The experience of those years has so thoroughly saturated American consciousness that the image of the starving young writer serving his apprenticeship in Paris has become one of our enduring literary myths.

It would be absurd to assume that each of these writers was directly influenced by the French. But it would be just

as absurd to assume that they went to Paris only because
it was a cheap place to live. In the most serious and energetic
magazine of the period, *transition*, American and French
writers were published side by side, and the dynamics of
this exchange led to what has probably been the most
fruitful period in our literature. Nor does absence from
Paris necessarily preclude an interest in things French. The
most Francophilic of all our poets, Wallace Stevens, never
set foot in France.

Since the twenties, American and British poets have been
steadily translating their French counterparts — not simply
as a literary exercise, but as an act of discovery and passion.
Consider, for example, these words from John Dos Passos's
preface to his translations of Cendrars in 1930: ". . . A young
man just starting to read verse in the year 1930 would have
a hard time finding out that this method of putting words
together has only recently passed through a period of
virility, intense experimentation and meaning in everyday
life. . . . For the sake of this hypothetical young man and
for the confusion of Humanists, stuffed shirts in editorial
chairs, anthology compilers and prize poets, sonnet writers
and readers of bookchats, I think it has been worth while
to attempt to turn these alive informal personal everyday
poems of Cendrars' into English . . ." Or T. S. Eliot, introducing his translation of *Anabasis* by Saint-John Perse that
same year: "I believe that this is a piece of writing of the
same importance as the later work of James Joyce, as
valuable as *Anna Livia Plurabelle*. And this is a high estimate
indeed." Or Kenneth Rexroth, in the preface to his translations of Reverdy in 1969: "Of all the modern poets in
Western European languages Reverdy has certainly been the

leading influence on my own work — incomparably more
than anyone in English or American — and I have known
and loved his work since I first read *Les Épaves du ciel* as
a young boy."

As the list of translators included in this book shows,
many of the most important contemporary American and
British poets have tried their hand at translating the French,
among them Pound, Williams, Eliot, Stevens, Beckett, Mac-
Neice, Spender, Ashbery, Blackburn, Bly, Kinnell, Levertov,
Merwin, Wright, Tomlinson, Wilbur — to mention just some
of the most familiar names. It would be difficult to imagine
their work had they not been touched in some way by the
French. And it would be even more difficult to imagine
the poetry of our own language if these poets had not been
a part of it. In a sense, then, this anthology is as much about
American and British poetry as it is about French poetry.
Its purpose is not only to present the work of French poets
in French, but to offer translations of that work as our own
poets have re-imagined and re-presented it. As such, it can
be read as a chapter in our own poetic history.

II

The French tradition and the English tradition in this epoch are
at opposite poles to each other. French poetry is more radical, more
total. In an absolute and exemplary way it has assumed the heritage
of European Romanticism, a romanticism which begins with
William Blake and the German romantics like Novalis, and via
Baudelaire and the Symbolists culminates in twentieth-century
French poetry, notably Surrealism. It is a poetry where the world
becomes writing and language becomes the double of the world.
                                                    — Octavio Paz

On the other hand, this much is also certain: If there has been a steady interest in French poetry for the past hundred years on the part of British and American poets, enthusiasm for the French has often been tempered by a certain wariness, even hostility, to literary and intellectual practices in France. This has been more true of the British than the Americans, but, nevertheless, the American literary establishment remains strongly Anglophilic in orientation. One has only to compare the dominant trends in philosophy, literary criticism, or novel-writing, to realize the enormous gulf between the two cultures.

Many of these differences reside in the disparities between the two languages. Although English is in large part derived from French, it still holds fast to its Anglo-Saxon origins. Against the gravity and substantiality to be found in the work of our greatest poets (Milton, say, or Emily Dickinson), which embodies an awareness of the contrast between the thick emphasis of Anglo-Saxon and the nimble conceptuality of French/Latin — and to play one repeatedly against the other — French poetry often seems almost weightless to us, to be composed of ethereal puffs of lyricism and little else. French is necessarily a thinner medium than English. But that does not mean it is weaker. If English writing has staked out as its territory the world of tangibility, of concrete presence, of surface accident, French literary language has largely been a language of essences. Whereas Shakespeare, for example, names more than five hundred flowers in his plays, Racine adheres to the single word "flower." In all, the French dramatist's vocabulary consists of roughly fifteen hundred words, while the word count in Shakespeare's plays runs upward of twenty-five thousand.

The contrast, as Lytton Strachey noted, is between "comprehension" and "concentration." "Racine's great aim," Strachey wrote, "was to produce, not an extraordinary nor a complex work of art, but a flawless one; he wished to be all matter and no impertinence. His conception of a drama was of something swift, inevitable; an action taken at the crisis, with no redundancies however interesting, no complications however suggestive, no irrelevances however beautiful — but plain, intense, vigorous, and splendid with nothing but its own essential force." More recently, the poet Yves Bonnefoy has described English as a "mirror" and French as a "sphere," the one Aristotelian in its acceptance of the given, the other Platonic in its readiness to hypothesize "a different reality, a different realm."

Samuel Beckett, who has spent the greater part of his life writing in both languages, translating his own work from French into English and from English into French, is no doubt our most reliable witness to the capacities and limitations of the two languages. In one of his letters from the mid-fifties, he complained about the difficulty he was having in translating *Fin de partie* (*Endgame*) into English. The line Clov addresses to Hamm, "Il n'y a plus de roues de bicyclette" was a particular problem. In French, Beckett contended, the line conveyed the meaning that bicycle wheels as a category had ceased to exist, that there were no more bicycle wheels in the world. The English equivalent, however, "There are no more bicycle wheels," meant simply that there were no more bicycle wheels available, that no bicycle wheels could be found in the place where they happened to be. A world of difference is embedded here beneath apparent similarity. Just as the Eskimos have more than twenty words for snow (a frequently cited example), which means they are able to experience snow in ways far more nuanced and elaborate than we are — literally to see things we cannot see — the French live inside their language in ways that are somewhat at odds with the way we live inside English. There is no judgment of any kind attached to this remark. If bad French poetry tends to drift off into almost mechanical abstractions, bad English and American poetry has tended to be too earthbound and leaden, sinking into triviality and inconsequence. Between the two bads there is probably little to choose from. But it is helpful to remember that a good French poem is not necessarily the same thing as a good English poem.

The French have had their Academy for more than three hundred years. It is an institution that at once expresses and helps to perpetuate a notion of literature far more grandiose than anything we have ever known in England or America. As an official point of view, it has had the effect of removing the literary from the realm of the everyday, whereas English and American writers have generally been more at home in the flux of the quotidian. But because they have an established tradition to react against, French poets — paradoxically — have tended to be more rebellious than their British and American counterparts. The pressures of conformity have had the net result of producing a vigorous anti-tradition, which in many ways has actually usurped the established tradition as the major current in French literature. Beginning with Villon and Rabelais, continuing on through Rousseau, Baudelaire, Rimbaud, and the cult of the *poète maudit*, and then on into the twentieth century with Apollinaire, the Dada movement and the

Surrealists, the French have systematically and defiantly attacked the accepted notions of their own culture — primarily because they have been secure in their knowledge that this culture exists. The lessons of this anti-tradition have been so thoroughly assimilated that today they are more or less taken for granted.

By contrast, the great interest shown by Pound and Eliot in French poetry (and, in Pound's case, the poetry of other languages as well) can be read not so much as an attack on Anglo-American culture as an effort to create a tradition, to manufacture a past that would somehow fill the vacuum of American newness. The impulse was essentially conservative in nature. With Pound, it degenerated into Fascist rantings; with Eliot, into Anglican pieties and an obsession with the notion of Culture. It would be wrong, however, to set up a simple dichotomy between radicalism and conservatism, and to put all things French in the first category and all things English and American in the second. The most subversive and innovative elements of our literature have frequently surfaced in the unlikeliest places and have then been absorbed into the culture at large. Nursery rhymes, which form an essential part of every English-speaking child's early education, do not exist as such in France. Nor do the great works of Victorian children's literature (Lewis Carroll, George Macdonald) have any equivalent in French. As for America, it has always had its own, homegrown Dada spirit, which has continued to exist as a natural force, without any need of manifestoes or theoretical foundations. The films of Buster Keaton and W. C. Fields, the skits of Ring Lardner, the drawings of Rube Goldberg surely match the corrosive exuberance of anything done in France during the same period. As Man Ray (a native American) wrote to Tristan Tzara from New York in 1921 about spreading the Dada movement to America: "Cher Tzara — Dada cannot live in New York. All New York is Dada, and will not tolerate a rival . . ."

Nor should one assume that twentieth-century French poetry is sitting out there as a convenient, self-contained entity. Far from being a unified body of work that resides neatly within the borders of France, French poetry of this century is various, tumultuous and contradictory. There is no typical case — only a horde of exceptions. For the fact is, a great number of the most original and influential poets were either born in other countries or spent a substantial part of their lives abroad. Apollinaire was born in Rome of mixed Polish and Italian parentage; Milosz was Lithuanian; Segalen spent his most productive years in China; Cendrars was born in Switzerland, composed his first major poem in New York and until he was over fifty rarely stayed in France long enough to collect his mail; Saint-John Perse was born in Guadeloupe, worked for many years in Asia as a diplomat and lived almost exclusively in Washington, D.C. from 1941 until his death in 1975; Supervielle was from Uruguay and for most of his life divided his time between Montevideo and Paris; Tzara was born in Rumania and came to Paris by way of the Dada adventures at the Cabaret Voltaire in Zurich, where he frequently played chess with Lenin; Jabès was born in Cairo and lived in Egypt until he was forty-five; Césaire is from Martinique; du Bouchet is part American and was educated at Amherst and Harvard; and nearly all the younger poets in this book have stayed for extended periods in either England or America. The stereotypical view of the French poet as a creature of Paris, as a xenophobic purveyor of French values, simply does not hold. The more intimately one becomes involved with the work of these poets, the more reluctant one becomes to make any generalizations about them. In the end, the only thing that can be said with any certainty is that they all write in French.

An anthology, therefore, is a kind of trap, tending to thwart our access to the poems even as it makes them available to us. By gathering the work of so many poets in one volume, the temptation is to consider the poets as a group, to drown them as individuals in the great pot of literature. Thus, even before it is read, the anthology becomes a kind of cultural dinner, a smattering of national dishes served up on a platter for popular consumption, as if to say, "Here is French poetry. Eat it. It's good for you." To approach poetry in that way is to miss the point entirely — for it allows one to avoid looking squarely at the poem on the page. And that, after all, is the reader's primary obligation. One must resist the notion of treating an anthology as the last word on its subject. It is no more than a first word, a threshold opening on to a new space.

III

In the end you are weary of this ancient world.
                                        — Guillaume Apollinaire

The logical place to begin this book is with Apollinaire. Although he is neither the first-born of the poets included nor the first to have written in a consciously modern idiom,

he, more than any other artist of his time, seems to embody
the aesthetic aspirations of the early part of the century.
In his poetry, which ranges from graceful love lyrics to bold
experiments, from rhyme to free verse to "shape" poems,
he manifests a new sensibility, at once indebted to the forms
of the past and enthusiastically at home in the world of
automobiles, airplanes and movies. As the tireless promoter
of the Cubist painters, he was the figure around whom many
of the best artists and writers gathered, and poets such as
Jacob, Cendrars and Reverdy formed an important part of
his circle. The work of these three, along with Apollinaire's,
has frequently been described as Cubist. While there are
vast differences among them, both in methods and tone,
they nevertheless share a certain point of view, especially
in the epistemogolical foundations of the work. Simul-
taneity, juxtaposition, an acute feeling for the jaggedness
of the real — these are traits to be found in all four, and
each exploits them to different poetic ends.

Cendrars, at once more abrasive and voluptuous than
Apollinaire, observed that "everything around me moves,"
and his work oscillates between the two solutions implicit
in this statement: on the one hand, the ebullient jangle of
sensations in works such as *Nineteen Elastic Poems*, and on the
other the snapshot realism of his travel poems (originally
entitled *Kodak*, but changed under pressure from the film
company of the same name, to *Documentaires*) — as if each
of these poems was the record of a single moment, lasting
no longer than it takes to click the shutter of a camera. With
Jacob, whose most enduring work is contained in his 1917
collection of prose poems, *The Dice Cup*, the impulse is
toward an anti-lyrical comedy. His language is continually

erupting into playfulness (puns, parody, satire) and takes its greatest delight in unmasking the deceptions of appearances: Nothing is ever what it seems to be, everything is subject to metamorphosis, and change always occurs unexpectedly, with lightning swiftness.

Reverdy, by contrast, uses many of these same principles, but with far more somber objectives. Here an accumulation of fragments is synthesized into an entirely new approach to the poetic image. "The image is a pure creation of the mind," wrote Reverdy in 1918. "It cannot be born from a comparison but from a juxtaposition of two more or less distant realities. The more the relationship between the two juxtaposed realities is both distant and true, the stronger the image will be — the greater its emotional power and poetic reality." Reverdy's strange landscapes, which combine an intense inwardness with a proliferation of sensual data, bear in them the signs of a continual search for an impossible totality. Almost mystical in their effect, his poems are nevertheless anchored in the minutiae of the everyday world; in their quiet, at times monotone music, the poet seems to evaporate, to vanish into the haunted country he has created. The result is at once beautiful and disquieting — as if Reverdy had emptied the space of the poem in order to let the reader inhabit it.

A similar atmosphere is sometimes produced by the prose poems of Fargue, whose work predates that of any other poet included here. Fargue is the supreme modern poet of Paris, and fully half his writings are about the city itself. In his delicate, lyrical configurations of memory and perception, which retain an echo of their Symbolist predecessors, there is an attentiveness to detail combined with a rigorous subjectivity that transforms the city into an immense interior landscape. The poem of witness is at the same time a poem of remembrance, as if, in the solitary act of seeing, the world were reflected back to its solitary source and then, once more, reflected outward as vision. With Larbaud, a close friend of Fargue's, one also finds a hint of the late nineteenth century. A. O. Barnabooth, the supposed author of Larbaud's finest book of poems (in the first edition of 1908 Larbaud's name was intentionally left off the title page), is a rich South American of twenty-four, a naturalized citizen of New York, an orphan, a world traveler, a highly sensitive and melancholy young man — a more sympathetic and humorous version of the traditional dandy hero. As Larbaud later explained, he wanted to invent a poet "sensitive to the diversity of races, people, and countries; who could find the exotic everywhere . . .; witty and 'international,' one, in a word, capable of writing like Whitman but in a light vein, and of supplying that note of comic, joyous irresponsibility which is lacking in Whitman." As in the poems of Apollinaire and Cendrars, Larbaud-Barnabooth expresses an almost euphoric delight in the sensations of travel: "I experienced for the first time all the joy of living / In a compartment of the Nord-Express . . ." Of Barnabooth André Gide wrote: "I love his haste, his cynicism, his gluttony. These poems, dated from here and there, and everywhere, are as thirst-making as a wine list . . . In this particular book, each picture of sensation, no matter how correct or dubious it may be, is made valid by the speed with which it is supplanted."

The work of Saint-John Perse also bears a definite resemblance to that of Whitman — both in the nature of his stanza and in the rolling, cumulative force of his long syntactic breaths. If Larbaud in some sense domesticates Whitman, Saint-John Perse carries him beyond universalism into a quest for great cosmic harmonies. The voice of the poet is mythical in its scope, as if, with its thunderous and sumptuous rhetoric, it had come into being for the sole purpose of conquering the world. Unlike most of the poets of his generation, who made their peace with temporality and used the notion of change as the premise of their work, Saint-John Perse's poems are quickened by an almost Platonic urge to seek out the eternal. In this respect, Milosz also stands to the side of his contemporaries. A student of the mystics and the alchemists, Milosz combines Catholicism, and cabalism with what Kenneth Rexroth has described as "apocalyptic sensualism," and his work draws much of its inspiration from numerological treatment of names, transpositions of letters, anagrammatic and acronymic combinations, and other linguistic practices of the occult. But, as with the poems of Yeats, the poetry itself transcends the restrictions of its sources, displaying, as John Peck has commented, "an obsessive range of feeling, in which personal melancholy is also melancholy for a crepuscular era, that long hour before first light 'when the shadows decompose.'"

Another poet who resists categorization is Segalen. Like Larbaud, who wrote his poems through an invented persona; like Pound, whose translations stand curiously among his best and most personal works, Segalen carried this impulse toward self-effacement one step further and wrote behind the mask of another culture. The poems to be found in *Stèles* are neither translations nor imitations, but French poems written by a French poet *as if he were Chinese.* There is no attempt to deceive on Segalen's part; he never pretended these poems were anything other than original works. What at first reading might appear to be a kind of literary exoticism on closer scrutiny holds up as a poetry of solid, universal interest. By freeing himself from the limitations of his own culture, by circumventing his own historical moment, Segalen was able to explore a much wider territory — to discover, in some sense, that part of himself that was a poet.

In many ways, the case of Jouve is no less unusual. A follower of the Symbolists as a young man, Jouve published a number of books of poetry between 1912 and 1923. What he described as a "moral, spiritual, and aesthetic crisis" in 1924 led him to break with all his early work, which he never allowed to be republished. Over the next forty years he produced a voluminous body of writing — his collected poems run well over a thousand pages. Deeply Christian in outlook, Jouve is primarily concerned with the question of sexuality, both as transgression and as creative force — "the beautiful power of human eroticism" — and his poetry is the first in France to have made use of the methods of Freudian psychoanalysis. It is a poetry without predecessors and without followers. If his work was somewhat forgotten during the period dominated by the Surrealists — which meant that recognition of Jouve's achievement was delayed for almost a generation — he is now widely considered to be one of the major poets of the half-century.

Supervielle was also influenced by the Symbolists as a young man, and of all the poets of his generation he is perhaps the most purely lyrical. A poet of space, of the

natural world, Supervielle writes from a position of supreme innocence. "To dream is to forget the materiality of
one's body," he wrote in 1951, "and to confuse to some
degree the outer and the inner world . . . People are
sometimes surprised over my marvelling at the world. This
arises as much from the permanency of my dreams as from
my bad memory. Both lead me from surprise to surprise,
and force me to be amazed at everything."

It is this sense of amazement, perhaps, that best describes
the work of these first eleven poets, all of whom began
writing before World War I. The poets of the next generation, however, who came of age during the war itself, were
denied the possibility of such innocent optimism. The war
was not simply a conflict between armies, but a profound
crisis of values that transformed European consciousness,
and the younger poets, while having absorbed the lessons
of Apollinaire and his contemporaries, were compelled to
respond to this crisis in ways that were without precedent.
As Hugo Ball, one of the founders of Dada, noted in his
diary in 1917: "A thousand-year-old culture disintegrates.
There are no columns and no supports, no foundations
anymore — they have all been blown up . . . The meaning
of the world has disappeared."

The Dada movement, which began in Zurich in 1916, was
the most radical response to this sense of spiritual collapse.
In the face of a discredited culture, the Dadaists challenged
every assumption and ridiculed every belief of that culture.
As artists, they attacked the notion of art itself, transforming
their rage into a kind of subversive doubt, filled with caustic
humor and willful self-contradiction. "The true Dadaists
are against Dada," wrote Tzara in one of his manifestoes.

The point was never to take anything at face value and never to take anything too seriously — especially oneself. The Socratic ironies of Marcel Duchamp's art are perhaps the purest expression of this attitude. In the realm of poetry, Tzara was no less sly or rambunctious. This is his recipe for writing a Dada poem: "Take a newspaper. Take a pair of scissors. Select an article as long as you want your poem to be. Cut out the article. Then carefully cut out each of the words that form this article and put them in a bag. Shake gently. Then take out each scrap, one after the other. Conscientiously copy them in the order they left the bag. The poem will resemble you. And there you are, an infinitely original writer, with a charming sensibility, beyond the understanding of the vulgar." If this is a poetry of chance, it should not be confused with the aesthetics of aleatory composition. Tzara's proposed method is an assault on the sanctity of Poetry, and it does not attempt to elevate itself to the status of an artistic ideal. Its function is purely negative. This is anti-art in its earliest incarnation, the "anti-philosophy of spontaneous acrobatics."

Tzara moved to Paris in 1919, introducing Dada to the French scene. Breton, Aragon, Éluard and Soupault all became participants in the movement. Inevitably, it did not last more than a few years. An art of total negation cannot survive, for its destructiveness must ultimately include itself. It was by drawing on the ideas and attitudes of Dada, however, that Surrealism became possible. "Surrealism is pure psychic automatism," Breton wrote in his first manifesto of 1924, "whose intention is to express, verbally, in writing, or by other means, the real process of thought and thought's dictation, in the absence of all control exercised by reason and outside all aesthetic or moral preoccupations. Surrealism rests on the belief in the superior reality of certain previously neglected forms of association; in the omnipotence of dream, and in the disinterested play of thought."

Like Dada, Surrealism did not offer itself as an aesthetic movement. Equating Rimbaud's cry to change life with Marx's injunction to change the world, the Surrealists sought to push poetry, in Walter Benjamin's phrase, "to the utmost limits of possibility." The attempt was to demystify art, to blur the distinctions between life and art, and to use the methods of art to explore the possibilities of human freedom. To quote Walter Benjamin again, from his prescient essay on the Surrealists published in 1929: "Since Bakunin, Europe has lacked a radical concept of freedom. The Surrealists have one. They are the first to liquidate the liberal-moral-humanistic ideal of freedom, because they are convinced that 'freedom, which on this earth can only be bought with a thousand of the hardest sacrifices, must be enjoyed unrestrictedly in its fullness, without any kind of programmatic calculation, as long as it lasts.'" For this reason, Surrealism associated itself closely with the politics of revolution (one of its magazines was even entitled *Surrealism in the Service of the Revolution*), flirting continually with the Communist Party and playing the role of fellow traveler during the era of the Popular Front — although refusing to submerge its identity in that of pure politics. Constant disputes over principles marked the history of the Surrealists, with Breton holding the middle ground between the activist and aesthetic wings of the group, frequently shifting positions in an effort to maintain a consistent program for Surrealism. Of all the poets associated with the movement, only Péret remained faithful to Breton over the long term. Soupault, by nature averse to the notion of literary movements, lost interest by 1927. Both Artaud and Desnos were excommunicated in 1929 — Artaud for opposing Surrealism's interest in politics and Desnos for supposedly compromising his integrity by working as a journalist. Aragon, Tzara and Éluard all joined the Communist Party in the thirties. Queneau and Prévert parted amicably after a brief association. Daumal, whose work was recognized by Breton as sharing the preoccupations of the Surrealists, declined an invitation to join the group. Char, ten or twelve years younger than most of the original members, was an early adherent but later broke with the movement and went on to do his best work during and after the war. Ponge's connection was peripheral, and Michaux, in some sense the most Surrealist of all French poets, never had anything to do with the group.

This same confusion exists when one examines the work of these poets. If "pure psychic automatism" is the underlying principle of Surrealist composition, only Péret seems to have stuck to it rigorously in the writing of his poems. Interestingly, his work is the least resonant of all the Surrealists — notable more for its comic effects than for any uncovering of the "convulsive beauty" that Breton envisaged as the goal of Surrealist writing. Even in Breton's poetry, with its abrupt shifts and unexpected associations, there is an undercurrent of consistent rhetoric that makes the poems cohere as densely reasoned objects of thought. With Tzara as well, automatism serves almost as a rhetorical device. It is a method of discovery, not an end in itself. In his best work — especially the long, multifaceted *Approx-*

imate Man — a torrent of images organizes itself into a nearly systematic argument by means of repetition and variation, propelling itself forward in the manner of a musical composition.

Soupault, on the other hand, is clearly a conscious crafts-man. While limited in range, his poetry displays a charm and a humility absent in the work of the other Surrealists. He is a poet of intimacy and pathos, at times strangely reminiscent of Verlaine, and if his poems have none of the flamboyance to be found in Tzara and Breton, they are more immediately accessible, more purely lyrical. By the same token, Desnos is a poet of plain speech, whose work often achieves a stunning lyrical intensity. His output extends from early experiments with language (dexterous, often dazzling exercises in word play) to free-verse love poems of great poignancy to longer, narrative poems and works in traditional forms. In an essay published just one year before his death, Desnos described his work as an effort "to fuse popular language, even the most colloquial, with an inex-pressible 'atmosphere'; with a vital use of imagery, so as to annex for ourselves those domains which . . . remain incom-patible with that fiendish, plaguing poetic dignity which endlessly oozes from tongues . . ."

With Éluard, arguably the greatest of the Surrealist poets, the love poem is accorded metaphysical status. His language, as limpid as anything to be found in Ronsard, is built on syntactic structures of extreme simplicity. Éluard uses the idea of love in his work to mirror the poetic process itself — as a way both to escape the world and to understand it. It is that irrational part of man which weds the inner to the outer, rooted in the physical and yet transcending matter, creating that uniquely human place in which man can discover his freedom. These same themes are present in Éluard's later work, particularly the poems written during the German Occupation, in which this notion of freedom is carried from the realm of the individual to that of an entire people.

If Éluard's work can be read as a continuous whole, Aragon's career as a poet divides into two distinct periods. Perhaps the most militant and provocative of the French Dadaists, he also played a leading role in the development of Surrealism and, after Breton, was the group's most active theorist. Attacked by Breton in the early thirties for the increasingly propagandist tone of his poetry, Aragon withdrew from the movement and joined the Communist Party. It was not until the war that he returned to the writing of poetry — and in a manner that bears almost no relation to his earlier work. His Resistance poems brought him national fame, and they are distinguished by their force and eloquence, but in their methods they are highly traditional, composed for the most part in alexandrines and rhyming stanzas.

Although Artaud was an early participant in Surrealism (for a time he even headed The Central Bureau for Surrealist Research) and although a number of his most important works were written during that period, he is a writer who stands so defiantly outside the traditional norms of literature that it is useless to label his work in any way. Properly speaking, Artaud is not a poet at all, and yet he has probably had a greater influence on the poets who came after him than any other writer of his generation. "Where others present their works," he wrote, "I claim to do no more than show my mind." His aim as a writer was never to create aesthetic objects — works that could be detached from their creator — but to record the state of mental and physical struggle in which "words rot at the unconscious summons of the brain." There is no division in Artaud between life and writing — and life not in the sense of biography, of external events, but life as it is lived in the intimacy of the body, of the blood that flows through one's veins. As such, Artaud is a kind of Ur-poet, whose work describes the processes of thought and feeling before the advent of language, before the possibility of speech. It is at once a cry of suffering and a challenge to all our assumptions about the purpose of literature.

In a totally different way from Artaud, Ponge also commands a unique place among the writers of his generation. He is a writer of supremely classical values, and his work — most of it has been written in prose — is pristine in its clarity, highly sensitive to nuance and the etymological origins of words, which Ponge has described as the "semantical thickness" of language. Ponge has invented a new kind of writing, a poetry of the object that is at the same time a method of contemplation. Minutely detailed in its descriptions, and everywhere infused with a fine ironic humor, his work proceeds as though the object being examined did not exist as a word. The primary act of the poet, therefore, becomes the act of seeing, as if no one had ever seen the thing before, so that the object might have "the good fortune to be born into words."

Like Ponge, who has frequently resisted the efforts of critics to classify him as a poet, Michaux is a writer whose work escapes the strictures of genre. Floating freely between prose and verse, his texts have a spontaneous, almost haphazard quality that sets them against the pretensions and platitudes of high art. No French writer has ever given greater rein to the play of his imagination. Much of his best writing is set in imaginary countries and reads as a bizarre kind of anthropology of inner states. Although often compared to Kafka, Michaux does not resemble the author of Kafka's novels and stories so much as the Kafka of the notebooks and parables. As with Artaud, there is an urgency of process in Michaux's writing, a sense of personal risk and necessity in the act of composition. In an early statement about his poetry he declared: "I write with transport and for myself. a) sometimes to liberate myself from an intolerable tension or from a no less painful abandonment. b) sometimes for an imaginary companion, for a kind of alter ego whom I would honestly like to keep up-to-date on an extraordinary transition in me or in the world, which I, ordinarily forgetful, all at once believe I rediscover in, so to speak, its virginity. c) deliberately to shake the congealed and established, to invent . . . Readers trouble me. I write, if you like, for the unknown reader."

An equal independence of approach is present in Daumal, a serious student of Eastern religions, whose poems deal obsessively with the rift between spiritual and physical life. "The Absurd is the purest and most basic form of metaphysical existence," he wrote, and in his dense, visionary work, the illusions of appearance fall away only to be transformed into further illusions. "The poems are haunted by a . . . consciousness of impending death," Michael Benedikt has commented, "seen as the poet's long-lost 'double'; and also by a personification of death as a sort of sinister mother, an exacting being avaricious in her search for beings to extinguish — but only so as to place upon them perversely the burden of further metamorphoses."

Daumal is considered one of the chief precursors of the "College of Pataphysics," a mock-secret literary organization inspired by Alfred Jarry that included both Queneau and Prévert among its members. Humor is the guiding principle in the work of these two poets. With Queneau, it is a linguistic humor, based on intricate word plays, parody, feigned stupidity and slang. In his well-known prose work of 1947, for example, *Exercices de style*, the same mundane event is given in ninety-nine different versions, each one written in a different style, each one presented from a different point of view. In discussing Queneau in *Writing Degree Zero*, Roland Barthes describes this style as "white writing" — in which literature, for the first time, has openly become a problem and question of language. If Queneau is an intellectual poet, Prévert, who also adheres closely to the patterns of ordinary speech in his work, is without question a popular poet — even a populist poet. Since World War II, no one has had a wider audience in France, and many of Prévert's works have been turned into highly successful songs. Anticlerical, antimilitaristic, rebellious in political attitude and extolling a rather sentimentalized form of love between man and woman, Prévert represents one of the more felicitous marriages between poetry and mass culture, and beyond the charm of his work, it is valuable as an indicator of popular French taste.

Although Surrealism continues to exist as a literary movement, the period of its greatest influence and most important creations came to an end by the beginning of World War II.

Of the second-generation Surrealists — or those poets who found inspiration in its methods — Césaire stands out as the most notable example. One of the first black writers to be recognized in France, founder of the *négritude* movement — which asserts the uniqueness and dignity of black culture and consciousness — Césaire, a native of Martinique, was championed by Breton, who discovered his work in the late thirties. As the South African poet Mazisi Kunene has written about Césaire: "Surrealism was for him a logical instrument with which to smash the restrictive forms of language which sanctified rationalized bourgeois values. The breaking up of language patterns coincided with his own desire to smash colonialism and all oppressive forms." More vividly perhaps than in the work of the Surrealists of France, Césaire's poetry embodies the twin aspirations of political and aesthetic revolution, and in such a way that they are inseparably joined.

For many of the poets who began writing in the thirties, however, Surrealism was never a temptation. Follain, for example, whose work has proved to be particularly amenable to American taste (of all recent French poets, he is the one who has been most frequently translated), is a poet of the everyday, and in his short, exquisitely crafted works one finds an examination of the object no less serious and challenging than Ponge's. At the same time, Follain is largely a poet of memory ("In the fields / of his eternal childhood / the poet wanders / wanting to forget nothing"), and his evocations of the world as seen through a child's eyes bear within them a shimmering, epiphanic quality of psychological truth. A similar kind of realism and attention to surface detail is also to be found in Guillevic. Materialist in his approach to the world, unrhetorical in his methods, Guillevic has also created a world of objects — but one in which the object is nevertheless problematical, a reality to be penetrated, to be striven for, but which is not necessarily given. Frénaud, on the other hand, although often grouped together with Follain and Guillevic, is a far more romantic poet than his two contemporaries. Effusive in his language, metaphysical in his concerns, he has been compared at times to the Existentialists in his insistence that man's world is a creation of man himself. Despairing of certainty (*There Is No Paradise*, reads the title of one of his collections), Frénaud's work draws its force not so much from a recognition of the absurd as from the attempt to find a basis for positive values within the absurd itself.

If World War I was the crucial event that marked the poetry of the twenties and thirties, World War II was no less decisive in determining the kind of poetry written in France during the late forties and fifties. The military defeat of 1940 and the Nazi Occupation that followed were among the darkest moments in French history. The country had been devastated both emotionally and economically. In the context of this disarray, the mature poetry of René Char came as a revelation. Aphoristic, fragmented, closely allied to the thought of Heraclitus and the pre-Socratics, Char's poetry is at once a lyrical summoning of natural correspondences and a meditation on the poetic process itself. Austere in its settings (for the most part the landscape is that of Char's native Provence) and roughly textured in its language, this is a poetry that does not attempt to record or evoke feelings so much as it seeks to embody the ongoing struggle of words to ground themselves in the world. Char writes from a position of deep existential commitment (he was an important field leader in the Resistance), and his work is permeated with a sense of new beginnings, of a necessary search to rescue life from the ruins.

The best poets of the immediate postwar generation share many of these same preoccupations. Bonnefoy, du Bouchet, Jaccottet, Giroux and Dupin, all born within four years of each other, manifest in their work a vigilant hermeticism that is characterized by a consciously reduced range of imagery, great syntactical inventiveness and a refusal to ask anything but essential questions. Bonnefoy, the most classical and philosophically oriented of the five, has largely been concerned in his work with tracking the reality that haunts "the abyss of concealed appearances." "Poetry does not interest itself in the shape of the world itself," he once remarked, "but in the world that this universe will become. Poetry speaks only of presences — or absences." Du Bouchet, by contrast, is a poet who shuns every temptation toward abstraction. His work, which is perhaps the most radical adventure in recent French poetry, is based on a rigorous attentiveness to phenomenological detail. Stripped of metaphor, almost devoid of imagery, and generated by a language of abrupt, paratactic brevity, his poems move through an almost barren landscape, a speaking "I" continually in search of itself. A du Bouchet page is the mirror of this journey, each one dominated by white space, the few words present as if emerging from a silence that will inevitably claim them again.

Of these poets, it is undoubtedly Dupin whose work holds the greatest verbal richness. Tightly sprung, calling upon an imagery that seethes with hidden violence, his poems are dazzling in both their energy and their anguish. "In this infinite unanimous dissonance," he writes, in a poem entitled "Lichens," "each ear of corn, each drop of blood, speaks its language and goes its way. The torch, which lights the abyss, which seals it up, is itself an abyss." Far gentler in approach are both Jaccottet and Giroux. Jaccottet's short nature poems, which in certain ways adhere to the aesthetics of Imagism, have an Oriental stillness about them that can flare at any moment into the brightness of epiphany. "For us living more and more surrounded by intellectual schemas and masks," Jaccottet has written, "and suffocating in the prison they erect around us, the poet's eye is the battering ram that knocks down these walls and gives back to us, if only for an instant, the real; and with the real, a possibility of life." Giroux, a poet of great lyrical gifts, died prematurely in 1973 and published only one book during his lifetime. The short poems in that volume are quiet, deeply meditated works about the nature of poetic reality, explorations of the space between the world and words, and they have had a considerable impact on the work of many of today's younger poets.

This hermeticism, however, is by no means present in the work of all the poets of the postwar period. Dadelsen, for example, is an effusive poet, monologic and varied in tone, who frequently launches into slang. There have been a number of distinguished Catholic poets in France during the twentieth century (La Tour du Pin, Emmanuel, Jean-Claude Renard and Mambrino are recent examples), but it is perhaps Dadelsen, less well known than the others, who in his tormented search for God best represents the limits and perils of religious consciousness. Marteau, on the other hand, draws much of his imagery from myth, and although his preoccupations often overlap with those of, say, Bonnefoy or Dupin, his work is less self-reflective than theirs, dwelling not so much on the struggles and paradoxes of expression as on uncovering the presence of archetypal forces in the world.

Of the new work that began to appear in the early sixties, the books of Jabès are the most notable. Since 1963, when *The Book of Questions* was published, Jabès has brought out ten volumes in a remarkable series of works, prompting comments such as Jacques Derrida's statement that "in the last ten years nothing has been written in France that does not have its precedent somewhere in the texts of Jabès." Jabès, an Egyptian Jew who published a number of books of poetry in the forties and fifties, has emerged as a writer of the first rank with his more recent work — all of it written in France after his expulsion from Cairo during the Suez crisis. These books are almost impossible to define. Neither novels nor poems, neither essays nor plays, they are a combination of all these forms, a mosaic of fragments, aphorisms, dialogues, songs and commentaries that endlessly move around the central question posed by each book: How to speak what cannot be spoken. The question is the Holocaust, but it is also the question of literature itself. By a startling leap of the imagination, Jabès treats them as one and the same: "I have talked to you about the difficulty of being Jewish, which is the same as the difficulty of writing. For Judaism and writing are but the same waiting, the same hope, the same wearing out."

This determination to carry poetry into uncharted territory, to break down the standard distinctions between prose and verse, is perhaps the most striking characteristic of the younger generation of poets today. In Deguy, for example, poetry can be made from just about anything at all, and his work draws on a broad range of material: from the technical language of science to the abstractions of philosophy to elaborate play on linguistic constructions. In Roubaud, the quest for new forms has led to books of highly intricate structures (one of his volumes, Σ, is based on the permutations of the Japanese game of go), and these invented shapes are exploited with great deftness, serving not as ends in themselves but as a means of ordering the fragments they encompass, of putting the various pieces in a larger context and investing them with a coherence they would not possess on their own.

Pleynet and Roche, two poets closely connected with the well-known review *Tel Quel*, have each carried the notion of antipoetry to a position of extreme combativeness. Pleynet's jocular, and at the same time deadly serious "Ars Poetica" of 1964 is a good example of this attitude. "I. ONE CANNOT KNOW HOW TO WRITE WITHOUT KNOWING WHY. II. THE AUTHOR OF THIS ARS POETICA DOES NOT KNOW HOW TO WRITE BUT HE WRITES. III. THE QUESTION 'HOW TO WRITE' ANSWERS THE QUESTION 'WHY WRITE' AND THE QUESTION 'WHAT IS WRITING'. IV. A QUESTION IS AN ANSWER." Roche's approach is perhaps even more disruptive of conventional assumptions about literature. "Poetry is inadmissible. Besides, it does not exist," he has written. And elsewhere: ". . . the logic of modern writing demands that one should take a vigorous hand in promoting the death agonies of [this] symbolist, outmoded ideology. Writing can only symbolize what it is in its functioning, in its 'society,' within the frame of its utilization. It must stick to that."

This is not to say, however, that short, lyric poems do not continue to be written in France. Delahaye and Denis, both still in their thirties, have created substantial bodies of work in this more familiar mode — mining a landscape that had first been mapped out by du Bouchet and Dupin. On the other hand, many of the younger poets, having absorbed and transmuted the questions raised by their predecessors, are now producing a kind of work that is both original and demanding in its insistence upon the textuality of the written word. Although there are significant differences among Albiach, Royet-Journoud, Daive, Hocquard and Veinstein, in one fundamental aspect of their work they share a common point of view. Their medium as writers is neither the individual poem nor even the sequence of poems, but the book. As Royet-Journoud stated in a recent interview: "My books consist only of a single text, the genre of which cannot be defined. . . . It's a *book* that I write, and I feel that the notion of genre obscures the book as such." This is as true of Daive's highly charged, psycho-erotic work, Hocquard's graceful and ironic narratives of memory, and Veinstein's minimal theaters of the creative process as it is of Royet-Journoud's obsessive "detective stories" of language. Most strikingly, this approach to composition can be found in Albiach's 1971 volume, *État*, undoubtedly the major work to be published thus far by a member of this younger generation. As Keith Waldrop has written: "The poem — it is a single piece — does not progress by images . . . or by plot. . . . The argument, if it were given, might include the following propositions: 1) everyday language is dependent on logic, but 2) in fiction, there is no necessity that any particular word should follow any other, so 3) it is possible at least to imagine a free choice, a syntax generated by desire. *État* is the 'epic' . . . of this imagination. To state such an argument . . . would be to renounce the whole project. But what is presented is not a series of emotions . . . the poem is composed mindfully; and if Anne-Marie Albiach rejects rationality, she quite obviously writes with full intelligence . . ."

IV

. . . with the conviction that, in the end, translating is madness.

— Maurice Blanchot

As I was about to embark on the project of editing this anthology, a friend gave me a piece of valuable advice. Jonathan Griffin, who served as British cultural attaché in Paris after the war, and has translated several books by De Gaulle, as well as poets ranging from Rimbaud to Pessoa, has been around long enough to know more about such things than I do. Every anthology, he said, has two types of readers: the critics, who judge the book by what is *not* included in it, and the general readers, who read the book for what it actually contains. He advised me to keep this second group uppermost in my thoughts. The critics, after all, are in business to criticize, and they are familiar with the material anyway. The important thing to remember is that most people will be reading the majority of these poets for the first time. They are the ones who will get the most out of the anthology.

During the two years it has taken for me to put this book together, I have often reminded myself of these words. Frequently, however, it has been difficult to take them to heart, since I myself am all too aware of what has not been included. My original plan for the anthology was to represent the work of almost a hundred poets. In addition to more familiar kinds of writing, I had wanted to use a number of eccentric works, provide examples of concrete and sound poetry, include several collaborative poems and, in a few instances, offer variant translations when more than one good version of a poem was available. As work progressed, it became apparent that this would not be possible. I was faced with the unhappy situation of trying to fit an elephant into a cage designed for a fox. Reluctantly, I changed my approach to the book. If my choice was between offering a smattering of poems by many poets or substantial selections of work by a reduced number of poets, there did not seem to be much doubt that the second solution was wiser and more coherent. Instead of imagining everything I would like to see in the anthology, I tried to think of the poets it would be inconceivable *not* to include. In this way, I gradually whittled the list down to forty-eight. These were difficult decisions for me, and though I stand by my final selection, it is with regret for those I was not able to include.*

---

*Among them are the following: Pierre Albert-Birot, Jean Cocteau, Raymond Roussel, Jean Arp, Francis Picabia, Arthur Cravan, Michel Leiris, Georges Bataille, Léopold Senghor, André Pieyre de Mandiargues, Jacques Audiberti, Jean Tardieu, Georges Schéhadé, Pierre Emmanuel, Joyce Mansour, Patrice de la Tour du Pin, René Guy Cadou, Henri Pichette, Christian Dotremont, Olivier Larronde, Henri Thomas, Jean Grosjean, Jean Tortel, Jean Laude, Pierre Torreilles, Jean-Claude Renard, Jean Joubert, Jacques Réda, Armen Lubin, Jean Pérol, Jude Stéfan, Marc Alyn, Jacqueline Risset, Michel Butor, Jean Pierre Faye, Alain Jouffroy, George Perros, Armand Robin, Boris Vian, Jean Mambrino, Lorand Gaspar, George Badin, Pierre Oster, Bernard Nöel, Claude Vigée, Joseph Gugliemi, Daniel Blanchard, Michel Couturier, Claude Esteban, Alain Sueid, Mathieu Bénézet.

There are no doubt some who will also wonder about certain other exclusions. In order to keep the book focused on poetry of the twentieth century, I decided on a fixed cut-off point to determine where the anthology should begin. The crucial year for my purposes turned out to be 1876: Any poet born before that year would not be considered. This allowed me, in good conscience, to forgo the problem posed by poets such as Valéry, Claudel, Jammes and Péguy, all of whom began writing in the late nineteenth century and went on writing well into the twentieth. Although their work overlaps chronologically with many of the poets in the book, it seems to belong in spirit to an earlier time. By the same token, 1876 was a convenient date for allowing me to include certain poets whose work is essential to the project — Fargue, Jacob and Milosz in particular.

As for the English versions of the poems, I have used already existing translations whenever possible. My motive has been to underscore the involvement, over the past fifty years, of American and British poets in the work of their French counterparts, and since there is abundant material to choose from (some of it hidden away in old magazines and out-of-print books, some of it readily available), there seemed to be no need to begin my search elsewhere. My greatest pleasure in putting this book together has been in rescuing a number of superb translations from the obscurity of library shelves and microfilm rooms: Nancy Cunard's Aragon, John Dos Passos' Cendrars, Paul Bowles's Ponge, and the translations by Eugene and Maria Jolas (the editors of *transition*), to mention just a few. Also to be noted are the translations that previously existed only in manuscript. Paul Blackburn's translations of Apollinaire, for example, were discovered among his papers after his death, and are published here for the first time.

Only in cases where translations did not exist or where the available translations seemed inadequate did I commission fresh translations. In each of these instances (Richard Wilbur's version of Apollinaire's "Le Pont Mirabeau," Lydia Davis's Fargue, Robert Kelly's Roubaud, Anselm Hollo's Dadelsen, Michael Palmer's Hocquard, Rosmarie Waldrop's Veinstein, Geoffrey Young's Aragon), I have tried to arrange the marriage with care. My aim was to bring together compatible poets — so that the translator would be able to exploit his particular strengths as a poet in rendering the original into English. The results of this matchmaking have been uniformly satisfying. Richard Wilbur's "Mirabeau Bridge," for instance, strikes me as the first acceptable version of this important poem we have had in English, the only translation that comes close to re-creating the subtle music of the original.

In general, I have followed no consistent policy about translation in making my choices. A few of the translations are hardly more than adaptations, although the vast majority are quite faithful to the originals. Translating poetry is at best an art of approximation, and there are no fixed rules to follow in deciding what works or does not. It is largely a matter of instinct, of ear, of common sense. Whenever I was faced with a choice between literalness and poetry, I did not hesitate to choose poetry. It seemed more important to me to give those readers who have no French a true sense of each poem *as a poem* than to strive for word-by-word exactness. The experience of a poem resides not only in each of its words, but in the interactions among

those words — the music, the silences, the shapes — and
if a reader is not somehow given the chance to enter the
totality of that experience, he will remain cut off from the
spirit of the original. It is for this reason, it seems to me,
that poems should be translated by poets.

1981

Mallarmé's Son

Mallarmé's second child, Anatole, was born on July 16, 1871, when the poet was twenty-nine. The boy's arrival came at a moment of great financial stress and upheaval for the family. Mallarmé was in the process of negotiating a move from Avignon to Paris, and arrangements were not finally settled until late November, when the family installed itself at 29 rue de Moscou and Mallarmé began teaching at the Lycée Fontanes.

Mme Mallarmé's pregnancy had been extremely difficult, and in the first months of his life Anatole's health was so fragile that it seemed unlikely he would survive. "I took him out for a walk on Thursday," Mme Mallarmé wrote to her husband on October 7. "It seemed to me that his fine little face was getting back some of its color . . . I left him very sad and discouraged, and even afraid that I would not see him anymore, but it's up to God now, since the doctor can't do anything more, but how sad to have so little hope of seeing this dear little person recover."

Anatole's health, however, did improve. Two years later, in 1873, he reappears in the family correspondence in a series of letters from Germany, where Mallarmé's wife had taken the children to meet her father. "The little one is like a blossoming flower," she wrote to Mallarmé. "Tole loves his grandfather, he does not want to leave him, and when he is gone, he looks for him all over the house." In that same letter, nine-year-old Geneviève added: "Anatole asks for

papa all the time." Two years later, on a second trip to
Germany, there is further evidence of Anatole's robust
health, for after receiving a letter from his wife, Mallarmé
wrote proudly to his friend Cladel: "Anatole showers stones
and punches on the little Germans who come back to attack
him in a group." The following year, 1876, Mallarmé was
absent from Paris for a few days and received this anecdote
from his wife: "Totol is a bad little boy. He did not notice
you were gone the night you left; it was only when I put
him to bed that he looked everywhere for you to say good-
night. Yesterday he did not ask for you, but this morning
the poor little fellow looked all over the house for you;
he even pulled back the covers on your bed, thinking he
would find you there." In August of that same year, during
another of Mallarmé's brief absences from the family,
Geneviève wrote to her father to thank him for sending her
presents and then remarked: "Tole wants you to bring him
back a whale."

Beyond these few references to Anatole in the Mallarmé
family letters, there are several mentions of him in C. L.
Lefèvre-Roujon's introduction to the *Correspondance inédite
de Stephane Mallarmé et Henry Roujon* — in particular, three
little incidents that give some idea of the boy's lively personality. In the first, a stranger saw Anatole attending to
his father's boat and asked him, "What is your boat called?"
Anatole answered with great conviction, "My boat isn't
called anything. Do you give a name to a carriage?" On
another occasion, Anatole was taking a walk through the
Fountainebleau forest with Mallarmé. "He loved the Fountainebleau forest and would often go there with Stéphane
. . . . [One day], running down a path, he came upon a very

pretty woman, politely stepped to the side, looked her over from top to bottom and, out of admiration, winked his eye at her, clicked his tongue, and then, this homage to beauty having been made, continued on his child's promenade." Finally, Lefèvre-Roujon reports the following: One day Mme Mallarmé boarded a Paris bus with Anatole and put the child on her lap in order to economize on the extra fare. As the bus jolted along, Anatole fell into a kind of trance, watching a gray-haired priest beside him who was .reading his breviary. He asked him sweetly: "Monsieur l'abbée, would you allow me to kiss you?" The priest, surprised and touched, answered: "But of course, my little friend." Anatole leaned over and kissed him. Then, in the suavest voice possible, he commanded: "And now, kiss mama!"

In the spring of 1879, several months before his eighth birthday, Anatole became seriously ill. The disease, diagnosed as child's rheumatism, was further complicated by an enlarged heart. The illness first attacked his feet and knees, and then, when the symptoms had apparently cleared up, his ankles, wrists, and shoulders. Mallarmé considered himself largely responsible for the child's suffering, feeling that he had given the boy "bad blood" through a hereditary weakness. At the age of seventeen, he had suffered terribly from rheumatic pain, with high fevers and violent headaches, and throughout his life rheumatism would remain a chronic problem.

In April, Mallarmé went off to the country for a few days with Geneviève. His wife wrote: "He's been a good boy, the poor little martyr, and from time to time asks me to dry his tears. He asks me often to tell little papa that he would

like to write to him, but he can't move his little wrists." Three day later, the pain had shifted from Anatole's hand to his legs, and he was able to write a few words: "I think of you always. If you knew, my dear Little Father, how my knees hurt."

Over the following months, things took a turn for the better. By August, the improvement had been considerable. On the tenth, Mallarmé wrote to Robert de Montesquiou, a recently made friend who had formed a special attachment to Anatole, to thank him for sending the child a parrot. "I believe that your delicious little animal . . . has distracted the illness of our patient, who is now allowed to go to the country. . . . Have you heard from where you are . . . all the cries of joy from our invalid, who never takes his eyes . . . away from the marvelous princess held captive in her marvelous palace, who is called Sémiramas because of the stone gardens she seems to reflect? I like to think that this satisfaction of an old and improbable desire has had something to do with the struggle of the boy's health to come back; to say nothing . . . of the secret influence of the precious stone that darts out continually from the cage's inhabitant on the child. . . . How charming and friendly you have been, you who are so busy with so much, during this recent time; and it is more than a pleasure for me to announce to you, before anyone else, that I feel all our worries will soon be over."

In this state of optimism, Anatole was taken by the family to Valvins in the country. After several days, however, his condition deteriorated drastically, and he nearly died. On August 22, Mallarmé wrote to his close friend Henry Roujon:

"I hardly dare to give any news because there are moments in this war between life and death that our poor little adored one is waging when I allow myself to hope, and repent of a too sad letter written the moment before, as of some messenger of bad tidings I myself have dispatched. I know nothing anymore and see nothing anymore . . . so much have I observed with conflicting emotions. The doctor, while continuing the Paris treatment, seems to act as though he were dealing with a condemned person who can only be comforted; and persists, when I follow him to the door, in not giving a glimmer of hope. The dear boy eats and sleep a little; breathes. Everything his organs could do to fight the heart problem they have done; after another enormous attack, that is the benefit he draws from the country. But the disease, the terrible disease, seems to have set in irremediably. If you lift the blanket, you see a belly so swollen you can't look at it!

"There it is. I do not speak to you of my pain; no matter where my thought tries to lead it, this pain recoils from seeing itself worsen! But what does suffering matter, even suffering like that: the horrible thing is . . . the misfortune in itself that this little being might vanish. . . . I confess that it is too much for me; I cannot bring myself to face this idea.

"When my wife looks at the darling, she seems to see a serious illness and nothing more; I must not rob her of the courage she has found to care for the child in this quietude. I am alone here then with the hatchet blow of the doctor's verdict."

A letter from Mallarmé to Montesquiou on September 9 offers further details: "Unfortunately, after several days [in the country], everything . . . grew dark: we have been

through the cruelest hours our darling invalid has caused us, for the symptoms we thought had disappeared forever have returned; they are taking hold now. The old improvements were a sham. . . . I am too tormented and too taken up with our poor little boy to do anything literary, except to jot down a few rapid notes. . . . *Tole* speaks of you, and even amuses himself in the morning by fondly imitating your voice. The parrot, whose auroral belly seems to catch fire with a whole orient of spices, is looking right now at the forest with one eye and at the bed with the other, like a thwarted desire for an excursion by her little master."

By late September there had been no improvement, and Mallarmé now centered his hopes on a return to Paris. On the twenty-fifth, he wrote to his oldest friend, Henri Cazalis: "The evening before your beautiful present came, the poor darling, for the second time since his illness began, was nearly taken from us. Three successive fainting fits in the afternoon did not, thank heaven, carry him off. . . . The belly disturbs us, as filled with water as ever. . . . The country has given us everything we could ask of it, assuming it could give us anything, milk, air, and peaceful surroundings for the invalid. We have only one idea now, to leave for a consultation with Doctor Peter. . . . I tell myself it is impossible that a great medical specialist cannot take advantage of the forces nature opposes so generously to a terrible disease. . . ."

After the return to Paris, there are two further letters about Anatole — both dated October 6. The first was to the English writer John Payne: "This is the reason for my long silence. . . . At Easter, already six hideous months ago, my son was attacked by rheumatism, which after a false convalescence has thrown itself on his poor heart with incredible violence, and holds him between life and death. The poor friend has twice almost been taken from us. . . . You can judge of our pain, knowing how much I live inside my family; then this child, so charming and exquisite, had captivated me to the point that I still include him in all my future projects and in my dearest dreams. . . ."

The other letter was to Montesquiou. "Thanks to immense precautions, everything went well [on the return to Paris] . . . but the darling paid for it with several bad days that drained his tiny energy. He is prey to a horrible and inexplicable nervous cough . . . it shakes him for a whole day and a whole night. . . . — Yes, I am quite beside myself, like someone on whom a terrible and endless wind is blowing. All-night vigils, contradictory emotions of hope and sudden fear, have supplanted all thought of repose. . . . My sick little boy smiles at you from his bed, like a white flower remembering the vanished sun."

After writing these two letters, Mallarmé went to the post office to mail them. Anatole died before his father managed to return home.

*

The 202 fragments that follow belonged to Mme E. Bonniot, the Mallarmé heir, and were deciphered, edited, and published in a scrupulously prepared volume by the literary scholar and critic Jean-Pierre Richard in 1961. In the preface to his book — which includes a lengthy study of the fragments — he describes his feelings on being handed the soft red box that contained Mallarmé's notes. On the

one hand: exaltation. On the other hand: wariness.
Although he was deeply moved by the fragments, he was
uncertain whether publication was appropriate, given the
intensely private nature of the work. He concluded, however, that anything that could enhance our understanding
of Mallarmé would be valuable. "And if these phrases are
no more than sighs," he wrote, "that makes them all the
more precious to us. It seemed to me that the very nakedness of these notes . . . made their distribution desirable.
It was useful in fact to prove once again to what extent the
famous Mallarméan serenity was based on the impulses of
a very vivid sensibility, at times even quite close to frenzy
and delirium. . . . Nor was it irrelevant to show, by means
of a precise example, how this impersonality, this vaunted
objectivity, was in reality connected to the most subjective
upheavals of a life."

A close reading of the fragments will clearly show that
they are no more than notes for a possible work: a long
poem in four parts with a series of very specific themes.
That Mallarmé projected such a work and then abandoned
it is indicated in a memoir written by Geneviève that was
published in a 1926 issue of the N.R.F.: "In 1879, we had
the immense sorrow of losing my little brother, an exquisite
child of eight. I was quite young then, but the deep and
silent pain I felt in my father made an unforgettable impression on me: 'Hugo,' he said, 'was happy to have been able
to speak (about the death of his daughter); for me, it's
impossible.'"

As they stand now, the notes are a kind of ur-text, the raw
data of the poetic process. Although they seem to resemble
poems on the page, they should not be confused with poetry

per se. Nevertheless, more than one hundred years after they were written, they are perhaps closer to what we today consider possible in poetry than at the time of their composition. For here we find a language of immediate contact, a syntax of abrupt, lightning shifts that still manages to maintain a sense, and in their brevity, the sparse presence of their words, we are given a rare and early example of isolate words able to span the enormous mental spaces that lie between them — as if intelligible links could be created by the brute force of each word or phrase, so densely charged that these tiny particles of language could somehow leap out of themselves and catch hold of the succeeding cliff-edge of thought. Unlike Mallarmé's finished poems, these fragments have a startlingly unmediated quality. Faithful not to the demands of art but to the jostling movement of thought — and with a speed and precision that astonish — these notes seem to emerge from such an interior place, it is as though we could hear the crackling of the wires in Mallarmé's brain, experience each synapse of thought as a physical sensation. If these fragments cannot be read as a work of art, neither, I think, should they be treated simply as a scholarly appendage to Mallarmé's collected writings. For, in spite of everything, the Anatole notes do carry the force of poetry, and in the end they achieve a stunning wholeness. They are a work in their own right — but one that cannot be categorized, one that does not fit into any preexistant literary form.

The subject matter of the fragments requires little comment. In general, Mallarmé's motivation seems to have been the following: feeling himself responsible for the disease that led to Anatole's death, for not giving his son a body strong enough to withstand the blows of life, he would take it upon himself to give the boy the one indomitable thing he was capable of giving: his thought. He would transmute Anatole into words and thereby prolong his life. He would, *literally*, resurrect him, since the work of building a tomb — a tomb of poetry — would obliterate the presence of death. For Mallarmé, death is the consciousness of death, not the physical act of dying. Because Anatole was too young to understand his fate (a theme that occurs repeatedly throughout the fragments), it was as though he had not yet died. He was still alive in his father, and it was only when Mallarmé himself died that the boy would die as well. This is one of the most moving accounts of a man trying to come to grips with modern death — that is to say, death without God, death without hope of salvation — and it reveals the secret meaning of Mallarmé's entire aesthetic: the elevation of art to the stature of religion. Here, however, the work could not be written. In this time of crisis even art failed Mallarmé.

It strikes me that the effect of the Anatole fragments is quite close to the feeling created by Rembrandt's last portrait of his son, Titus. Bearing in mind the radiant and adoring series of canvasses the artist made of the boy throughout his childhood, it is almost impossible for us to look at that last painting: the dying Titus, barely twenty years old, his face so ravaged by disease that he looks like an old man. It is important to imagine what Rembrandt must have felt as he painted that portrait; to imagine him staring into the face of his dying son and being able to keep his hand steady enough to put what he saw onto the canvas. If fully imagined, the act becomes almost unthinkable.

In the natural order of things, fathers do not bury their sons. The death of a child is the ultimate horror of every parent, an outrage against all we believe we can expect of life, little though it is. For everything, at that point, is taken away from us. Unlike Ben Jonson, who could lament the fact of his fatherhood as an impediment to understanding that his son had reached "the state he should envie," Mallarmé could find no support for himself, only an abyss, no consolation, except in the plan to write about his son — which, in the end, he could not bring himself to do. The work died along with Anatole. It is all the more moving to us, all the more important, for having been left unfinished.

1982

On the High Wire

The first time I saw Philippe Petit was in 1971. I was in Paris, walking down the Boulevard Montparnasse, when I came upon a large circle of people standing silently on the sidewalk. It seemed clear that something was happening in-side that circle, and I wanted to know what it was. I elbowed my way past several onlookers, stood on my toes, and caught sight of a smallish young man in the center. Everything he wore was black: his shoes, his pants, his shirt, even the battered silk top hat he wore on his head. The hair jutting out from under the hat was a light red-blonde, and the face below it was so pale, so devoid of color, that at first I thought he was in whiteface.

The young man juggled, rode a unicycle, performed little magic tricks. He juggled rubber balls, wooden clubs, and burning torches, both standing on the ground and sitting on his one-wheeler, moving from one thing to the next without interruption. To my surprise, he did all this in silence. A chalk circle had been drawn on the sidewalk, and scrupulously keeping any of the spectators from entering that space — with a persuasive mime's gesture — he went through his performance with such ferocity and intelligence that it was impossible to stop watching.

Unlike other street performers, he did not play to the crowd. Rather, it was somehow as though he had allowed the audience to share in the workings of his thoughts, had made us privy to some deep, inarticulate obsession within him. Yet there was nothing overtly personal about what he did. Everything was revealed metaphorically, as if at one remove, through the medium of the performance. His juggling was precise and self-involved, like some conversation he was holding with himself. He elaborated the most complex combinations, intricate mathematical patterns, arabesques of nonsensical beauty, while at the same time keeping his gestures as simple as possible. Through it all, he managed to radiate a hypnotic charm, oscillating somewhere between demon and clown. No one said a word. It was as though his silence were a command for others to be silent as well. The crowd watched, and after the performance was over, everyone put money in the hat. I realized that I had never seen anything like it before.

The next time I saw Philippe Petit was several weeks later. It was late at night — perhaps one or two in the morning — and I was walking along a quai of the Seine not far from Nôtre-Dame. Suddenly, across the street, I spotted several young people moving quickly through the darkness. They were carrying ropes, cables, tools, and heavy satchels. Curious as ever, I kept pace with them from my side of the street and recognized one of them as the juggler from the Boulevard Montparnasse. I knew immediately that something was going to happen. But I could not begin to imagine what it was.

The next day, on the front page of the *International Herald Tribune*, I got my answer. A young man had strung a wire between the towers of Nôtre-Dame Cathedral and walked and juggled and danced on it for three hours, astounding the crowds of people below. No one knew how he had rigged up his wire nor how he had managed to elude the attention of the authorities. Upon returning to the ground, he had been arrested, charged with disturbing the peace and sundry other offenses. It was in this article that I first learned his name: Philippe Petit. There was not the slightest doubt in my mind that he and the juggler were the same person.

This Nôtre-Dame escapade made a deep impression on me, and I continued to think about it over the years that followed. Each time I walked past Nôtre-Dame, I kept seeing the photograph that had been published in the newspaper: an almost invisible wire stretched between the enormous towers of the cathedral, and there, right in the middle, as if suspended magically in space, the tiniest of human figures, a dot of life against the sky. It was impossible for me not to add this remembered image to the actual cathedral before my eyes, as if this old monument of Paris, built so long ago to the glory of God, had been transformed into something else. But what? It was difficult for me to say. Into something more human, perhaps. As though its stones now bore the mark of a man. And yet, there was no real mark. I had made the mark with my own mind, and it existed only in memory. And yet, the evidence was irrefutable: my perception of Paris had changed. I no longer saw it in the same way.

It is, of course, an extraordinary thing to walk on a wire so high off the ground. To see someone do this triggers an almost palpable excitement in us. In fact, given the necessary courage and skill, there are probably very few people who would not want to do it themselves. And yet, the art of high-wire walking has never been taken very seriously. Because wire walking generally takes place in the circus, it is automatically assigned marginal status. The circus, after all, is for children, and what do children know about art? We grownups have more important things to think about. There is the art of music, the art of painting, the art of sculpture, the art of poetry, the art of prose, the art of theater, the art of dancing, the art of cooking, the art of living. But the art of high-wire walking? The very term seems laughable. If people stop to think about the high-wire at all, they usually categorize it as some minor form of athletics.

There is, too, the problem of showmanship. I mean the crazy stunts, the vulgar self-promotion, the hunger for publicity that is everywhere around us. We live in an age when people seem willing to do anything for a little attention. And the public accepts this, granting notoriety or fame to anyone brave enough or foolish enough to make the effort. As a general rule, the more dangerous the stunt, the greater the recognition. Cross the ocean in a bathtub, vault forty burning barrels on a motorcycle, dive into the East River from the top of the Brooklyn Bridge, and you are sure to get your name in the newspapers, maybe even an interview on a talk show. The idiocy of these antics is obvious. I'd much rather spend my time watching my son ride his bicycle, training wheels and all.

Danger, however, is an inherent part of high-wire walking. When a man walks on a wire two inches off the ground, we do not respond in the same way as when he walks on a wire two hundred feet off the ground. But danger is only half of it. Unlike the stuntman, whose performance is calculated to emphasize every hair-raising risk, to keep his audience panting with dread and an almost sadistic antici-pation of disaster, the good high-wire walker strives to make his audience forget the dangers, to lure it away from thoughts of death by the beauty of what he does on the wire itself. Working under the greatest possible constraints, on a stage no more than an inch across, the high-wire walker's job is to create a sensation of limitless freedom. Juggler, dancer, acrobat, he performs in the sky what other men are content to perform on the ground. The desire is at once far-fetched and perfectly natural, and the appeal of it, finally, is its utter uselessness. No art, it seems to me, so clearly emphasizes the deep aesthetic impulse inside us all. Each time we see a man walk on the wire, a part of us is up there with him. Unlike performances in the other arts, the experience of the high wire is direct, unmediated, simple, and it requires no explanation whatsoever. The art is the thing itself, a life in its most naked delineation. And if there is beauty in this, it is because of the beauty we feel inside ourselves.

There was another element of the Nôtre-Dame spectacle that moved me: the fact that it was clandestine. With the thoroughness of a bank robber preparing a heist, Philippe had gone about his business in silence. No press conferences, no publicity, no posters. The purity of it was impressive. For what could he possibly hope to gain? If the wire had snapped, if the installation had been faulty, he would have died. On the other hand, what did success bring? Certainly he did not earn any money from the venture. He did not even try to capitalize on his brief moment of glory. When all was said and done, the only tangible result was a short stay in a Paris jail.

Why did he do it, then? For no other reason, I believe, than to dazzle the world with what he could do. Having seen his stark and haunting juggling performance on the street, I sensed intuitively that his motives were not those of other men — not even those of other artists. With an ambition and an arrogance fit to the measure of the sky, and placing on himself the most stringent internal demands, he wanted, simply, to do what he was capable of doing.

After living in France for four years, I returned to New York in July of 1974. For a long time I had heard nothing about Philippe Petit, but the memory of what had happened in Paris was still fresh, a permanent part of my inner mythology. Then, just one month after my return, Philippe was in the news again — this time in New York, with his now-famous walk between the towers of the World Trade Center. It was good to know that Philippe was still dreaming his dreams, and it made me feel that I had chosen the right moment to come home. New York is a more generous city than Paris, and the people here responded enthusiastically to what he had done. As with the aftermath of the Nôtre-Dame adventure, however, Philippe kept faith with his vision. He did not try to cash in on his new celebrity; he managed to resist the honky-tonk temptations America is all too willing to offer. No books were published, no films were made, no entrepeneur took hold of him for packaging. The fact that the World Trade Center did not make him rich was almost as remarkable as the event itself. But the proof of this was there for all New Yorkers to see: Philippe continued to make his living by juggling in the streets.

The streets were his first theater, and he still takes his performances there as seriously as his work on the wire. It all started very early for him. Born into a middle-class French family in 1949, he taught himself magic at the age of six, juggling at the age of twelve, and high-wire walking a few years later. In the meantime, while immersing himself in such varied activities as horseback riding, rock-climbing, art, and carpentry, he managed to get himself expelled from nine schools. At sixteen, he began a period of incessant travels all over the world, performing as a street juggler in Western Europe, Russia, India, Australia, and the United States. "I learned to live by my wits," he has said of those years. "I offered juggling shows everywhere, for everyone — traveling around like a troubadour with my old leather sack. I learned to escape the police on my unicycle. I got hungry like a wolf; I learned how to control my life."

But it is on the high-wire that Philippe has concentrated his most important ambitions. In 1973, just two years after the Nôtre-Dame walk, he did another renegade performance in Sydney, Australia: stretching his wire between the northern pylons of the Harbour Bridge, the largest steel arch bridge in the world. Following the World Trade Center Walk in 1974, he crossed the Great Falls of Paterson, New Jersey, appeared on television for a walk between the spires of the Cathedral in Laon, France, and also crossed the Superdome in New Orleans before 80,000 people. This last performance took place just nine months after a forty-foot fall from an inclined wire, from which he suffered several broken ribs, a collapsed lung, a shattered hip, and a smashed pancreas.

Philippe has also worked in the circus. For one year he was a featured attraction with Ringling Brothers Barnum and Bailey, and from time to time he has served as a guest performer with The Big Apple Circus in New York. But the traditional circus has never been the right place for

Philippe's talents, and he knows it. He is too solitary and unconventional an artist to fit comfortably into the strictures of the commercial big top. Far more important to him are his plans for the future: to walk across Niagara Falls; to walk from the top of the Sydney Opera House to the top of the Harbour Bridge — an inclined walk of more than half a mile. As he himself explains it: "To talk about records or risks is to miss the point. All my life I have looked for the most amazing places to cross — mountains, waterfalls, buildings. And if the most beautiful walks also happen to be the longest or most dangerous — that's fine. But I didn't look for that in the first place. What interests me is the performance, the show, the beautiful gesture."

When I finally met Philippe in 1980, I realized that all my feelings about him had been correct. This was not a daredevil or a stuntman, but a singular artist who could talk about his work with intelligence and humor. As he said to me that day, he did not want people to think of him as just another "dumb acrobat." He talked about some of the things he had written — poems, narratives of his Nôtre-Dame and World Trade Center adventures, film scripts, a small book on high-wire walking — and I said that I would be interested in seeing them. Several days later, I received a bulky package of manuscripts in the mail. A covering note explained that these writings had been rejected by eighteen different publishers in France and America. I did not consider this to be an obstacle. I told Philippe that I would do all I could to find him a publisher and also promised to serve as translator if necessary. Given the pleasure I had received from his performances on the street and wire, it seemed the least I could do.

On the High-Wire is in my opinion a remarkable book. Not only is it the first study of high-wire walking ever written, but it is also a personal testament. One learns from it both the art and the science of wire walking, the lyricism and the technical demands of the craft. At the same time, it should not be misconstrued as a "how to" book or an instruction manual. High-wire walking cannot really be taught: it is something you learn by yourself. And certainly a book would be the last place to turn if you were truly serious about doing it.

The book, then, is a kind of parable, a spiritual journey in the form of a treatise. Through it all, one feels the presence of Philippe himself: it is his wire, his art, his personality that inform the entire discourse. No one else, finally, has a place in it. This is perhaps the most important lesson to be learned from the treatise: the high-wire is an art of solitude, a way of coming to grips with one's life in the darkest, most secret corner of the self. When read carefully, the book is transformed into the story of a quest, an exemplary tale of one man's search for perfection. As such, it has more to do with the inner life than the high-wire. It seems to me that anyone who has ever tried to do something well, anyone who has ever made personal sacrifices for an art or an idea, will have no trouble understanding what it is about.

Until two months ago, I had never seen Philippe perform on the high-wire outdoors. A performance or two in the circus, and of course films and photographs of his exploits, but no outdoor walk in the flesh. I finally got my chance during the recent inauguration ceremony at the Cathedral of Saint John the Divine in New York. After a hiatus of

several decades, construction was about to begin again
on the cathedral's tower. As a kind of homage to the wire
walkers of the Middle Ages — the *joglar* from the period
of the great French cathedrals — Philippe had conceived
of the idea of stretching a steel cable from the top of a
tall apartment building on Amsterdam Avenue to the top
of the Cathedral across the street — an inclined walk of
several hundred yards. He would go from one end to the
other and then present the Bishop of New York with a silver
trowel, which would be used to lay the symbolic first stone
of the tower.

The preliminary speeches lasted a long time. One after
the other, dignitaries got up and spoke about the Cathedral
and the historic moment that was about to take place.
Clergymen, city officials, former Secretary of State Cyrus
Vance — all of them made speeches. A large crowd had
gathered in the street, mostly school children and neighborhood people, and it was clear that the majority of them had
come to see Philippe. As the speeches droned on, there was
a good deal of talking and restlessness in the crowd. The
late September weather was threatening: a raw, pale gray
sky; the wind beginning to rise; rain clouds gathering in
the distance. Everyone was impatient. If the speeches went
on any longer, perhaps the walk would have to be canceled.

Fortunately, the weather held, and at last Philippe's turn
came. The area below the cable had to be cleared of people,
which meant that those who a moment before had held
center stage were now pushed to the side with the rest of
us. The democracy of it pleased me. By chance, I found
myself standing shoulder to shoulder with Cyrus Vance on
the steps of the Cathedral. I, in my beat-up leather jacket,

and he in his impeccable blue suit. But that didn't seem
to matter. He was just as excited as I was. I realized later
that at any other time I might have been tongue-tied to be
standing next to such an important person. But none of that
even occurred to me then. We talked about the high-wire
and the dangers Philippe would have to face. He seemed
to be genuinely in awe of the whole thing and kept looking
up at the wire — as I did, as did the hundreds of children
around us. It was then that I understood the most important
aspect of the high wire: it reduces us all to our common
humanity. A Secretary of state, a poet, a child: we became
equal in each other's eyes, and therefore a part of each other.

A brass band played a Renaissance fanfare from some
invisible place behind the Cathedral facade, and Philippe
emerged from the roof of the building on the other side
of the street. He was dressed in a white satin medieval
costume, the silver trowel hanging from a sash at his side.
He saluted the crowd with a graceful, bravura gesture, took
hold of his balancing-pole firmly in his two hands, and
began his slow ascent along the wire. Step by step, I felt
myself walking up there with him, and gradually those
heights seemed to become habitable, human, filled with
happiness. He slid down to one knee and acknowledged
the crowd again; he balanced on one foot; he moved
deliberately and majestically, exuding confidence. Then,
suddenly, he came to a spot on the wire far enough away
from his starting-point that my eyes lost contact with all
surrounding references: the apartment building, the street,
the other people. He was almost directly overhead now, and
as I leaned backward to take in the spectacle, I could see
no more than the wire, Philippe, and the sky. There was

nothing else. A white body against a nearly white sky, as if free. The purity of that image burned itself into my mind and is still there today, wholly present.

From beginning to end, I did not once think that he might fall. Risk, fear of death, catastrophe: these were not part of the performance. Philippe had assumed full respon-sibility for his own life, and I sensed that nothing could possibly shake that resolve. High-wire walking is not an art of death, but an art of life — and life lived to the very extreme of life. Which is to say, life that does not hide from death, but stares it straight in the face. Each time he sets foot on the wire, Philippe takes hold of that life and lives it in all its exhilarating immediacy, in all its joy.

May he live to be a hundred.

1982

III

— — —

Interviews

Translation

An Interview with Stephen Rodefer

STEPHEN RODEFER: When did you begin doing translations?

PAUL AUSTER: Back when I was nineteen or twenty years
old, as an undergraduate at Columbia. They gave us various
poems to read in French class — Baudelaire, Rimbaud,
Verlaine — and I found them terribly exciting, even if I
didn't always understand them. The foreignness was daunting to me — as though a work written in a foreign language
was somehow not real — and it was only by trying to put
them into English that I began to penetrate them. At that
point, it was a strictly private activity for me, a method
to help me understand what I was reading, and I had no
thoughts about trying to publish what I did. I suppose
you could say that I started doing translations because I
was such a slow learner. I couldn't imagine a linguistic
reality other than English, and I was driven by a need
to appropriate these works, to make them part of my own
world.

SR: Were you writing poetry of your own at that time, too?

PA: Yes. But like most young people, I had no idea what
I was doing. One's ambitions at that stage are so enormous,
but you don't necessarily have the tools to carry them out.
It leads to frustration, a deep sense of your own inadequacy.

I struggled along during those years to find my own way, and in the process I discovered that translation was an extremely helpful exercise. Pound recommends translation for young poets, and I think that shows great understanding on his part. You have to begin slowly. Translation allows you to work on the nuts and bolts of your craft, to learn how to live intimately with words, to see more clearly what you are actually doing. That is the positive benefit, but there is also a negative one. Working on translations removes the pressure of composition. There is no need to be brilliant and original, no need to attempt things that you are finally not capable of doing. You learn how to feel more comfortable with yourself in the act of writing, and that is probably the most crucial thing for a young person. You submit yourself to someone else's work — someone who is necessarily more accomplished than you are — and you begin to read more profoundly and intelligently than you ever have before. Scholarly analysis of poetry serves an important function, but this kind of practical experience is irreplaceable. A young poet will learn more about how Rilke wrote sonnets by trying to translate one than by writing an essay about it.

SR: How does translation relate to your own work now?

PA: At this point hardly at all. In the beginning, it occupied a central place for me, but then, as time went on, it became more and more marginal. My first translations years ago of modern French poets were real acts of discovery, labors of love. Then I went through a long period when I earned my living by doing transations. That was a completely dif-

ferent matter. I had nothing to do with choosing the texts.
The publishers would tell me that they needed a translation of such and such a book, and I would do it. It was
very draining work and had nothing to do with literature
or my own writing. History books, anthropology books,
art books. You grind out so many pages a day, and it puts
bread on the table. Eventually, I stopped doing it to save
my sanity. For the past five or six years, I've tried to limit
myself to things that I am passionately interested in —
works that I have discovered and want to share with other
people. Joubert's notebooks, for example, or the Anatole
fragments by Mallarmé. I find both those works extraordinary, unlike anything I have ever read. The same with
the book about high-wire walking by Philippe Petit, which
was published last summer. I did it because Philippe is
a friend and because he is one of the most remarkable
artists I know. If those books are not exactly connected
to my writing, they still belong to my inner world. But
the act of translating in itself is no longer the adventure
for me that it once was. There are sublimely talented translators out there in America today — Manheim, Rabassa,
Wilbur, Mandelbaum, to name just a few. But I don't think
of myself as belonging to the fraternity of translators. I'm
just someone who likes to follow his nose, and more often
than not this leads me into some odd corners. Occasionally,
I will stumble onto something that excites me enough to
want to translate it, but these generally seem to be eccentric
and peculiar works — works that correspond to my own
eccentric and peculiar tastes!

1985

Interview with Joseph Mallia

JOSEPH MALLIA: In your book of essays *The Art of Hunger* you cite Samuel Beckett as saying, "There will be a new form." Is your work an example of that new form?

PAUL AUSTER: It seems that everything comes out a little strangely and my books don't quite resemble other books, but whether they're "new" in any sense, I really can't say. It's not my ambition to think about it. So I suppose the answer is yes and no. At this point I'm not even thinking about anything beyond doing the books themselves. They impose themselves on me, so it's not my choice. The only thing that really matters, it seems to me, is saying the thing that has to be said. If it really has to be said, it will create its own form.

JM: All of your early work, from the 1970s, is poetry. What brought about this switch in genres, what made you want to write prose?

PA: Starting from a very early age, writing novels was always my ambition. When I was a student in college, in fact, I spent a great deal more time writing prose than poetry. But the projects and ideas that I took on were too large for me, too ambitious, and I could never get a grip on them. By concentrating on a smaller form I felt that I was able to make more progress. Years went by, and writing poetry became such an obsession that I stopped thinking about anything else. I wrote very short, compact lyrical poems that usually took me months to complete. They were very dense, especially in the beginning — coiled in on themselves like fists — but over the years they gradually began to open up, until I finally felt that they were heading in the direction of narrative. I don't think of myself as having made a break from poetry. All my work is of a piece, and the move into prose was the last step in a slow and natural evolution.

JM: As a younger writer, who were the modern writers you were interested in?

PA: Of prose writers, unquestionably Kafka and Beckett. They both had a tremendous hold over me. In the same sense, the influence of Beckett was so strong that I couldn't see my way beyond it. Among poets, I was very attracted to contemporary French poetry and the American Objectivists, particularly George Oppen, who became a close friend. And the German poet Paul Celan, who in my opinion is the finest post-War poet in any language. Of older writers, there were Hölderlin and Leopardi, the essays of Montaigne, and Cervantes' *Don Quixote*, which has remained a great source for me.

JM: But in the '70s you also wrote a great number of articles and essays about other writers.

PA: Yes, that's true. There was a period in the middle '70s in particular when I found myself eager to test my own ideas about writers in print. It's one thing to read and admire somebody's work, but it's quite another to marshal your thoughts about that writer into something coherent. The people I wrote about — Laura Riding, Edmond Jabès, Louis Wolfson, Knut Hamsun, and others — were writers I felt a need to respond to. I never considered myself a reviewer, but simply one writer trying to talk about others. Having to write prose for publication disciplined me, I think, and convinced me that ultimately I was able to write prose. So in some sense those little pieces of literary journalism were the training ground for the novels.

JM: Your first prose book was *The Invention of Solitude*, which was an autobiographical book.

PA: I don't think of it as an autobiography so much as a meditation about certain questions, using myself as the central character. The book is divided into two sections, which were written separately, with a gap of about a year between the two. The first, *Portrait of an Invisible Man*, was written in response to my father's death. He simply dropped dead one day, unexpectedly, after being in perfect health, and the shock of it left me with so many unanswered questions about him that I felt I had no choice but to sit down and try to put something on paper. In the act of trying to write about him, I began to realize how problematical it is to presume to know anything about anyone else. While that piece is filled with specific details, it still seems to me not so much an attempt at biography but an exploration of how one might begin to speak about another person, and whether or not it is even possible.

The second part grew out of the first and was a response

to it. It gave me a great deal of trouble, especially in terms of organization. I began writing it in the first person, as the first part had been written, but couldn't make any head-way with it. This part was even more personal than the first, but the more deeply I descended into the material, the more distanced I became from it. In order to write about myself, I had to treat myself as though I were someone else. It was only when I started all over again in the third person that I began to see my way out of the impasse. The astonishing thing, I think, is that at the moment when you are most truly alone, when you truly enter a state of solitude, that is the moment when you are not alone anymore, when you start to feel your connection with others. I believe I even quote Rimbaud in that book, "Je est un autre" — I is another — and I take that sentence quite literally. In the process of writing or thinking about yourself, you actually become someone else.

JM: Not only is the narrative voice of *The Book of Memory* different, but the structure is different as well.

PA: The central question in the second part was memory. So in some sense everything that happens in it is simul-taneous. But writing is sequential, it unfolds over time. So my greatest problem was in trying to put things in the correct order.

The point was to be as honest as possible in every sen-tence. I wanted to write a work that was completely exposed. I didn't want to hide anything. I wanted to break down for myself the boundary between living and writing as much as I could. That's not to say that a lot of literary effort didn't

go into the book, but the impulses are all very immediate
and pressing. With everything I do, it seems that I just get
so inside it, I can't think about anything else. And writing
the book becomes real for me. I was talking about myself
in *The Book of Memory*, but by tracking specific instances of
my own mental process, perhaps I was doing something that
other people could understand as well.

JM: Yes, that's how it worked for me. *The Book of Memory*
dwells on coincidences, strange intersections of events in
the world. This is also true in the novels of *The New York
Trilogy*.

PA: Yes, I believe the world is filled with strange events.
Reality is a great deal more mysterious than we ever give
it credit for. In that sense, the *Trilogy* grows directly out of
The Invention of Solitude. On the most personal level, I think
of *City of Glass* as an homage to my wife. It's a kind of
fictitious subterranean autobiography, an attempt to imagine what my life would have been like if I hadn't met her.
That's why I had to appear in the book as myself, but at
the same time Auster is also Quinn, but in a different
universe. . . .

    The opening scene in the book is something that actually
happened to me. I was living alone at the time, and one
night the telephone rang and the person on the other end
asked for the Pinkerton Detective Agency. I told him that
he had the wrong number, of course, but the same person
called back the next night with the same question. When
I hung up the phone the second time, I asked myself what
would have happened if I had said "Yes." That was the

genesis of the book, and I went on from there.

JM: Reviews of the book seem to emphasize the mystery elements of *The New York Trilogy*, making it out to be a gloss on the mystery genre. Did you feel that you were writing a mystery novel?

PA: Not at all. Of course I used certain elements of detective fiction. Quinn, after all, writes detective novels, and takes on the identity of someone he thinks is a detective. But I felt I was using those elements for such different ends, for things that had so little to do with detective stories, and I was somewhat disappointed by the emphasis that was put on them. That's not to say that I have anything against the genre. The mystery, after all, is one of the oldest and most compelling forms of storytelling, and any number of works can be placed in that category: *Oedipus Rex, Crime and Punishment*, a whole range of twentieth-century novels. In America, there's no question that people like Raymond Chandler and James M. Cain are legitimate writers, writers who have contributed something important to the language. It's a mistake to look down on the popular forms. You have to be open to everything, to be willing to take inspiration from any and all sources. In the same way that Cervantes used chivalric romances as the starting point for *Don Quixote*, or the way that Beckett used the standard vaudeville routine as the framework for *Waiting for Godot*, I tried to use certain genre conventions to get to another place, another place altogether.

JM: The problem of identity, right?

PA: Exactly. The question of who is who and whether or not we are who we think we are. The whole process that Quinn undergoes in that book — and the characters in the other two, as well — is one of stripping away to some barer condition in which we have to face up to who we are. Or who we aren't. It finally comes to the same thing.

JM: And the detective is somebody who's supposed to deal with the problems we have in maintaining a conventional identity. He deals with the messy edges of reality. Like, "My wife, she's not doing what she's supposed to —"

PA: Right, exactly — or, "Somebody's missing." So the detective really is a very compelling figure, a figure we all understand. He's the seeker after truth, the problem-solver, the one who tries to figure things out. But what if, in the course of trying to figure it out, you just unveil more mysteries? I suppose maybe that's what happens in the books.

The books have to do with the idea of mystery in several ways. We're surrounded by things we don't understand, by mysteries, and in the books these are people who suddenly come face to face with them. It becomes more apparent that they're surrounded by things they don't know or understand. So in that sense there might be some psychological resonance. Even though the situations aren't strictly realistic, they might follow some realistic psychology. These are things that we all feel — that confusion, that lack of knowing what it is that surrounds us.

JM: I saw the protagonists dropping into a kind of necessity, suddenly, and putting personal life aside, driven by some extraordinary hunger. It has almost religious undertones to it. I remember reading a review by Fanny Howe in the *Boston Globe*, and she said that the book is about a kind of gnosis — "grace among the fallen."

PA: "Religious" might not be the word I would use, but I agree that these books are mostly concerned with spiritual questions, the search for spiritual grace. At some point or another, all three characters undergo a form of humiliation, of degradation, and perhaps that is a necessary stage in discovering who we are.

Each novel in the *Trilogy*, I suppose, is about a kind of passionate excess. Quinn's story in *City of Glass* alludes to *Don Quixote*, and the questions raised in the two books are very similar: what is the line between madness and creativity, what is the line between the real and the imaginary, is Quinn crazy to do what he does or not? For a time, I toyed with the idea of using an epigraph at the beginning of *City of Glass*. It comes from Wittgenstein: "And it also means something to talk of 'living in the pages of a book.'"

In *Ghosts*, the spirit of Thoreau is dominant — another kind of passionate excess. The idea of living a solitary life, of living with a kind of monastic intensity — and all the dangers that entails. Walden Pond in the heart of the city. In his *American Notebook*, Hawthorne wrote an extraordinary and luminous sentence about Thoreau that has never left me. "I think he means to live like an Indian among us." That sums up the project better than anything else I've read. The determination to reject everyday American life, to go against the grain, to discover a more solid foundation for oneself

. . . In *The Locked Room*, by the way, the name Fanshawe is a direct reference to Hawthorne. *Fanshawe* was the title of Hawthorne's first novel. He wrote it when he was very young, and not long after it was published, he turned against it in revulsion and tried to destroy every copy he could get his hands on. Fortunately, a few of them survived . . .

JM: In *Ghosts*, Blue, in effect, loses his whole life in taking the case, and the narrator in *The Locked Room* goes through that terrible experience in Paris —

PA: But in the end, he manages to resolve the question for himself — more or less. He finally comes to accept his own life, to understand that no matter how bewitched or haunted he is, he has to accept reality as it is, to tolerate the presence of ambiguities within himself. That's what happens to him with relation to Fanshawe. He hasn't slain the dragon, he's let the dragon move into the house with him. That's why he destroys the notebook in the last scene.

JM: And the reader feels it. We're inside him.

PA: The one thing I try to do in all my books is to leave enough room in the prose for the reader to inhabit it. Because I finally believe it's the reader who writes the book and not the writer. In my own case as a reader (and I've certainly read more books than I've written!), I find that I almost invariably appropriate scenes and situations from a book and graft them onto my own experiences — or vice versa. In reading a book like *Pride and Prejudice*, for example, I realized at a certain point that all events were set in the house I grew up in as a child. No matter how specific a writer's description of a place might be, I always seem to twist it into something I'm familiar with. I've asked a number of my friends if this happens to them when they read fiction as well. For some yes, for others no. I think this probably has a lot to do with one's relation to language, how one responds to words printed on a page. Whether the words are just symbols, or whether they are passageways into our unconscious.

There's a way in which a writer can do too much, overwhelming the reader with so many details that he no longer has any air to breathe. Think of a typical passage in a novel. A character walks into a room. As a writer, how much of that room do you want to talk about? The possibilities are infinite. You can give the color of the curtains, the wallpaper pattern, the objects on the coffee table, the reflection of the light in the mirror. But how much of this is really necessary? Is the novelist's job simply to reproduce physical sensations for their own sake? When I write, the story is always uppermost in my mind, and I feel that everything must be sacrificed to it. All the elegant passages, all the curious details, all the so-called beautiful writing — if they are not truly relevant to what I am trying to say, then they have to go. It's all in the voice. You're telling a story, after all, and your job is to make people want to go on listening to your tale. The slightest distraction or wandering leads to boredom, and if there's one thing we all hate in books, it's losing interest, feeling bored, not caring about the next sentence. In the end, you don't only write the books you need to write, but you write the books you would like to read yourself.

JM: Is there a method to it?

PA: No. The deeper I get into my own work, the less engaging theoretical problems have become. When you look back
on the works that have moved you, you find that they have
always been written out of some kind of necessity. There's
something calling out to you, some human call, that makes
you want to listen to the work. In the end, it probably has
very little to do with literature.

George Bataille wrote about this in his preface to *Le Bleu
du Ciel*. I refer to it in *The Art of Hunger*, in an essay on the
schizophrenic Wolfson. He said that every real book comes
from a moment of rage, and then he asked: "How can we
read works that we don't feel compelled to read?" I believe
he's absolutely correct: there's always some indefinable
something that makes you attend to a writer's work — you
can never put your finger on it, but that something is what
makes all the difference.

JM: In other words the writer has to be haunted by his story
before he can write it.

PA: In my own experience I've often lived for years with
the ideas for books before I could manage to write them.
In The Country of Last Things is a novel I started writing back
in the days when I was a college student. The idea of a
unknowable place . . . it got under my skin and I couldn't
let go of it. I would pick up the manuscript, work on it for
a while, and then put it down. The essential thing was to
capture her voice, and when I couldn't hear it anymore, I
would have to stop. I must have started the book thirty times.

Each time it was somewhat different than the time before, but the essential situation was always the same.

JM: In the same way that some reviewers classified *The New York Trilogy* as a mystery, there were many articles about this book that classified it as apocalyptic science fiction.

PA: That was the farthest thing from my mind while I was writing it. In fact, my private, working subtitle for the book was "Anna Blume Walks Through the 20th Century." I feel that it's very much a book about our own moment, our own era, and many of the incidents are things that have actually happened. For example, the pivotal scene in which Anna is lured into a human slaughterhouse is based on something I read about the siege of Leningrad during World War II. These things actually happened. And in many cases, reality is far more terrible than anything we can imagine. Even the garbage system that I describe at such length was inspired by an article I once read about the present-day garbage system in Cairo. Admittedly, the book takes on these things from a somewhat oblique angle, and the country Anna goes to might not be immediately recognizable, but I feel that this is where we live. It could be that we've become so accustomed to it that we no longer see it.

JM: What are you working on now?

PA: I'm coming close to the end of a novel called *Moon Palace*. It's the longest book I've ever written and probably the one most rooted in a specific time and place. The action begins in 1969 and doesn't get much beyond 1971.

At bottom, I suppose it's a story about families and generation, a kind of *David Copperfield* novel, and it's something
that I've been wanting to write for a long time. As with the
last book, it's gone through many changes. The pages pile
up, but God knows what it will look like when it's finished
. . . Whenever I complete a book, I'm filled with a feeling
of immense disgust and disappointment. It's almost a
physical collapse. I'm so disappointed by my feeble efforts
that I can't believe I've actually spent so much time and
accomplished so little. It takes years before I'm able to
accept what I've done — to realize that this was the best
I could do. But I never like to look at the things I've written.
The past is the past, and there's nothing I can do about it
any more. The only thing that counts is the project I'm
working on now.

JM: Beckett once said in one of his stories, "No sooner is
the ink dry than it revolts me."

PA: You can't say it any better than that.

1987

Interview with Larry McCaffery

and Sinda Gregory

LARRY McCAFFERY: At one point in *Moon Palace*, Marco Fogg says that art's purpose is "penetrating the world and finding one's place in it." Is that what writing does for you?

PAUL AUSTER: Sometimes. I often wonder why I write. It's not simply to create beautiful objects or entertaining stories. It's an activity I seem to need in order to stay alive. I feel terrible when I'm not doing it. It's not that writing brings me a lot of pleasure — but *not* doing it is worse.

SINDA GREGORY: Your books have always relied more on chance and synchronicity to move their plots forward than the sorts of causality found in most fiction: this is even more apparent in your two new novels, *Moon Palace* and *The Music of Chance*. Is this foregrounding of chance a result of your own sense of how life operates (your "personal philosophy")? Or does it have more to do with your sense that this approach has interesting aesthetic applications?

PA: From an aesthetic point of view, the introduction of chance elements in fiction probably creates as many problems as it solves. I've come in for a lot of abuse from critics because of it. In the strictest sense of the word, I consider myself a realist. Chance is a part of reality: we are continually shaped by the forces of coincidence, the unexpected occurs with almost numbing regularity in all our lives. And yet there's a widely held notion that novels shouldn't stretch the imagination too far. Anything that appears "implausible" is necessarily taken to be forced, artificial, "unrealistic." I don't know what reality these people have been living in, but it certainly isn't my reality. In some perverse way, I believe they've spent too much time reading books. They're so immersed in the conventions of so-called realistic fiction that their sense of reality has been distorted. Everything's been smoothed out in these novels, robbed of its singularity, boxed into a predictable world of cause and effect. Anyone with the wit to get his nose out of his book and study what's actually in front of him will understand that this realism is a complete sham. To put it another way: truth is stranger than fiction. What I am after, I suppose, is to write fiction as strange as the world I live in.

LM: I'd say your books don't use coincidence in an effort to "smooth things over" or to create the usual realist's manipulated illusion that everything can be explained. Your books seem more fundamentally "about" mystery and coincidence, so that these operate almost as governing principles that are constantly clashing with causality and rationality.

PA: Precisely. When I talk about coincidence, I'm not referring to a desire to manipulate. There's a good deal of that in bad eighteenth- and nineteenth-century fiction: mechanical plot devices, the urge to tie everything up, the happy endings in which everyone turns out to be related to everyone else. No, what I'm talking about is the presence of the unpredictable, the utterly bewildering nature of human experience. From one moment to the next, anything can happen. Our life-long certainties about the world can be demolished in a single second. In philosophical terms, I'm talking about the powers of contingency. Our lives don't really belong to us, you see — they belong to the world, and in spite of our efforts to make sense of it, the world is a place beyond our understanding. We brush up against these mysteries all the time. The result can be truly terrifying — but it can also be comical.

SG: What sorts of things are you thinking of — a small thing, like someone getting a phone call to the wrong number (which sets the plot of *City of Glass* in motion)? Or something more outlandish, like meeting your long-lost father by accident in *Moon Palace*?

PA: I'm thinking of both small things and large things. Meeting three people named George on the same day. Or checking into a hotel and being given a room with the same number as your address at home. Seven or eight years ago, my wife and I were invited to a dinner party in New York, and there was an exceedingly charming man at the table — very urbane, full of intelligence and humor, a dazzling talker who had all the guests captivated with his stories. My wife had grown up in a small town in Minnesota, and at one point she actually said to herself: this is why I moved to New York, to meet people like this. Later on in the evening, we all started talking about our childhoods and where we had grown up. As it turned out, the man who had so enthralled her, the man who had struck her as the very embodiment of New York sophistication, came from the same little town in Minnesota that she did. The same town! It was astonishing — like something straight out of an O. Henry story.

These are coincidences, and it's impossible to know what to make of them. You think of a long-lost friend, someone you haven't seen in ten years, and two hours later you run into him on the street. Things like that happen to me all the time. Just two or three years ago, a woman who had been reading my books wrote to me to say that she was going to be in New York and would like to meet me. We had been corresponding for some time, and I welcomed the chance to talk to her in person. Unfortunately, there was a conflict. I already had an appointment with someone else for that day, and I couldn't make it. I was supposed to meet my friend at three or four o'clock in a delicatessen in midtown Manhattan. So I went to the restaurant — which was rather empty at that hour, since it was neither lunchtime nor dinnertime — and not fifteen minutes after we sat down, a woman with an absolutely startled expression on her face walked up to me and asked if I was Paul Auster. It turned out to be the same woman from Iowa who had written me those letters, the same woman I hadn't been able to meet with because I was going to this restaurant. And so I wound up meeting her anyway — in the very place where I hadn't been able to meet her!

Chance? Destiny? Or simple mathematics, an example of probability theory at work? It doesn't matter what you call it. Life is full of such events. And yet there are critics who would fault a writer for using that episode in a novel. Too bad for them. As a writer of novels, I feel morally obligated to incorporate such events into my books, to write about the world as I experience it — not as someone else tells me it's supposed to be. The unknown is rushing in on top of us at every moment. As I see it, my job is to keep myself open to these collisions, to watch out for all these mysterious goings-on in the world.

LM: When you say that your job as a writer is to open yourself to these collisions that are really occurring around you, does this imply that your works are usually inspired in some fairly direct way from the mysteries you've actually experienced — or is the autobiographical basis of your work less literal?

PA: Essentially, I'm a very intuitive writer, which makes it difficult for me to talk about my work in any coherent way. There's no question that my books are full of references to my own life, but more often than not, I don't become aware of these references until after the fact. *Moon Palace* is a good case in point. It sounds more like an autobiography than any of my other novels, but the truth is that it's probably the least autobiographical novel I've ever written. Still, there are a number of private allusions buried in the story, but it was only after the book was finished that I began to see them.

The business about the boxes of books in the beginning, for example. Fogg receives these boxes from his Uncle Victor, and after his uncle dies, Fogg sells off the books to keep himself afloat. Well, it turns out that the image of those boxes must have been planted in my head way back in my early childhood. My mother's sister is married to Allen Mandelbaum, who is widely known now as the translator

of Virgil and Dante. When I was five or six, my aunt and
uncle went off to live in Italy and wound up staying there
for twelve years. My uncle had an enormous library, and
since we lived in a large house, he left his books with us
for all the years he was gone. At first, they were stored in
boxes in the attic, but after a while (I must have been nine
or ten at that point), my mother began to worry that the
books might get damaged up there. So one fine day she and
I carried the boxes downstairs, opened them up, and put
the books on shelves in the living room. Until then, our
household had been largely devoid of books. Neither of
my parents had gone to college, and neither of them was
particularly interested in reading. Now, quite suddenly,
literally overnight, I had a magnificent library at my dis-
posal: all the classics, all the great poets, all the major novels.
It opened up a whole new world to me. When I think back
on it now, I realize that these boxes of books probably
changed my life. Without them, I doubt I ever would have
dreamed of becoming a writer.

The Edison material has deep roots in my past as well.
Our house wasn't far from the Seton Hall University cam-
pus, and every two weeks I would go for a haircut at Rocco's
Barbershop, which did a brisk business with the college
students and the boys from the town. This was the late fifties,
and everyone walked around in crewcuts then, which meant
that you wound up going to the barbershop quite often.
Anyway, it so happened that Rocco had been Thomas
Edison's barber for many years, and hanging on a wall of
the shop was a large framed portrait of Edison, along with
a handwritten message from the great man himself. "To my
good friend Rocco," it said. "Genius is 1% inspiration, 99%

perspiration. Thomas A. Edison." I found it tremendously exciting that my barber was the same man who had once cut the hair of the inventor of the lightbulb. It was ennobling, somehow — to imagine that the hands touching my head had once touched the head of America's greatest genius. I used to think that ideas from Edison's brain had been transferred to Rocco's fingers — which meant that those ideas were now going into my brain! Edison became the hero of childhood, and each time I went for a haircut, I'd stare at his portrait and feel as though I were worshipping at a shrine.

Some years later, this beautiful myth of my boyhood shattered to pieces. It turned out that my father had once worked as an assistant in Edison's lab at Menlo park. He had been hired straight out of high school in 1929, but just a few weeks after he started the job, Edison discovered that he was Jewish and fired him. My idol turned out to be a vicious anti-Semite, a scoundrel who had done my father a terrible injustice. None of this is mentioned in *Moon Palace*, of course, but the unflattering references to Edison no doubt come from the personal animosity I developed for him. I won't bore you by citing other examples, but in some way the whole book is impregnated with subliminal connections of this sort. There's nothing unusual about that. All writers draw on their own lives to write their books; to a greater or lesser degree, every novel is autobiographical. What *is* interesting, however, is how the work of the imagination intersects with reality.

SG: Do you mean that eerie sense that Borges kept writing about — the author who begins to find evidence of his

writing somehow finding its way into the world? A big
responsibility . . .

PA: It can become quite disturbing at times, utterly uncanny.
The very day I finished writing *The Music of Chance* — which
is a book about walls and slavery and freedom — the Berlin
Wall came down. There's no conclusion to be drawn from
this, but every time I think of it, I start to shake.

Back in 1984, when I was in the middle of writing *The
Locked Room*, I had to go to Boston for a few days. I already
knew that the final scene in the book was going to take place
in a house in Boston, at 9 Columbus Square, which happens
to be a real address. The house is owned by good friends
of mine, and I have slept there on many occasions over the
past fifteen years or so. That's where I was going to stay this
time as well, and I remember thinking how odd it would
be to visit this house again now that I had fictionalized it
for myself, had appropriated it into the realm of the imagination. I took the train to Boston, and when I arrived
at South Station, I climbed into a cab and asked the driver
to take me to 9 Columbus Square. The moment I gave him
the address, he started to laugh. It turned out that he had
once lived there himself — back in the 1940's, at a time
when the building had been used as a boarding house. Not
only that, but he had lived in the very room where my friend
now had his study. For the rest of the ride, he told me stories
about the people who had lived there, the woman who had
owned it, and all the mischief that had gone on in the rooms
I knew so well. Prostitution, pornographic films, drugs,
crimes of every sort. It was all so odd, so mysterious. Even
today, it's hard for me not to feel that I invented this cab

driver myself, that he didn't materialize out of the pages
of my own book. It was as if I had met the spirit of the place
I was writing about. The ghost of 9 Columbus Square!

LM: You told me once that in a certain way you felt all of
your books were really "the same book." What book *is* that?

PA: The story of my obsessions, I suppose. The saga of the
things that haunt me. Like it or not, all my books seem to
revolve around the same set of questions, the same human
dilemmas. Writing is no longer an act of free will for me,
it's a matter of survival. An image surges up inside me, and
after a time I begin to feel cornered by it, to feel that I have
no choice but to embrace it. A book starts to take shape
after a series of such encounters.

SG: Have you tried to figure out the specific source of these
encounters?

PA: Frankly, I'm never really certain where any of it comes
from. I'm sure there are deep psychological explanations
for most of it, but I'm not terribly interested in trying to
track down the source of my ideas. Writing, in some sense,
is an activity that helps me to relieve some of the pressure
caused by these buried secrets. Hidden memories, traumas,
childhood scars — there's no question that novels emerge
from those inaccessible parts of ourselves.
     Every once in a while, however, I'll have a glimmer or a
sudden intuition about where something came from. But,
as I said before, it always happens after the fact, after the
book is finished, at a moment when the book no longer

belongs to me. Just recently, as I was going through the manuscript of *The Music of Chance* for typographical errors, I had a revelation about one of the scenes that takes place toward the end of the novel: the moment when Nashe opens the door of the trailer and discovers Pozzi lying on the ground. As I read that passage — which goes on to describe how Nashe bends over the body and examines Pozzi to see if he is alive or dead — I understood that I was writing about something that had happened to me many years before. It was one of the most terrible moments of my life, an episode that has stayed with me ever since, and yet I wasn't aware of it at the time I composed that scene.

I was thirteen or fourteen years old and had been sent to a summer camp in upstate New York. One day, a group of about twenty of us went for a hike in the woods, accompanied by one or two counselors. We trekked for several miles, I remember, all of us in good spirits, when it suddenly began to rain. A moment later, the sky opened up, and we found ourselves in the middle of a ferocious downpour, a summer lightning storm punctuated by tremendous claps of thunder. It wasn't just some passing cloud. It was an out-and-out tempest, a monumental attack from the heavens. Lightning bolts were shooting down all around us, and there we were, stuck in the woods, with no shelter in sight. It became very terrifying, as though we had suddenly been caught in an aerial bombardment. One of the boys said that we would be safer if we got away from the trees, and so we began to scramble back toward a clearing we had passed a little while before. He was right, of course. In a lightning storm, you have to protect yourself by going to open ground. The problem in this case was that in order to enter the clearing, we had to crawl under a barbed wire fence. So, one by one, we crawled under the fence and made our way to what we thought would be safety. I was somewhere in the middle of the line, behind a boy named Ralph. Just as he was crawling under the fence, an enormous bolt of lightning struck the wire. I couldn't have been more than two feet away from him. He stopped, apparently stunned by the lightning, and I remember that I crawled under the fence at that point, inching under the wire to Ralph's left. Once I got through, I turned around and dragged him into the meadow to make room for the other boys. It didn't occur to me that he was seriously hurt. I figured that he had received a shock and would soon recover from it. Once we were all in the clearing, the lightning attack continued; the bolts were dancing around us like spears. Several of the boys were hit, and they lay there weeping and moaning on the ground. It was an awful scene, truly awful. Another boy and I stayed with Ralph the whole time, rubbing his hands to keep him warm, holding his tongue to make sure he didn't swallow it. His lips were turning blue, his skin was turning cold, but still, I kept thinking he would start coming around at any moment. He was dead, of course. He had been killed the instant the lightning had hit the fence — electrocuted, with an eight-inch burn across his back. But I didn't learn that until afterward, until after the storm had stopped.

LM: That's the kind of experience you never leave behind completely.

PA: No, never. I can't tell you how deeply it affected me. Not just the tragedy of a young boy losing his life like that —

but the absolute suddenness of it, the fact that I could easily have been the one crawling under the fence when the lightning struck. Speaking about it now, I understand how crucial it was to me. In some sense, my entire attitude toward life was formed in those woods in upstate New York.

SG: In retrospect, is that why *Moon Palace* winds up having those two critical scenes involving lightning?

PA: There's no question that those storms refer to the storm I lived through, I'm certain of it. And there are other traces of that event in *Moon Palace*. The passage when Effing watches over Byrne's body in the Utah desert. Clearly I was reliving the experience of watching over the dead boy's body in the woods . . .

What I am trying to say, I suppose, is that the material that haunts me, the material that I feel compelled to write about, is dredged up from the depths of my own memories. But even after that material is given to me, I can't always be sure where it comes from.

LM: How do you balance this sense of feeling *compelled* to write about these things, your desire to leave yourself open, creatively, to these powerful resonances, versus your goal as an artist to *control* them, to shape them into an aesthetic arrangement?

PA: I don't mean to imply that my books are nothing but an outpouring of my unconscious. There's art involved as well, and effort, and a very precise sense of the kinds of feelings I am trying to convey. To say that "all my books are the same book" is probably too simple. What I mean is that all my books are connected by their common source, by the preoccupations they share. But each book belongs to its central character: Quinn, Blue, the narrator of *The Locked Room*, Anna Blume, Fogg, Nashe. Each one of these people thinks differently, speaks differently, writes differently from all the others. But each one is also a part of myself — which probably goes without saying. If all these books were put together in one volume, they would form the book of my life so far, a multi-faceted picture of who I am. But there's still more to come, I hope. If you think of the imagination as a continent, then each book would be an individual country. The map is still quite sketchy at this point, with many gaps and unexplored territories. But if I'm able to keep going long enough, perhaps all the blanks will eventually be filled in.

SG: On the other hand, you frequently seem to return to the same "terrain," even if it's located on different literary continents. For example, there's a recurrent motif in several of your books (I'm thinking of *City of Glass, Moon Palace* and *The Music of Chance*) of the windfall or inheritance that creates a suspension of the daily routine for the main character, followed by a gradual dissipation of the money until the character is left with nothing. This sounds almost like a starving artist's fantasy, but since the process is described so vividly and convincingly, I wonder if it might have a basis in your autobiography . . .

PA: As a matter of fact, I did receive an inheritance after my father died eleven years ago. It wasn't a tremendous amount of money as far as inheritances go, but it made a huge difference, it was enough to change my life entirely. I was pushing thirty-two at the time, and in the ten years since graduating from college I had been scraping along as best I could, often in very miserable circumstances. There were long stretches of time when I had nothing, when I was literally on the brink of catastrophe. The year before my father died was a particularly bad period. I had a small child, a crumbling marriage, and a minuscule income that amounted to no more than a fraction of what we needed. I became desperate, and for more than a year I wrote almost nothing. I couldn't think about anything but money. Half-crazed by the pressure of it all, I began devising various get-rich-quick schemes. I invented a game (a card baseball game — which was actually quite good) and spent close to six months trying to sell it. When that failed, I sat down and wrote a pseudonymous detective novel in record time, about three months. It was eventually published, but it only brought in about two thousand dollars, which was hardly the kind of money I had been hoping for.

At another point, I made some inquiries about getting a job as a sports writer, but nothing came of that either. As a last resort, I even broke down and applied for a job as a teacher. A full load of freshman composition courses at Dutchess Community College for $8000 a year. This was the worst thing I could imagine, but I swallowed my pride and took the plunge. I thought my credentials were decent. I had an M.A. from Columbia, I had published two or three books of poetry, I had translated quite a bit, had written articles for *The New York Review of Books, Harper's,* and so on. But it turned out that there were three hundred applicants for that miserable job, and without any prior experience, I didn't have a chance. I was rejected on the spot. I don't think I've ever been closer to feeling that I was at the end of my rope. Then, out of nowhere, with absolutely no warning at all, my father dropped dead of a heart attack and I inherited some money. That money changed everything for me; it set my life on an entirely different course.

LM: Your early published creative works were nearly all poems. Wasn't it just after the death of your father that you first started writing prose — the materials that eventually became *The Invention of Solitude*?

PA: Not exactly. Although you might say that it was only then that I began to think of myself as a prose writer. But the fact is that I had always dreamed of writing novels. My first published works were poems, and for ten years or so I published only poems, but all along I spent nearly as much time writing prose. I wrote hundred and hundreds of pages, I filled up dozens of notebooks. It's just that I wasn't satisfied with it, and I never showed it to anyone. But the ideas for several of the novels I eventually published — at least in some kind of preliminary form — came to me back then, as far back as 1969 and 1970. I'm thinking particularly of *In The Country of Last Things* and *Moon Palace*, but also certain parts of *City of Glass*. The crazy speech about *Don Quixote*, the maps of Stillman's footsteps, the crackpot theories about America and the Tower Of Babel — all that was cooked up when I was still in my early twenties.

SG: But at some point you fairly consciously decided to shift your focus away from prose to poetry. What was behind this decision?

PA: It was like someone trying to will himself to break a bad habit. By about the mid-Seventies, I stopped writing fiction altogether. I felt that I was wasting my time, that I would never get anywhere with it, and so I decided to restrict myself exclusively to poetry.

LM: Was it really so exclusive, though? Wasn't this about the time your first critical essays began appearing?

PA: Yes, I suppose I failed to break the habit. I continued writing prose anyway, quite a bit of it, in fact. Critical prose, articles, book reviews. Between 1974 and 1979, I must have written twenty-five or thirty pieces. It started right after I returned to New York. I had just spent four years living in France, and right before I left, an American friend of mine in Paris who knew Bob Silvers of *The New York Review of Books* suggested that I contact him once I returned. I eventually did, and when I proposed writing an article about Louis Wolfson's book *Le Schizo et les Langues*, he said go ahead. He made no promises, of course, but I remember that he offered to pay me something even if they didn't publish it, which I found very generous and uncalled-for. It turned out that he liked the article, and I wound up writing a number of others for him. They were mostly on poets — Laura Riding, Jabès, Ungaretti, and so on. Bob Silvers was an excellent editor — tough, respectful, very businesslike and very enthusiastic — and I'm still grateful to him for having given me a chance.

LM: Did you find any of the same kinds of pleasures writing those critical articles that you received from your creative work?

PA: I never thought of myself as a critic or literary journalist, even when I was doing a lot of critical pieces. Eventually, I started doing articles for other magazines as well. *Harper's, Saturday Review, Parnassus, The San Francisco Review of Books*, I can't remember all of them. I never accepted assignments or did pieces to order. I only wrote about writers who interested me, and in nearly every case I was the one who suggested the article to the editor — not the other way around. I looked on those pieces as an opportunity to articulate some of my ideas about writing and literature, to map out some kind of aesthetic position. In effect, I could have accomplished the same thing by keeping a journal, but I felt it was more interesting and challenging to throw my thoughts out into a public arena. I wasn't able to cheat. Everything had to be stated with absolute clarity: there was no room for vague impressions. All in all, I feel it was a useful apprenticeship. I wasn't writing fiction, but I was writing prose, and the experience of working on those articles proved to me that I was gradually learning how to express myself.

SG: How was your poetry evolving during this period?

PA: It was beginning to change, beginning to open up. I had started out by writing poems that resembled clenched fists; they were short and dense and obscure, as compact and hermetic as Delphic oracles. But by the mid-Seventies I could feel them taking on a new direction. The breath became somewhat longer, the propositions became some-what more discursive. At times, a certain prose tonality began to creep in. In 1976 and 1977, I wrote four one-act plays, wondering if this wouldn't be the proper medium for these new urges that were growing inside me. One of them, to my everlasting regret, was even performed. There's no point in talking about that now — except to say that the memory of that performance still pains me. But another of those plays eventually came to life again. Six years later, I went back to it and reworked it into a piece of prose fiction. That was where *Ghosts* came from, the second novel of *The New York Trilogy*.

LM: Was there any particular breakthrough moment for you in terms of your prose — something that made you realize you could work in this form? Or was it more a matter of one thing leading to another — the essays, the plays, and so on — until you felt comfortable with it?

PA: It was both, I think, if such a thing is possible. But first came all the emotional and financial hardships I mentioned before. I barely wrote anything for close to a year. My wife and I were grinding out translations to put food on the table, and the rest of the time I was pursuing my half-baked money schemes. There were moments when I thought I was finished, when I thought I would never write another word. Then, in December of 1978, I happened to go to an open rehearsal of a dance piece choreographed by the friend of a friend, and something happened to me. A revelation, an epiphany — I don't know what to call it. Something

happened, and a whole world of possibilities suddenly
opened up to me. I think it was the absolute fluidity of what
I was seeing, the continual motion of the dancers as they
moved around the floor. It filled me with immense happiness. The simple fact of watching men and women moving
through space filled me with something close to euphoria.
The very next day, I sat down and started writing *White
Spaces*, a little work of no identifiable genre — which was
an attempt on my part to translate the experience of that
dance performance into words. It was a liberation for me,
a tremendous letting go, and I look back on it now as the
bridge between writing poetry and writing prose. That was
the piece that convinced me I still had it in me to be a writer.
But everything was going to be different now. A whole new
period of my life was about to begin.

It's very strange, but I remember finishing that piece on
January fourteenth. I went to sleep very late that night,
around two or three in the morning. At eight o'clock the
phone rang, and there was one of my uncles on the other
end of the line, telling me that my father had died during
the night. . . .

LM: And along with that news came the inheritance.

PA: Yes, then came the inheritance. The money gave me a
cushion, and for the first time in my life I had the time to
write, to take on long projects without worrying about how
I was going to pay the rent. In some sense, all the novels
I've written have come out of that money my father left me.
It gave me two or three years, and that was enough to get
me on my feet again. It's impossible to sit down and write

without thinking about it. It's a terrible equation, finally. To think that my father's death saved my life.

SG: The way you describe this movement — from initially writing prose, to abandoning it in favor of poetry when you felt you had failed at prose, to returning to it almost trium- phantly during this moment of conversion — it almost sounds as if all along you had strong personal and aesthetic preferences for prose forms. If that's the case, how do you feel about the poetry you wrote during that period?

PA: What it boils down to, I think, is a question of scope. It was a gradual process, but at the same time there was also a leap, a last little jump right at the end.

I remain very attached to the poetry I wrote, I still stand by it. In the final analysis, it could even be the best work I've ever done. But there's a fundamental difference between the two activities, at least in the way I've approached them. In some sense, poetry is like taking still photographs, whereas prose is like filming with a movie camera. Film is the medium for both those arts — but the results are totally different. In the same way, words are the medium for both poetry and prose, but they create entirely different experi- ences, both for the writer and the reader.

SG: In other words, prose is able to encompass a lot more for you.

PA: That's essentially it. My poems were a quest for what I would call a uni-vocal expression. They expressed what I felt at any given moment, as if I'd never felt anything before

and would never feel anything again. They were concerned
with essences, with bedrock beliefs, and their aim was always
to achieve a purity and consistency of language. Prose, on
the other hand, gives me a chance to articulate my conflicts
and contradictions. Like everyone else, I am a multiple
being, and I embody a whole range of attitudes and
responses to the world. Depending on my mood, the same
event can make me laugh or make me cry; it can inspire
anger or compassion or indifference. Writing prose allows
me to include all of these responses. I no longer have to
choose among them.

LM: That sounds like Bakhtin's notion of "the dialogic imagination," with the novel arising out of this welter of conflicting but dynamic voices and opinions. Heteroglossia. . .

PA: Exactly. Of all the theories of the novel, Bakhtin's strikes
me as the most brilliant, the one that comes closest to
understanding the complexity and the magic of the form.
    It probably also explains why it's so rare for a young
person to write a good novel. You have to grow into yourself
before you can take on the demands of fiction. I've been
talking about it in theoretical and literary terms, but there's
also the simple fact of growing older, of acquiring a better
sense of who you are.

SG: I know you had started other books before *City of Glass*,
but one thing that struck me in reading that book was how
fully formed this literary sensibility seemed to be for somebody just publishing his first novel. Were there some private,
personal factors at work, beyond the death of your father,

that helped you mature as a writer and as an individual,
so that you were in fact ready to write that first novel?

PA: I'm certain that having children has had a lot to do with
it. Becoming a parent connects you to a world beyond yourself, to the continuum of generations, to the inevitability
of your own death. You understand that you exist in time,
and after that you can no longer look at yourself in the same
way. It's impossible to take yourself as seriously as you once
did. You begin to let go, and in that letting go — at least
in my case — you find yourself wanting to tell stories.

   When my son was born twelve years ago, Charlie Simic,
who's been a close friend for a long time, wrote me a letter
of congratulations in which he said, "Children are wonderful. If I didn't have kids, I'd walk around thinking I was
Rimbaud all the time." He put his finger right on the heart
of the experience.

   This past summer, something funny happened to me that
threw this whole question of children and writing into very
sharp focus. We rented a house in Vermont for two months,
an old fallen-down place in the middle of nowhere, a
wonderful refuge. I was still writing *The Music of Chance* then,
and every morning I'd walk over to a little outbuilding on
the property to work on the book. It was about twenty or
thirty yards from the house, and the kids and their friends
would often play in the area between the two buildings.
Right at the end of the summer, I was coming to the end
of the first draft. As it happened, I finished on the day
before we were supposed to head back to New York. I wrote
the last sentence at about twelve or twelve-thirty in the afternoon, and I remember standing up from the table and

saying to myself: "You've finally done it, old man. For once in your life, you've written something halfway decent." I felt good, really very good — which is something that almost never happens to me when I think about my work. I lit a cigar and opened the door to step out into the sun, wanting to savor the triumph for a few minutes before I returned to the house. So there I was, standing on the steps of my little shack, telling myself what a genius I was, when all of sudden I looked up and saw my two-year old daughter in front of the house. She was stark naked (she scarcely wore any clothes all summer) and at that moment she was squatting over some stones and taking a shit. She saw me looking at her and began shouting very happily: "Look at me, daddy! Look at what I'm doing!" So, rather than being able to bask in my own brilliance, I had to clean up my daughter's mess. That was the first thing I did after finishing my book [Laughs]. Thirty seconds of glory, and then right back to earth. I can't be sure if Sophie was offering me a not-so-subtle form of literary criticism, or if she was simply making a philosophical statement about the equality of all creative acts. One way or the other, she knocked me off my cloud, and I was very grateful to her for it.

LM: You mentioned earlier that all of your books are finally about yourself, that they are all exploring parts of your inner terrain. *City of Glass* supplies a lot of hints that it is in fact very much a book about you: not only do "you" literally appear by name in the book, but everyone Quinn meets—all these doubles and mirrors of his lost wife and family—seem to reflect back to us Quinn's psychic dilemmas. And presumably yours. Had the experience of writing about yourself so prismatically in *The Invention of Solitude* helped prepare you, in a sense, for writing about yourself in the way you did in your novel?

PA: I think so. Yes, most definitely. In some sense, *City of Glass* was a direct response to *The Invention of Solitude*, particularly the second part, the section called "The Book of Memory." But, in spite of the evidence, I wouldn't actually say that I was "writing about myself" in either book. *The Invention of Solitude* is autobiographical, of course, but I don't feel that I was telling the story of my life so much as using myself to explore certain questions that are common to us all: how we think, how we remember, how we carry our pasts around with us at every moment. I was looking at myself in the same way a scientist studies a laboratory animal. I was no more than a little gray rat, a guinea pig stuck in the cage of my own consciousness. The book wasn't written as a form of therapy; it was an attempt to turn myself inside-out and examine what I was made of. Myself, yes — but myself as anyone, myself as everyone. Even the first part, which is ostensibly about my father, is finally concerned with something larger than one man's life. It's about the question of biography, about whether it's in fact possible for one person to talk to another person. *The Locked Room* picks up this problem again and approaches it from a somewhat different angle.

SG: Given what you've just said, I would have assumed you would have tried to prevent your audience from reading *City of Glass* as a disguised autobiography. Instead you introduce this possibility, and play with it in various ways. Why?

PA: I think it stemmed from a desire to implicate myself in the machinery of the book. I don't mean my autobiographical self, I mean my author self, that mysterious other who lives inside me and puts my name on the covers of books. What I was hoping to do, in effect, was to take my name off the cover and put it inside the story. I wanted to open up the process, to break down walls, to expose the plumbing. There's a strange kind of trickery involved in the writing and reading of novels, after all. You see Leo Tolstoy's name on the cover of *War and Peace*, but once you open the book, Leo Tolstoy disappears. It's as though no one has really written the words you're reading. I find this "no one" terribly fascinating — for there's finally a profound truth to it. On the one hand, it's an illusion: on the other hand, it has everything to do with how stories are written. For the author of a novel can never be sure where any of it comes from. The self that exists in the world — the self whose name appears on the covers of books — is finally not the same self who writes the book.

SG: And of course it turns out that the "Paul Auster" whom Quinn visits in the novel isn't the author of the book we've been reading — which literalizes this idea.

PA: Right. Paul Auster appears as a character in *City of Glass*, but in the end the reader learns that he is not the author. It's someone else, an anonymous narrator who comes in on the last page and walks off with Quinn's red notebook. So the Auster on the cover and the Auster in the story are not the same person. They're the same and yet not the same. Just as the author of *War and Peace* is both Tolstoy and not Tolstoy.

LM: Was there a specific incident or impulse that started *City of Glass?*

PA: About a year after my first marriage broke up, I moved to an apartment in Brooklyn. It was early 1980, and I was working on "The Book of Memory" then — and also editing an anthology of twentieth-century French poetry for Random House. One day, a couple of months after I moved in, the telephone rang, and the person on the other end asked if he had reached Pinkerton Agency. I said no, you've got the wrong number, and hung up. I probably would have forgotten all about it, but the very next day another person called and asked the same question. "Is this the Pinkerton Agency?" Again I said no, told him he'd dialed the wrong number, and hung up. But the instant after I hung up, I began to wonder what would have happened if I had said yes. Would it have been possible for me to pose as a Pinkerton agent? And if so, how far could I have taken it? The book grew out of those telephone calls, but more than a year went by before I actually began to write it. The wrong numbers were the starting point, but there's no question that they influenced some of the other elements of the book as well — the private detective element, for example, and the idea of involving myself in the action of the story.

LM: There's a scene in *City of Glass* where Quinn says that writing his Max Work mystery novels under the pen name of William Wilson made him feel he was writing these books at one step removed, so that "Wilson served as a kind of ventriloquist. Quinn himself was the dummy, and Work was the animated voice that gave purpose to the enterprise."

Since I know that you also wrote a detective novel under a pseudonym, I was wondering if you shared some of Quinn's feelings about this process.

PA: It was exactly the same. All through the months I worked on that book, I felt as though I were writing with a mask on my face. It was an odd experience, but I can't say that it was unenjoyable. Posing as someone else was quite a bit of fun, in fact — but at the same time disturbing and provocative. If I hadn't gone through that experience of pseudonymity myself, I never would have been able to develop Quinn in the way I did.

SG: You must have had mixed feelings about finding yourself labeled so often (at least initially) as a "detective writer."

PA: Yes, I must say I've found it rather galling at times. Not that I have anything against detective fiction — it's just that my work has very little to do with it. I refer to it in the three novels of the *Trilogy*, of course, but only as a means to an end, as a way to get somewhere else entirely. If a true follower of detective fiction ever tried to read one of those books, I'm sure he would be bitterly disappointed. Mystery novels always give answers; my work is about asking questions.

In the long run, it probably doesn't matter. People can say whatever they want; they're entitled to misread books in any way they choose. It takes time for the dust to settle, and every writer has to be prepared to listen to a lot of stupidities when his work is discussed. The reviewing situa-

tion is particularly bad here after all. Not only do we have
the worst infant mortality rate in the western world, but we
probably have the lowest standard of literary journalism anywhere. Some of the people who review books strike me as
quasi-illiterate, out-and-out morons. And theirs are the opinions that circulate, at least at the beginning of a book's life.

SG: And yet, there are certain aspects about detective
writing that are enormously attractive and compelling —
things you point to in *City of Glass* about nothing being
wasted in a good mystery novel, that "the center of the
book shifts with each event that propels it forward," its
potential for having everything come to life, seething with
possibilities.

PA: Of course. At its best, detective fiction can be one of
the purest and most engaging forms of story-telling. The
idea that every sentence counts, that every word can make a
difference — it creates a tremendous narrative propulsion.
It's on that level that the form has been most interesting
to me.

   In the end, though, I would say that the greatest influence
on my work has been fairy tales, the oral tradition of story-
telling. The Brothers Grimm, the Thousand and One Nights
— the kinds of stories you read out loud to children. These
are bare-bones narratives, narratives largely devoid of
details, yet enormous amounts of information are commu-
nicated in a very short space, with very few words. What fairy
tales prove, I think, is that it's the reader — or the listener
— who actually tells the story to himself. The text is no more
than a springboard for the imagination. "Once upon a time

there was a girl who lived with her mother in a house at the edge of a large wood." You don't know what the girl looks like, you don't know what color the house is, you don't know if the mother is tall or short, fat or thin, you know next to nothing. But the mind won't allow these things to remain blank; it fills in the details itself, it creates images based on its own memories and experiences — which is why these stories resonate so deeply inside us. The listener becomes an active participant in the story.

LM: A lot of the contemporary writers who have also acknowledged a fascination with fairy tales (I'm thinking of people like Barth, Coover, Calvino, Borges) seem to share the sense that the fairy tale offers a method of communicating with readers that the novel basically ignores because it wants to provide all the details, the background, the explanation.

PA: I'd certainly agree that novel-writing has strayed very far from these open-ended structures — and from oral traditions as well. The typical novel of the past two hundred years has been crammed full of details, descriptive passages, local color — things that might be excellent in themselves, but which often have little to do with the heart of the story being told, that can actually block the reader's access to that story. I want my books to be all heart, all center, to say what they have to say in as few words as possible. This ambition seems so contrary to what most novelists are trying to accomplish that I often have trouble thinking of myself as a novelist at all.

SG: In "The Book of Memory" you described your reaction to the breakup of your first marriage and your separation from your son by saying, "Each day would drag a little more of the pain out into the open." Was writing *City of Glass* one way for you to work through or (or at least get at) that pain?

PA: That was the emotional source of the book, yes. My first wife and I split up in 1979, and for a year-and-a-half after that I lived in a kind of limbo — first on Varick Street in Manhattan, then in that apartment in Brooklyn. But once the arrangements were worked out, my son was with me half the time. He was just three back then, and we lived together like a couple of old bachelors. It was a strange existence, I suppose, but not without its pleasures, and I assumed that life would go on like that for a long time. Then, early in 1981 (February 23rd, to be exact, it's impossible for me to forget the date) I met Siri Hustvedt, the person I'm married to now. We took each other by storm, and nothing has ever been the same since. For the past nine years, she's meant everything to me, absolutely everything. . .

So, by the time I started writing *City of Glass*, my life had undergone a dramatic improvement. I was in love with an extraordinary woman; we were living together in a new apartment; my inner world had been utterly transformed. In many ways, I think of *City of Glass* as an homage to Siri, as a love letter in the form of a novel. I tried to imagine what would have happened to me if I hadn't met her, and what I came up with was Quinn. Perhaps my life would have been something like his. . . .

SG: Let's talk a bit about the question of "solitude." It's a

word that comes up often in your works — and of course
it appears in the title of your first book of prose, *The Invention of Solitude*. It's a concept that seems to contain a lot of
different resonances for you, both personal and aesthetic.

PA: Yes, I suppose there's no getting rid of it. But solitude
is a rather complex term for me; it's not just a synonym for
loneliness or isolation. Most people tend to think of solitude as a rather gloomy idea, but I don't attach any negative
connotations to it. It's simply a fact, one of the conditions
of being human, and even if we're surrounded by others,
we essentially live our lives alone: real life takes place inside
us. We're not dogs, after all. We're not driven solely by
instincts and habits; we can think, and because we think,
we're always in two places at the same time. Even in the
throes of physical passion, thoughts come pouring through
our head. At the very height of sexual arousal, a person can
be thinking about an unanswered letter on the dining room
table or about standing on a street in a foreign city twenty
years ago — or anything, anything at all . . .
    What it boils down to is the old mind-body problem.
Descartes. Solipsism. Self and other, all the old philosophical questions. In the end, we know who we are because
we can think about who we are. Our sense of self is formed
by the pulse of consciousness within us — the endless
monologue, the life-long conversation we have with ourselves. And this takes place in absolute solitude. It's impossible to know what someone else is thinking. We can only
see the surfaces: the eyes, the face, the body. But we can't
see another person's thoughts, can we? We can't hear them
or touch them; they're utterly walled off from us.

Oliver Sacks, the neurologist, has made some astute observations about such things. Every whole person, he says, every person with a coherent identity, is in effect narrating the story of his life to himself at every moment — following the thread of his own story. For brain-damaged people, however, this thread has been snapped. And once that happens, it's no longer possible to hold yourself together.

But there's more to it than that. We live alone, yes, but at the same time everything we are comes from the fact that we have been made by others. I'm not just referring to biology — mothers and fathers, uterine birth, and so on. I'm thinking about psychology and the formation of the human personality. The infant feeding at the mother's breast looks up into the mother's eyes and sees her looking at him, and from that experience of being seen, the baby begins to learn that he is separate from his mother, that he is a person in his own right. We literally acquire a self from this process. Lacan calls it the "mirror-stage," which strikes me as a beautiful way of putting it. Self-consciousness in adulthood is merely an extension of those early experiences. It's no longer the mother who's looking at us then — we're looking at ourselves. But we can only see ourselves because someone else has seen us first. In other words, we learn our solitude from others. In the same way that we learn language from others.

LM: "Solitude," then, is the essential condition of being locked inside one's own head — but also something that only comes into our awareness because of other people. This sounds like a paradox . . .

PA: It does, but I don't know how else to express it. What is so startling to me, finally, is that you don't begin to understand your connection to others until you are alone. And the more intensely you are alone, the more deeply you plunge into a state of solitude, the more deeply you feel that connection. It isn't possible for a person to isolate himself from other people. No matter how apart you might find yourself in a physical sense — whether you've been marooned on a desert island or locked up in solitary confinement — you discover that you are inhabited by others. Your language, your memories, even your sense of isolation — every thought in your head has been born from your connection with others. This is what I was trying to explore in "The Book of Memory," to examine both sides of the word "solitude." I felt as though I were looking down to the bottom of myself, and what I found there was more than just myself — I found the world. That's why that book is filled with so many references and quotations, in order to pay homage to all the others inside me. On the one hand, it's a work about being alone; on the other hand, it's about community. That book has dozens of authors, and I wanted them all to speak through me. In the final analysis, "The Book of Memory" is a collective work.

SG: Earlier, when we were talking about your pseudonymous mystery novel, you said you felt like you were "wearing a mask" while writing that book. Could you talk a bit about the different relationships you have with your characters when you're writing a book from the first person, as opposed to a third-person persepctive? For example, do you feel less that you're wearing this mask when you're writing

in the first person? Or do you feel a more abstract relationship to all your characters?

PA: This is a fundamental question for me. Some of my
books have been written in the first person, others have
been written in the third, and in each case the entire story
has developed out of the particular narrative voice I've
chosen. Yes, obviously a novel written in the first person
is going to sound more intimate than one written in the
third person. But there's a vast range within those two
categories, and it's possible to bring the boundaries of first-
person and third-person so close to teach other that they
touch, even overlap.

SG: How does this overlap work in your own books? Do you
mean by confusing the distinction between who the reader
thinks the narrator is and who finally is revealed to actually
be telling the story, as you did in *City of Glass*?

PA: That's probably where the overlap is most obvious,
because in *City of Glass* you have a book written in the third
person throughout, and then, right at the end, the narrator
appears and announces himself in the first-person — which
colors the book in retrospect somehow, turning the whole
story into a kind of oblique, first-person narrative. But I've
been interested in pursuing different ranges of effects that
can be produced with this sort of thing in most of my books.
Even in *Ghosts*, which reads something like a fable, you feel
the presence of the narrator lurking behind each sentence.
The storyteller is a part of the story, even though he never
uses the word "I." In the few places where he breaks in, he

always refers to himself in the plural — as if addressing the reader directly, including him in what is finally a very personal "we." *The Locked Room* is written in the first person, but so much of it is about trying to understand someone else that certain sections of it are actually written in the third person. The same holds true for *In the Country of Last Things*. The little phrases that appear a few times at the beginning — "she wrote" or "her letter continued" — put the whole book in a third-person perspective. Someone has read Anna Blume's book notebook; somehow or other, her letter has arrived. *Moon Palace* functions a bit like *The Locked Room* in that it's an intimate, first-person narrative that veers off into the third person. There are long passages in that book where Fogg literally disappears. When it comes right down to it, *The Music of Chance* is the only one of my novels that doesn't combine first- and third-person narration. It's written strictly in the third person.

LM: Your handling of the narrative perspective in *The Music of Chance* reminded me of what we find in several of Kafka's best works — your narrator is "outside" the character but somehow manages to convey very directly Nashe's intensely subjective, emotionally charged "inner" life. It's a delicate balance: the seemingly objective representation of an emotionally charged, psychological landscape.

PA: Yes, that third person is so close to the first person, is so deeply imagined from Nashe's point of view, that there's hardly any difference at all. It was a very wrenching experience to write that book — utterly grueling and exhausting. For weeks after I finished it, I felt like a dead man.

LM: You chose to present the two sections of *The Invention of Solitude* through two different narrative perspectives, with "Portrait of an Invisible Man" being writtten in the first person, while "The Book of Memory" is in the third person. What was involved in that choice?

PA: The opening part was written very naturally in the first person. I didn't question it; it just came to me that way, and I went with it. When I started the next section, I assumed it would be written in the first person as well. I worked on it for six or eight months in that form but something about it disturbed me, something wasn't right. Eventually, after groping in the dark with it for a long time, I understood that the book could only be written in the third person. Rimbaud: "Je est un autre." It opened a door for me, and after that I worked in a kind of fever, as though my brain had caught fire.

What it came down to was creating a distance between myself and myself. If you're too close to the thing you're trying to write about, the perspective vanishes, and you begin to smother. I had to objectify myself in order to explore my own subjectivity — which gets us back to what we were talking about before: the multiplicity of the singular. The moment I think about the fact that I'm saying "I," I'm actually saying "he." It's the mirror of self-consciousness, a way of watching yourself think.

SG: Were there any particular difficulties in writing from a woman's perspective, as you did with Anna in *In the Country of Last Things*?

PA: Not really. But something in me resisted it for a long time. In many ways, writing that book was like taking dictation. I *heard* her voice speaking to me — and that voice was utterly distinct from my own. In that sense, there was almost no difficulty at all.

But when you consider that I first heard that voice in 1970 and didn't finish the book until 1985, it's safe to conclude that it was a very difficult book to write. I didn't want to do it. I felt it was presumptuous to write from the viewpoint of a woman, and so every time I started working on it again, I'd stop. I'd cross my fingers and hope that the voice had talked itself out, that at last I'd be free of it. A year or two would go by, and then I'd start hearing her again. I'd write for a while, then stop again. This went on for years and years. Finally, some time in the early Eighties, right when I was in the middle of *The New York Triology* (I think I was between the second and third books), she came back to me in full force, and I wrote the first thirty or forty pages as they stand now. Still not sure of myself, I showed them to Siri and asked her what she thought. She said those pages were the best work I had ever done and that I had to finish the book. I had to finish the book as a present to her. "It's my book," she said, and she's continued to refer to it in that way ever since.

Still, there was a pause after writing those initial pages. I wanted to finish the *Trilogy* first, so more time went by before I returned to it. But in that interval, I published what I had already written in *The Paris Review*. It's the only time I've ever published a piece of a novel, but in this case it seemed to make sense. I did it as a kind of promise to myself, as a guarantee that I would actually finish it.

LM: There's an obvious way that *In the Country of Last Things* is grounded in the dystopian or post-holocaust tradition of science fiction. But I was mostly struck with how palpably real this urban nightmare scene is. It seems not too differ- ent, in fact, from what you can find right here in New York.

PA: As far as I'm concerned, the book has nothing to do with science fiction. It's quite fantastical at times, of course, but that doesn't mean it's not firmly anchored in historical realities. It's a novel about the present and the immediate past, not about the future. "Anna Blume walks through the twentieth century." That's the phrase I carried around in my head while I was working on the book.

LM: What sorts of historical realities do you mean — the massive devastations caused in the two world wars?

PA: Among other things, yes. There are specific references to the Warsaw ghetto and the siege of Leningrad, but also to events taking place in the Third World today — not to speak of New York, which is rapidly turning into a Third World city before our eyes. The garbage system, which I describe at such great length in the novel, is loosely based on the present-day garbage system in Cairo. All in all, there's very little invented material in the book. The characters, yes, but not the circumstances. Even the pivotal event in the story — when Anna, hoping to buy a pair of shoes, is lured into a human slaughterhouse — even that scene is based on historical fact. Precisely that kind of thing happened in Leningrad in World War II. The city was surrounded by the Germans for two and a half years, and in that time

500,000 people lost their lives. 500,000 people in one city. Just stop for a moment and try to imagine what it must have been like. Once you begin to think about such things, it's difficult to think about anything else.

I realize that many people found this book depressing, but there's nothing I can do about that. In the end, I find it the most hopeful book I've ever written. Anna Blume survives, at least to the extent that her words survive. Even in the midst of the most brutal realities, the most terrible social conditions, she struggles to remain a human being, to keep her humanity intact. I can't imagine anything more noble and courageous than that. It's a struggle that millions of people have had to face in our time, and not many of them have been as tenacious as she is. I think of Anna Blume as a true heroine.

SG: Earlier in the interview you referred to yourself as basically an "intuitive writer" in terms of the way your writing process operates. Maybe we could have you discuss the relationship between your conscious intentionality versus your intuition by having you discuss the way a specific image in your work develops. For instance the moon image in *Moon Palace* appears in dozens of different contexts that occasionally dovetail or coalesce into groupings — Barber's legends of the Indians (with their origins on the moon), the way the Utah desert is described as a lunar landscape, the fortune cookie that says, "The sun is the past, the earth is the present, the moon is the future" (and which turns out to be a quote from Tesla), the restaurant named "Moon Palace," and so on. Is the unfolding of these connections and resonances the product of conscious design or happy accident?

PA: If you think about any one thing long enough or hard enough, it's going to begin to reverberate for you. Once that happens, waves are emitted, and those waves travel through space and bounce off other things, which in turn emit their own waves. It's an associative process, and if you stick with it conscientiously enough, large portions of the world will eventually be touched by your thoughts. It's not really a question of accident or design. This is the way the mind works. It just happens, but you have to be watching attentively for it to go on happening. Pick any object in front of you — a coffee cup, or a box of cigars, or a telephone — and try to think about where it comes from. Within ten minutes, you're onto any number of other things — geology, history, labor problems, biology, God knows what — a whole range of subjects. "To see the world in a grain of sand." If you're capable of doing that, imagine how much can be seen in the moon!

LM: There's also a certain sense in which those elaborate connections and metaphorical associations being developed grow naturally out of the kind of sensibility you project for Fogg.

PA: Precisely. Fogg is a bookish young man, an intellectual, and he has a penchant for this kind of thing. It's something he inherits from his Uncle Victor, a man who is constantly searching the world for hidden connections. The moon imagery comes from Fogg — I wasn't trying to impose it on him. At the same time, remember, he's telling the story of his youth from the distance of middle age, and he often pokes fun at himself. He's looking back on the way he *used* to think, the way he *used* to interpret the world. It's one of the many follies of his adolescence, a symptom of the madness of those times. But Fogg is a unique case. Other characters I've written about have none of these tendencies; they don't indulge in such elaborate mental gymnastics. Nashe, for example, the hero of *The Music of Chance*, has nothing in common with Fogg. He's a much more straight-forward kind of person, and consequently the book he appears in is a much simpler story.

LM: Let's go back for a second to your comment about seeing the world in a grain of sand. What made it seem so much a part of what you were doing in the novel? And how did this fit in with the "follies" of Fogg's adolescence?

PA: The moon is many things all at once, a touchstone. It's the moon as myth, as "radiant Diana, image of all that is dark within us"; the imagination, love, madness. At the same time, it's the moon as object, as celestial body, as lifeless stone hovering in the sky. But it's also the longing for what is not, the unattainable, the human desire for transcendence. And yet it's history as well, particularly American history. First there's Columbus, then there was the discovery of the West, then finally there is outer space: the moon as the last frontier. But Columbus had no idea that he'd discovered America. He thought he had sailed to India, to China. In some sense, *Moon Palace* is the embodiment of that misconception, an attempt to think of America as China. But the moon is also repetition, the cyclical nature of human experience. There are three stories in the book, after all, and each one is finally the same. Each generation repeats the mistakes of the previous generation. So it's also a critique of the notion of progress. And if America is the land of progress, what are we to make of ourselves then? And so on and so on and so on. Fogg wends his way among all these ideas, this pinball machine of associations, struggling to find a place for himself. By the end of the book I think he manages to get somewhere. But he only reaches the beginning, the brink of his adult life. And that's where we leave him — getting ready to begin.

SG: You've described how emotionally exhausting it was for you to write your latest novel, *The Music of Chance*. Did you realize when you started it that it was going to be such a wrenching book to write?

PA: It's never possible to predict what it's going to be like. With my other books, I've usually known the general shape of the story before beginning to write it, but in this case a number of crucial elements were altered as I went along. I began with a different ending in mind, but at a certain point I realized that I had been wrong, that the book was heading for a much darker conclusion than I had originally planned. This revelation came as a shock to me, it stopped me cold in my tracks. But there was no getting around it, and after thinking it over for several days, I understood that I had no choice.

SG: Do you recall what the origins of the book were?

PA: At the end of *Moon Palace*, Fogg is driving out west in a car. The car is stolen, and he winds up continuing the journey on foot. I realized that I wanted to get back inside that car, to give myself a chance to go on driving around America. So there was that very immediate and visceral impulse, which is how *The Music of Chance* begins — with Nashe sitting behind the wheel of a car.

At the same time, I wanted to explore the implications of the windfall I had received after my father's death — which is something we discussed before. This led me to start thinking about the question of freedom, which is ultimately the true subject of the book.

As for the wall — those stones had been standing inside me for years. The play that I mentioned earlier, the one that was performed in the Seventies, was about two men building a wall. The whole play consists of them lugging stones around the stage, and by the end they're completely blocked off from the audience. I was never satisfied by it, but at the same time I couldn't get rid of the idea. It plagued me and haunted me for all those years. So this was my attempt to improve on what I had done with it the first time. Those are three elements of the novel that I was able to think about before I wrote it. The conscious material, so to speak. Everything else is shrouded in obscurity.

When I was about two-thirds of the way through the first draft, it occurred to me that the story had the same structure as a fairy tale. Up until then, I had only thought about the book in concrete terms, the reality of the action. But if you reduce the book to its skeleton, then you wind up with something that resembles a typical story by the Brothers Grimm, don't you? A wanderer stumbles onto an oppor-

tunity to make his fortune; he travels to the ogre's castle
to test his luck, is tricked into staying there, and can win
his freedom only by performing a series of absurd tasks that
the ogre invents for him.

I don't know if I want to make too much out of this, but
is was an interesting discovery anyway. Another example of
how elusive the whole activity of writing is. Yet another
testimony to my own ignorance.

1989-90

IV

The Red Notebook

1

In 1972, a close friend of mine ran into trouble with the law. She was in Ireland that year, living in a small village not far from the town of Sligo. As it happened, I was visiting on the day a plainclothes detective drove up to her cottage and presented her with a summons to appear in court. The charges were serious enough to require a lawyer. My friend asked around and was given a name, and the next morning we bicycled into town to meet with this person and discuss the case. To my astonishment, he worked for a firm called Argue and Phibbs.

This is a true story. If there are those who doubt me, I challenge them to visit Sligo and see for themselves if I have made it up or not. I have reveled in these names for the past twenty years, but even though I can prove that Argue and Phibbs were real men, the fact that the one name should have been coupled with the other (to form an even more delicious joke, an out-and-out sendup of the legal profession) is something I still find hard to believe.

According to my latest information (three or four years ago), the firm continues to do a thriving business.

2

The following year (1973), I was offered a job as caretaker of a farmhouse in the south of France. My friend's legal troubles were well behind her, and since our on-again off-again romance seemed to be on again, we decided to join forces and take the job together. We had both run out of money by then, and without this offer we would have been compelled to return to America—which neither one of us was prepared to do just yet.

It turned out to be a curious year. On the one hand, the place was beautiful: a large, eighteenth-century stone house bordered by vineyards on one side and a national forest on the other. The nearest village was two kilometers away, but it was inhabited by no more than forty people, none of whom was under sixty or seventy years old. It was an ideal spot for two young writers to spend a year, and L. and I both worked hard there, accomplishing more in that house than either one of us would have thought possible.

On the other hand, we lived on the brink of permanent catastrophe. Our employers, an American couple who lived in Paris, sent us a small monthly salary (fifty dollars), a gas allowance for the car, and money to feed the two Labrador retrievers who were part of the household. All in all, it was a generous arrangement. There was no rent to pay, and even if our salary fell short of what we needed to live on, it gave us a head start on each month's expenses. Our plan was to earn the rest by doing translations. Before leaving Paris and settling in the country, we had set up a number of jobs to see us through the year. What we had neglected to take into account was that publishers are often slow to pay their bills. We had also forgotten to consider that checks sent from one country to another can take weeks to clear, and that once they do, bank charges and exchange fees cut into the amounts of those checks. Since L. and I had left no margin for error or miscalculation, we often found ourselves in quite desperate straits.

I remember savage nicotine fits, my body numb with need as I scrounged among sofa cushions and crawled behind cupboards in search of loose coins. For eighteen centimes (about three and a half cents), you could buy a brand of cigarettes called Parisiennes, which were sold in packs of four. I remember feeding the dogs and thinking that they ate better than I did. I remember conversations with L. when we seriously considered opening a can of dog food and eating it for dinner.

Our only other source of income that year came from a man named James Sugar. (I don't mean to insist on metaphorical names, but facts are facts, and there's nothing I can do about it.) Sugar worked as a staff photographer for *National Geographic*, and he entered our lives because he was collaborating with one of our employers on an article about the region. He took pictures for several months, crisscrossing Provence in a rented car provided by his magazine, and whenver he was in our neck of the woods he would spend the night with us. Since the magazine also provided him with an expense account, he would very graciously slip us the money that had been allotted for his hotel costs. If I remember correctly, the sum came to fifty francs a night. In effect, L. and I became his private innkeepers, and since Sugar was an amiable man into the bargain, we were always glad to see him. The only problem was that we never knew when he was going to turn up. He never called in advance, and more often than not weeks would go by between his visits. We therefore learned not to count on Mr. Sugar. He would arrive out of nowhere, pulling up in front of the house in his shiny blue car, stay for a night or two, and then disappear again. Each time he left, we assumed that was the last time we would ever see him.

The worst moments came for us in the late winter and early spring. Checks failed to arrive, one of the dogs was stolen, and little by little we ate our way through the stockpile of food in the kitchen. In the end, we had nothing left but a bag of onions, a bottle of cooking oil, and a packaged pie crust that someone had bought before we ever moved into the house—a stale remnant from the previous summer. L. and I held out all morning and into the afternoon, but by two-thirty hunger had gotten the better of us, and so we went into the kitchen to prepare our last meal. Given the paucity of elements we had to work with, an onion pie was the only dish that made sense.

After our concoction had been in the oven for what seemed a sufficient length of time, we took it out, set it on the table, and dug in. Against all our expectations, we both found it delicious. I think we even went so far as to say that it was the best food we had ever tasted, but no doubt that was a ruse, a feeble attempt to keep our spirits up. Once we had chewed a little more, however, disappointment set in. Reluctantly—ever so reluctantly—we were forced to admit that the pie had not yet cooked through, that the center was still too cold to eat. There was nothing to be done but put it back in the oven for another ten or fifteen minutes. Considering how hungry we were, and considering that our salivary glands had just been activated, relinquishing the pie was not easy.

To stifle our impatience, we went outside for a brief stroll, thinking the time would pass more quickly if we removed ourselves from the good smells in the kitchen. As I remember it, we circled the house once, perhaps twice. Perhaps we drifted into a deep conversation about something (I can't remember), but however it happened, and however long we were gone, by the time we entered the house again the kitchen was filled with smoke. We rushed to the oven and pulled out the pie, but it was too late. Our meal was dead. It had been incinerated, burned to a charred and blackened mass, and not one morsel could be salvaged.

It sounds like a funny story now, but at the time it was anything but funny. We had fallen into a dark hole, and neither one of us could think of a way to get out. In all my years of struggling to be a man, I doubt there has ever been a moment when I felt less inclined to laugh or crack jokes. This was really the end, and it was a terrible and frightening place to be.

That was at four o'clock in the afternoon. Less than an hour later, the errant Mr. Sugar suddenly appeared, driving up to the house in a cloud of dust, gravel and dirt crunching all around him. If I think about it hard enough, I can still see the naive and goofy smile on his face as he bounced out of the car and said hello. It was a miracle. It was a genuine miracle, and I was there to witness it with my own eyes, to live it in my own flesh. Until that moment, I had thought those things happened only in books.

Sugar treated us to dinner that night in a two-star res-

taurant. We ate copiously and well, we emptied several
bottles of wine, we laughed our heads off. And yet, delicious as that food must have been, I can't remember a
thing about it. But I have never forgotten the taste of the
onion pie.

3

Not long after I returned to New York (July 1974), a friend told me the following story. It is set in Yugoslavia, during what must have been the last months of the Second World War.

S.'s uncle was a member of a Serbian partisan group that fought against the Nazi occupation. One morning, he and his comrades woke up to find themselves surrounded by German troops. They were holed up in a farmhouse somewhere in the country, a foot of snow lay on the ground, and there was no escape. Not knowing what else to do, the men decided to draw lots. Their plan was to burst out of the farmhouse one by one, dash through the snow, and see if they couldn't make it to safety. According to the results of the draw, S.'s uncle was supposed to go third.

He watched through the window as the first man ran out into the snow-covered field. There was a barrage of machine-gun fire from across the woods, and the man was cut down. A moment later, the second man ran out, and the same thing happened. The machine guns blasted, and he fell down dead in the snow.

Then it was my friend's uncle's turn. I don't know if he hesitated at the doorway, I don't know what thoughts were pounding through his head at that moment. The only thing I was told was that he started to run, charging through the snow for all he was worth. It seemed as if he ran forever. Then, suddenly, he felt pain in his leg. A second after that, an overpowering warmth spread through his body, and a second after that he lost consciousness.

When he woke up, he found himself lying on his back
in a peasant's cart. He had no idea how much time had
elapsed, no idea of how he had been rescued. He had
simply opened his eyes—and there he was, lying in a cart
that some horse or mule was pulling down a country road,
staring up at the back of a peasant's head. He studied the
back of that head for several seconds, and then loud ex-
plosions began to erupt from the woods. Too weak to
move, he kept looking at the back of the head, and suddenly it was gone. It just flew off the peasant's body, and
where a moment before there had been a whole man,
there was now a man without a head.

More noise, more confusion. Whether the horse went
on pulling the cart or not I can't say, but within minutes,
perhaps even seconds, a large contingent of Russian
troops came rolling down the road. Jeeps, tanks, scores of
soldiers. When the commanding officer took a look at S.'s
uncle's leg, he quickly dispatched him to an infirmary that
had been set up in the neighborhood. It was no more than
a rickety wooden shack—a henhouse, maybe, or an outbuilding on some farm. There the Russian army doctor
pronounced the leg past saving. It was too severely damaged, he said, and he was going to have to cut it off.

My friend's uncle began to scream. "Don't cut off my
leg," he cried. "Please, I beg of you, don't cut off my leg!"
But no one listened to him. The medics strapped him to
the operating table, and the doctor picked up the saw.
Just as he was about to pierce the skin of the leg, there
was another explosion. The roof of the infirmary collapsed, the walls fell down, the entire place was obliterated.
And once again, S.'s uncle lost consciousness.

When he woke up this time, he found himself lying in a bed. The sheets were clean and soft, there were pleasant smells in the room, and his leg was still attached to his body. A moment later, he was looking into the face of a beautiful young woman. She was smiling at him and feeding him broth with a spoon. With no knowledge of how it had happened, he had been rescued again and carried to another farmhouse. For several minutes after coming to, S.'s uncle wasn't sure if he was alive or dead. It seemed possible to him that he had woken up in heaven.

He stayed on in the house during his recovery and fell in love with the beautiful young woman, but nothing ever came of that romance. I wish I could say why, but S. never filled me in on the details. What I do know is that his uncle kept his leg—and that once the war was over, he moved to America to begin a new life. Somehow or other (the circumstances are obscure to me), he wound up as an insurance salesman in Chicago.

4

L. and I were married in 1974. Our son was born in 1977, but by the following year our marriage had ended. None of that is relevant now—except to set the scene for an incident that took place in the spring of 1980.

We were both living in Brooklyn then, about three or four blocks from each other, and our son divided his time between the two apartments. One morning, I had to stop by L.'s house to pick up Daniel and walk him to nursery school. I can't remember if I went inside the building or if Daniel came down the stairs himself, but I vividly recall that just as we were about to walk off together, L. opened the window of her third-floor apartment to throw me some money. Why she did that is also forgotten. Perhaps she wanted me to replenish a parking meter for her, perhaps I was supposed to do an errand, I don't know. All that remains is the open window and the image of a dime flying through the air. I see it with such clarity, it's almost as if I have studied photographs of that instant, as if it's part of a recurring dream I've had ever since.

But the dime hit the branch of a tree, and its downward arc into my hand was disrupted. It bounced off the tree, landed soundlessly somewhere nearby, and then it was gone. I remember bending down and searching the pavement, digging among the leaves and twigs at the base of the tree, but the dime was nowhere to be found.

I can place that event in early spring because I know that later the same day I attended a baseball game at Shea Stadium—the opening game of the season. A friend of mine had been offered tickets, and he had generously invited me to go along with him. I had never been to an opening game before, and I remember the occasion well.

We arrived early (something about collecting the tickets at a certain window), and as my friend went off to complete the transaction, I waited for him outside one of the entrances to the stadium. Not a single soul was around. I ducked into a little alcove to light a cigarette (a strong wind was blowing that day), and there, sitting on the ground not two inches from my feet, was a dime. I bent down, picked it up, and put it in my pocket. Ridiculous as it might sound, I felt certain that it was the same dime I had lost in Brooklyn that morning.

5

In my son's nursery school, there was a little girl whose
parents were going through a divorce. I particularly liked
her father, a struggling painter who earned his living by
doing architectural renderings. His paintings were quite
beautiful, I thought, but he never had much luck in con-
vincing dealers to support his work. The one time he did
have a show, the gallery promptly went out of business.

B. was not an intimate friend, but we enjoyed each
other's company, and whenever I saw him I would return
home with renewed admiration for his steadfastness and
inner calm. He was not a man who grumbled or felt sorry
for himself. However gloomy things had become for him
in recent years (endless money problems, lack of artistic
success, threats of eviction from his landlord, difficulties
with his ex-wife), none of it seemed to throw him off
course. He continued to paint with the same passion as
ever, and unlike so many others, he never expressed any
bitterness or envy toward less talented artists who were
doing better than he was.

When he wasn't working on his own canvasses, he would
sometimes go to the Metropolitan Museum and make copies of the old masters. I remember a Caravaggio he once
did that struck me as utterly remarkable. It wasn't a copy
so much as a replica, an exact duplication of the original.
On one of those visits to the museum, a Texas millionaire
spotted B. at work and was so impressed that he commissioned him to do a copy of a Renoir painting—which
he then presented to his fiancée as a gift.

B. was exceedingly tall (six-five or six-six), good-looking,
and gentle in his manner—qualities that made him es-

pecially attractive to women. Once his divorce was behind him and he began to circulate again, he had no trouble finding female companions. I only saw him about two or three times a year, but each time I did, there was another woman in his life. All of them were obviously mad for him. You had only to watch them looking at B. to know how they felt, but for one reason or another, none of these affairs lasted very long.

After two or three years, B.'s landlord finally made good on his threats and evicted him from his loft. B. moved out of the city, and I lost touch with him.

Several more years went by, and then one night B. came back to town to attend a dinner party. My wife and I were also there, and since we knew that B. was about to get married, we asked him to tell us the story of how he had met his future wife.

About six months earlier, he said, he had been talking to a friend on the phone. This friend was worried about him, and after a while he began to scold B. for not having married again. You've been divorced for seven years now, he said, and in that time you could have settled down with any one of a dozen attractive and remarkable women. But no one is ever good enough for you, and you've turned them all away. What's wrong with you, B.? What in the world do you want?

There's nothing wrong with me, B. said. I just haven't found the right person, that's all.

At the rate you're going, you never will, the friend answered. I mean, have you ever met one woman who comes close to what you're looking for? Name one. I dare you to name just one.

Startled by his friend's vehemence, B. paused to consider the question carefully. Yes, he finally said, there was one. A woman by the name of E., whom he had known as a student at Harvard more than twenty years ago. But she had been involved with another man at the time, and he had been involved with another woman (his future ex-wife), and nothing had developed between them. He had no idea where E. was now, he said, but if he could meet someone like her, he knew he wouldn't hesitate to get married again.

That was the end of the conversation. Until mentioning her to his friend, B. hadn't thought about this woman in over ten years, but now that she had resurfaced in his mind, he had trouble thinking about anything else. For the next three or four days, he thought about her constantly, unable to shake the feeling that his one chance for happiness had been lost many years ago. Then, almost as if the intensity of these thoughts had sent a signal out into the world, the phone rang one night, and there was E. on the other end of the line.

B. kept her on the phone for more than three hours. He scarcely knew what he said to her, but he went on talking until past midnight, understanding that something momentous had happened and that he mustn't let her escape again.

After graduating from college, E. had joined a dance company, and for the past twenty years she had devoted herself exclusively to her career. She had never married, and now that she was about to retire as a performer, she was calling old friends from her past, trying to make contact with the world again. She had no family (her parents had been killed in a car crash when she was a small girl) and had been raised by two aunts, both of whom were now dead.

B. arranged to see her the next night. Once they were together, it didn't take long for him to discover that his feelings for her were just as strong as he had imagined. He fell in love with her all over again, and several weeks later they were engaged to be married.

To make the story even more perfect, it turned out that E. was independently wealthy. Her aunts had been rich, and after they died she had inherited all their money—which meant that not only had B. found true love, but the crushing money problems that had plagued him for so many years had suddenly vanished. All in one fell swoop.

A year or two after the wedding, they had a child. At last report, mother, father, and baby were doing just fine.

6

In much the same spirit, although spanning a shorter
period of time (several months as opposed to twenty
years), another friend, R., told me of a certain out-of-the-
way book that he had been trying to locate without success,
scouring bookstores and catalogues for what was supposed
to be a remarkable work that he very much wanted to
read, and how, one afternoon as he made his way through
the city, he took a shortcut through Grand Central Station,
walked up the staircase that leads to Vanderbilt Avenue,
and caught sight of a young woman standing by the mar-
ble railing with a book in front of her: the same book he
had been trying so desperately to track down.

Although he is not someone who normally speaks to
strangers, R. was too stunned by the coincidence to remain
silent. "Believe it or not," he said to the young woman,
"I've been looking everywhere for that book."

"It's wonderful," the young woman answered. "I just
finished reading it."

"Do you know where I could find another copy?" R.
asked. "I can't tell you how much it would mean to me."

"This one is for you," the woman answered.

"But it's yours," R. said.

"It *was* mine," the woman said, "but now I'm finished
with it. I came here today to give it to you."

7

Twelve years ago, my wife's sister went off to live in Taiwan. Her intention was to study Chinese (which she now
speaks with breathtaking fluency) and to support herself
by giving English lessons to native Chinese speakers in
Taipei. That was approximately one year before I met my
wife, who was then a graduate student at Columbia
University.

One day, my future sister-in-law was talking to an American friend, a young woman who had also gone to Taipei
to study Chinese. The conversation came around to the
subject of their families back home, which in turn led to
the following exchange:

"I have a sister who lives in New York," my future sister-
in-law said.

"So do I," her friend answered.

"My sister lives on the Upper West Side."

"So does mine."

"My sister lives on West 109th Street."

"Believe it or not, so does mine."

"My sister lives at 309 West 109th Street."

"So does mine!"

"My sister lives on the second floor of 309 West 109th
Street."

The friend took a deep breath and said, "I know this
sounds crazy, but so does mine."

It is scarcely possible for two cities to be farther apart
than Taipei and New York. They are at opposite ends of
the earth, separated by a distance of more than ten thousand miles, and when it is day in one it is night in the

other. As the two young women in Taipei marveled over
the astounding connection they had just uncovered, they
realized that their two sisters were probably asleep at that
moment. On the same floor of the same building in northern Manhattan, each one was sleeping in her own apartment, unaware of the conversation that was taking place
about them on the other side of the world.

Although they were neighbors, it turned out that the
two sisters in New York did not know each other. When
they finally met (two years later), neither one of them was
living in that building anymore.

Siri and I were married then. One evening, on our way
to an appointment somewhere, we happened to stop in
at a bookstore on Broadway to browse for a few minutes.
We must have wandered into different aisles, and because
Siri wanted to show me something, or because I wanted
to show her something (I can't remember), one of us spoke
the other's name out loud. A second later, a woman came
rushing up to us."You're Paul Auster and Siri Hustvedt,
aren't you?" she said. "Yes," we said, "that's exactly who
we are. How did you know that?" The woman then explained that her sister and Siri's sister had been students
together in Taiwan.

The circle had been closed at last. Since that evening
in the bookstore ten years ago, this woman has been one
of our best and most loyal friends.

8

Three summers ago, a letter turned up in my mailbox. It came in a white oblong envelope and was addressed to someone whose name was unfamiliar to me: Robert M. Morgan of Seattle, Washington. Various post office markings were stamped across the front: *Not Deliverable, Unable to Forward, Return to Writer*. Mr. Morgan's name had been crossed out with a pen, and beside it someone had written *Not at this address*. Drawn in the same blue ink, an arrow pointed to the upper left-hand corner of the envelope, accompanied by the words *Return to sender*. Assuming that the post office had made a mistake, I checked the upper left-hand corner to see who the sender was. There, to my absolute bewilderment, I discovered my own name and my own address. Not only that, but this information was printed on a custom-made address label (one of those labels you can order in packs of two hundred from advertisements on matchbook covers). The spelling of my name was correct, the address was my address—and yet the fact was (and still is) that I have never owned or ordered a set of printed address labels in my life.

Inside, there was a single-spaced typewritten letter that began: "Dear Robert, In response to your letter dated July 15, 1989, I can only say that, like other authors, I often receive letters concerning my work." Then, in a bombastic, pretentious style, riddled with quotations from French philosophers and oozing with a tone of conceit and self-satisfaction, the letter-writer went on to praise "Robert" for the ideas he had developed about one of my books in a college course on the contemporary novel. It was a contemptible letter, the kind of letter I would never dream of writing to anyone, and yet it was signed with my name. The handwriting did not resemble mine, but that was small comfort. Someone was out there trying to impersonate me, and as far as I know he still is.

One friend suggested that this was an example of "mail art." Knowing that the letter could not be delivered to Robert Morgan (since there was no such person), the author of the letter was actually addressing his remarks to me. But that would imply an unwarranted faith in the U.S. Postal Service, and I doubt that someone who would go to the trouble of ordering address labels in my name and then sitting down to write such an arrogant, high-flown letter would leave anything to chance. Or would he? Perhaps the smart alecks of this world believe that everything will always go their way.

I have scant hope of ever getting to the bottom of this little mystery. The prankster did a good job of covering his tracks, and he has not been heard from since. What puzzles me about my own behavior is that I have not thrown away the letter, even though it continues to give me chills every time I look at it. A sensible man would have tossed the thing in the garbage. Instead, for reasons I do not understand, I have kept it on my work table for the past three years, allowing it to become a permanent fixture among my pens and notebooks and erasers. Perhaps I keep it there as a monument to my own folly. Perhaps it is a way to remind myself that I know nothing, that the world I live in will go on escaping me forever.

9

One of my closest friends is a French poet by the name
of C. We have known each other for more than twenty
years now, and while we don't see each other often (he
lives in Paris and I live in New York), the bond between
us remains strong. It is a fraternal bond, somehow, as if
in some former life we had actually been brothers.

C. is a man of manifold contradictions. He is both open
to the world and shut off from it, a charismatic figure with
scores of friends everywhere (legendary for his kindness,
his humor, his sparkling conversation) and yet someone
who has been wounded by life, who struggles to perform
the simple tasks that most other people take for granted.
An exceptionally gifted poet and thinker about poetry, C.
is nevertheless hampered by frequent writing blocks,
streaks of morbid self-doubt, and surprisingly (for someone who is so generous, so profoundly lacking in mean-
spiritedness), a capacity for long-standing grudges and
quarrels, usually over some trifle or abstract principle. No
one is more universally admired than C., no one has more
talent, no one so readily commands the center of attention,
and yet he has always done everything in his power to
marginalize himself. Since his separation from his wife
many years ago, he has lived alone in a number of small,
one-room apartments, subsisting on almost no money and
only fitful bouts of employment, publishing little, and refusing to write a single word of criticism, even though he
reads everything and knows more about contemporary
poetry than anyone in France. To those of us who love
him (and we are many), C. is often a cause of concern.

To the degree that we respect him and care about his well-being, we also worry about him.

He had a rough childhood. I can't say to what extent that explains anything, but the facts should not be overlooked. His father apparently ran off with another woman when C. was a little boy, and after that my friend grew up with his mother, an only child with no family life to speak of. I have never met C.'s mother, but by all accounts she is a bizarre character. She went through a series of love affairs during C.'s childhood and adolescence, each with a man younger than the man before him. By the time C. left home to enter the army at the age of twenty-one, his mother's boyfriend was scarcely older than he was. In more recent years, the central purpose of her life has been a campaign to promote the canonization of a certain Italian priest (whose name eludes me now). She has besieged the Catholic authorities with countless letters defending the holiness of this man, and at one point she even commissioned an artist to create a life-size statue of the priest—which now stands in her front yard as an enduring testament to her cause.

Although not a father himself, C. became a kind of pseudo-father seven or eight years ago. After a falling out with his girlfriend (during which they temporarily broke up), his girlfriend had a brief affair with another man and became pregnant. The affair ended almost at once, but she decided to have the baby on her own. A little girl was born, and even though C. is not her real father, he has devoted himself to her since the day of her birth and adores her as if she were his own flesh and blood.

One day about four years ago, C. happened to be visiting a friend. In the apartment there was a *Minitel*, a small computer given out free by the French telephone company. Among other things, the *Minitel* contains the address and phone number of every person in France. As C. sat there playing with his friend's new machine, it suddenly occurred to him to look up his father's address. He found it in Lyon. When he returned home later that day, he stuffed one of his books into an envelope and sent it off to the address in Lyon—initiating the first contact with his father in over forty years. None of it made any sense to him. Until he found himself doing these things, it had never even crossed his mind that he wanted to do them.

That same night, he ran into another friend in a café —a woman psychoanalyst—and told her about these strange, unpremeditated acts. It was as if he had felt his father calling out to him, he said, as if some uncanny force had unleashed itself inside him. Considering that he had absolutely no memories of the man, he couldn't even begin to guess when they had last seen each other.

The woman thought for a moment and said, "How old is L.?" referring to C.'s girlfriend's daughter.

"Three and a half," C. answered.

"I can't be sure," the woman said, "but I'd be willing to bet that you were three and a half the last time you saw your father. I say that because you love L. so much. Your identification with her is very strong, and you're reliving your life through her."

Several days after that, there was a reply from Lyon— a warm and perfectly gracious letter from C.'s father. After thanking C. for the book, he went on to tell him how proud he was to learn that his son had grown up to

become a writer. By pure coincidence, he added, the package had been mailed on his birthday, and he was very
moved by the symbolism of the gesture.

None of this tallied with the stories C. had heard
throughout his childhood. According to his mother, his
father was a monster of selfishness who had walked out
on her for a "slut" and had never wanted anything to do
with his son. C. had believed these stories, and therefore
he had shied away from any contact with his father. Now,
on the strength of this letter, he no longer knew what to
believe.

He decided to write back. The tone of his response was
guarded, but nevertheless it was a response. Within days
he received another reply, and this second letter was just
as warm and gracious as the first had been. C. and his
father began a correspondence. It went on for a month
or two, and eventually C. began to consider traveling down
to Lyon to meet his father face to face.

Before he could make any definite plans, he received a
letter from his father's wife informing him that his father
was dead. He had been in ill health for the past several
years, she wrote, but the recent exchange of letters with
C. had given him great happiness, and his last days had
been filled with optimism and joy.

It was at this moment that I first heard about the incredible reversals that had taken place in C.'s life. Sitting
on the train from Paris to Lyon (on his way to visit his
"stepmother" for the first time), he wrote me a letter that
sketched out the story of the past month. His handwriting
reflected each jolt of the tracks, as if the speed of the train
were an exact image of the thoughts racing through his

head. As he put it somewhere in that letter: "I feel as if I've become a character in one of your novels."

His father's wife could not have been friendlier to him during the visit. Among other things, C. learned that his father had suffered a heart attack on the morning of his last birthday (the same day that C. had looked up his address on the *Minitel*) and that, yes, C. had been precisely three and a half years old at the time of his parents' divorce. His stepmother then went on to tell him the story of his life from his father's point of view—which contradicted everything his mother had ever told him. In this version, it was his mother who had walked out on his father; it was his mother who had forbidden his father from seeing him; it was his mother who had broken his father's heart. She told C. how his father would come around to the schoolyard when he was a little boy to look at him through the fence. C. remembered that man, but not knowing who he was, he had been afraid.

C.'s life had now become two lives. There was Version A and Version B, and both of them were his story. He had lived them both in equal measure, two truths that cancelled each other out, and all along, without even knowing it, he had been stranded in the middle.

His father had owned a small stationery store (the usual stock of paper and writing materials, along with a rental library of popular books). The business had earned him a living, but not much more than that, and the estate he left behind was quite modest. The numbers are unimportant, however. What counts is that C.'s stepmother (by then an old woman) insisted on splitting the money with him half and half. There was nothing in the will that

required her to do that, and morally speaking she needn't
have parted with a single penny of her husband's savings.
She did it because she wanted to, because it made her
happier to share the money than to keep it for herself.

10

In thinking about friendship, particularly about how some friendships endure and others don't, I am reminded of the fact that in all my years of driving I have had just four flat tires, and that on each of these occasions the same person was in the car with me (in three different countries, spread out over a period of eight or nine years). J. was a college friend, and though there was always an edge of unease and conflict in our relations, for a time we were close. One spring while we were still undergraduates, we borrowed my father's ancient station wagon and drove up into the wilderness of Quebec. The seasons change more slowly in that part of the world, and winter was not yet over. The first flat tire did not present a problem (we were equipped with a spare), but when a second tire blew out less than an hour later, we were stranded in the bleak and frigid countryside for most of the day. At the time, I shrugged off the incident as a piece of bad luck, but four or five years later, when J. came to France to visit the house where L. and I were working as caretakers (in miserable condition, inert with depression and self-pity, unaware that he was overstaying his welcome with us), the same thing happened. We went to Aix-en-Provence for the day (a drive of about two hours), and coming back late that night on a dark, back-country road, we had another flat. Just a coincidence, I thought, and then pushed the event out of my mind. But then, four years after that, in the waning months of my marriage to L., J. came to visit us again—this time in New York State, where L. and I were living with the infant Daniel. At one point, J. and

I climbed into the car to go to the store and shop for
dinner. I pulled the car out of the garage, turned it around
in the rutted dirt driveway, and advanced to the edge of
the road to look left, right, and left before going on. Just
then, as I waited for a car to pass by, I heard the unmis-
takable hiss of escaping air. Another tire had gone flat,
and this time we hadn't even left the house. J. and I both
laughed, of course, but the truth is that our friendship
never really recovered from that fourth flat tire. I'm not
saying that the flat tires were responsible for our drifting
apart, but in some perverse way they were an emblem of
how things had always stood between us, the sign of some
impalpable curse. I don't want to exaggerate, but even
now I can't quite bring myself to reject those flat tires as
meaningless. For the fact is that J. and I have lost contact,
and we have not spoken to each other in more than ten
years.

11

In 1990, I found myself in Paris again for a few days. One
afternoon, I stopped by the office of a friend to say hello
and was introduced to a Czech woman in her late forties
or early fifties—an art historian who happened to be a
friend of my friend. She was an attractive and vivacious
person, I remember, but since she was on the point of
leaving when I walked in, I spent no more than five or
ten minutes in her company. As usually happens in such
situations, we talked about nothing of any importance: a
town we both knew in America, the subject of a book she
was reading, the weather. Then we shook hands, she
walked out the door, and I have never seen her again.

After she was gone, the friend I had come to visit leaned
back in her chair and said, "Do you want to hear a good
story?"

"Of course," I said. "I'm always interested in good
stories."

"I like my friend very much," she continued, "so don't
get the wrong idea. I'm not trying to spread gossip about
her. It's just that I feel you have a right to know this."

"Are you sure?"

"Yes, I'm sure. But you have to promise me one thing.
If you ever write the story, you mustn't use anyone's
name."

"I promise," I said.

And so my friend let me in on the secret. From start to
finish, it couldn't have taken her more than three minutes
to tell the story I am about to tell now.

The woman I had just met was born in Prague during

the war. When she was still a baby, her father was captured, impressed into the German army, and shipped off
to the Russian front. She and her mother never heard
from him again. They received no letters, no news to tell
them if he was alive or dead, nothing. The war just swallowed him up, and he vanished without a trace.

Years passed. The girl grew up. She completed her studies at the university and became a professor of art history.
According to my friend, she ran into trouble with the
government during the Soviet crackdown in the late sixties, but exactly what kind of trouble was never made clear
to me. Given the stories I know about what happened to
other people during that time, it is not very difficult to
guess.

At some point, she was allowed to begin teaching again.
In one of her classes, there was an exchange student from
East Germany. She and this young man fell in love, and
eventually they were married.

Not long after the wedding, a telegram arrived an-
nouncing the death of her husband's father. The next
day, she and her husband traveled to East Germany to
attend the funeral. Once there, in whatever town or city
it was, she learned that her now dead father-in-law had
been born in Czechoslovakia. During the war he had been
captured by the Nazis, impressed into the German army,
and shipped off to the Russian front. By some miracle, he
had managed to survive. Instead of returning to Czechoslovakia after the war, however, he had settled in Germany
under a new name, had married a German woman, and
had lived there with his new family until the day of his
death. The war had given him a chance to start all over
again, and it seems that he had never looked back.

When my friend's friend asked what this man's name had been in Czechoslovakia, she understood that he was her father.

Which meant, of course, that insofar as her husband's father was the same man, the man she had married was also her brother.

12

One afternoon many years ago, my father's car stalled at a red light. A terrible storm was raging, and at the exact moment his engine went dead, lighting struck a large tree by the side of the road. The trunk of the tree split in two, and as my father struggled to get the car started again (unaware that the upper half of the tree was about to fall), the driver of the car behind him, seeing what was about to happen, put his foot on the accelerator and pushed my father's car through the intersection. An instant later, the tree came crashing to the ground, landing in the very spot where my father's car had just been. What was very nearly the end of him proved to be no more than a close call, a brief episode in the ongoing story of his life.

A year or two after that, my father was working on the roof of a building in Jersey City. Somehow or other (I wasn't there to witness it), he slipped off the edge and started falling to the ground. Once again, he was headed for certain disaster, and once again he was saved. A clothesline broke his fall, and he walked away from the accident with only a few bumps and bruises. Not even a concussion. Not a single broken bone.

That same year, our neighbors across the street hired two men to paint their house. One of the workers fell off the roof and was killed.

The little girl who lived in that house happened to be my sister's best friend. One winter night, the two of them went to a costume party (they were six or seven years old, and I was nine or ten). It had been arranged that my father would pick them up after the party, and when the time came I went along to keep him company in the car. It was bitter cold that night, and the roads were covered with treacherous sheets of ice. My father drove carefully, and we made the journey back and forth without incident. As we pulled up in front of the little girl's house, however, a number of unlikely events occurred all at once.

My sister's friend was dressed as a fairy princess. To complete the outfit, she had borrowed a pair of her mother's high heels, and because her feet swam in those shoes, every step she took was turned into an adventure. My father stopped the car and climbed out to accompany her to the front door. I was in the back with the girls, and in order to let my sister's friend out, I had to get out first. I remember standing on the curb as she disentangled herself from the seat, and just as she stepped into the open air, I noticed that the car was rolling slowly in reverse—either because of the ice or because my father had forgotten to engage the emergency brake (I don't know)—but before I could tell my father what was happening, my sister's friend touched the curb with her mother's high heels and slipped. She went skidding under the car—which was still moving—and there she was, about to be crushed to death by the wheels of my father's Chevy. As I remember it, she didn't make a sound. Without pausing to think, I bent down from the curb, grabbed hold of her right hand, and in one quick gesture yanked her to the sidewalk. An instant later, my father finally noticed that the car was moving. He jumped back into the driver's seat, stepped on the brake, and brought the machine to a halt. From start to finish, the whole chain of misadventures couldn't have taken more than eight or ten seconds.

For years afterward, I walked around feeling that this had been my finest moment. I had actually saved someone's life, and in retrospect I was always astonished by how quickly I had acted, by how sure my movements had been at the critical juncture. I saw the rescue in my mind again and again; again and again I relived the sensation of pulling that little girl out from under the car.

About two years after that night, our family moved to another house. My sister fell out of touch with her friend, and I myself did not see her for another fifteen years.

It was June, and my sister and I had both come back to town for a short visit. Just by chance, her old friend dropped by to say hello. She was all grown up now, a young woman of twenty-two who had graduated from college earlier that month, and I must say that I felt some pride in seeing that she had made it to adulthood in one piece. In a casual sort of way, I mentioned the night I had pulled her out from under the car. I was curious to know how well she remembered her brush with death, but from the look on her face when I asked the question, it was clear that she remembered nothing. A blank stare. A slight frown. A shrug. She remembered nothing!

I realized then that she hadn't known the car was moving. She hadn't even known that she was in danger. The whole incident had taken place in a flash: ten seconds of her life, an interval of no account, and none of if had left the slightest mark on her. For me, on the other hand, those seconds had been a defining experience, a singular event in my internal history.

Most of all, it stuns me to acknowledge that I am talking about something that happened in 1956 or 1957—and that the little girl of that night is now over forty years old.

13

My first novel was inspired by a wrong number. I was alone in my apartment in Brooklyn one afternoon, sitting at my desk and trying to work when the telephone rang. If I am not mistaken, it was the spring of 1980, not many days after I found the dime outside Shea Stadium.

I picked up the receiver, and the man on the other end asked if he was talking to the Pinkerton Agency. I told him no, he had dialed the wrong number, and hung up. Then I went back to work and promptly forgot about the call.

The next afternoon, the telephone rang again. It turned out to be the same person asking the same question I had been asked the day before: "Is this the Pinkerton Agency?" Again I said no, and again I hung up. This time, however, I started thinking about what would have happened if I had said yes. What if I had pretended to be a detective from the Pinkerton Agency? I wondered. What if I had actually taken on the case?

To tell the truth, I felt that I had squandered a rare opportunity. If the man ever called again, I told myself, I would at least talk to him a little bit and try to find out what was going on. I waited for the telephone to ring again, but the third call never came.

After that, wheels started turning in my head, and little by little an entire world of possibilities opened up to me. When I sat down to write *City of Glass* a year later, the wrong number had been transformed into the crucial event of the book, the mistake that sets the whole story in motion. A man named Quinn receives a phone call from someone who wants to talk to Paul Auster, the private detective. Just as I did, Quinn tells the caller he has dialed the wrong number. It happens again the next night, and again Quinn hangs up. Unlike me, however, Quinn is given another chance. When the phone rings again on the third night, he plays along with the caller and takes on the case. Yes, he says, I'm Paul Auster—and at that moment the madness begins.

Most of all, I wanted to remain faithful to my original impulse. Unless I stuck to the spirit of what had really happened, I felt there wouldn't have been any purpose to writing the book. That meant implicating myself in the action of the story (or at least someone who resembled me, who bore my name), and it also meant writing about detectives who were not detectives, about impersonation, about mysteries that cannot be solved. For better or worse, I felt I had no choice.

All well and good. I finished the book ten years ago, and since then I have gone on to occupy myself with other projects, other ideas, other books. Less than two months ago, however, I learned that books are never finished, that it is possible for stories to go on writing themselves without an author.

I was alone in my apartment in Brooklyn that afternoon, sitting at my desk and trying to work when the telephone rang. This was a different apartment from the one I had in 1980—a different apartment with a different telephone number. I picked up the receiver, and the man on the other end asked if he could speak to Mr. Quinn. He had a Spanish accent and I did not recognize the voice. For a moment I thought it might be one of my friends trying to pull my leg. "Mr. Quinn?" I said. "Is this some kind of joke or what?"

No, it wasn't a joke. The man was in dead earnest. He had to talk to Mr. Quinn, and would I please put him on the line. Just to make sure, I asked him to spell out the name. The caller's accent was quite thick, and I was hoping that he wanted to talk to Mr. Queen. But no such luck. "Q-U-I-N-N," the man answered. I suddenly grew scared, and for a moment or two I couldn't get any words out of my mouth. "I'm sorry," I said at last, "there's no Mr. Quinn here. You've the dialed the wrong number." The man apologized for disturbing me, and then we both hung up.

This really happened. Like everything else I have set down in this red notebook, it is a true story.

1992

FOR THE BEST IN PAPERBACKS, LOOK FOR THE

In every corner of the world, on every subject under the sun, Penguin represents quality and variety—the very best in publishing today.

For complete information about books available from Penguin—including Pelicans, Puffins, Peregrines, and Penguin Classics—and how to order them, write to us at the appropriate address below. Please note that for copyright reasons the selection of books varies from country to country.

In the United Kingdom: For a complete list of books available from Penguin in the U.K., please write to *Dept E.P., Penguin Books Ltd, Harmondsworth, Middlesex, UB7 0DA.*

In the United States: For a complete list of books available from Penguin in the U.S., please write to *Consumer Sales, Penguin USA, P.O. Box 999—Dept. 17109, Bergenfield, New Jersey 07621-0120.* VISA and MasterCard holders call 1-800-253-6476 to order all Penguin titles.

In Canada: For a complete list of books available from Penguin in Canada, please write to *Penguin Books Canada Ltd, 10 Alcorn Avenue, Suite 300, Toronto, Ontario, Canada M4V 3B2.*

In Australia: For a complete list of books available from Penguin in Australia, please write to the *Marketing Department, Penguin Books Ltd, P.O. Box 257, Ringwood, Victoria 3134.*

In New Zealand: For a complete list of books available from Penguin in New Zealand, please write to the *Marketing Department, Penguin Books (NZ) Ltd, Private Bag, Takapuna, Auckland 9.*

In India: For a complete list of books available from Penguin, please write to *Penguin Overseas Ltd, 706 Eros Apartments, 56 Nehru Place, New Delhi, 110019.*

In Holland: For a complete list of books available from Penguin in Holland, please write to *Penguin Books Nederland B.V., Postbus 195, NL-1380AD Weesp, Netherlands.*

In Germany: For a complete list of books available from Penguin, please write to *Penguin Books Ltd, Friedrichstrasse 10-12, D-6000 Frankfurt Main I, Federal Republic of Germany.*

In Spain: For a complete list of books available from Penguin in Spain, please write to *Longman, Penguin España, Calle San Nicolas 15, E-28013 Madrid, Spain.*

In Japan: For a complete list of books available from Penguin in Japan, please write to *Longman Penguin Japan Co Ltd, Yamaguchi Building, 2-12-9 Kanda Jimbocho, Chiyoda-Ku, Tokyo 101, Japan.*